Disrupting Political Science

SUNY series in Black Women's Wellness
───────────
Stephanie Y. Evans, editor

Disrupting Political Science
Black Women Re-Imagining the Discipline

Edited by

ANGELA K. LEWIS-MADDOX

Published by State University of New York Press, Albany

© 2025 State University of New York

All rights reserved

Printed in the United States of America

No part of this book may be used or reproduced in any manner whatsoever without written permission. No part of this book may be stored in a retrieval system or transmitted in any form or by any means including electronic, electrostatic, magnetic tape, mechanical, photocopying, recording, or otherwise without the prior permission in writing of the publisher.

Links to third-party websites are provided as a convenience and for informational purposes only. They do not constitute an endorsement or an approval of any of the products, services, or opinions of the organization, companies, or individuals. SUNY Press bears no responsibility for the accuracy, legality, or content of a URL, the external website, or for that of subsequent websites.

For information, contact State University of New York Press, Albany, NY
www.sunypress.edu

Library of Congress Cataloging-in-Publication Data

Name: Lewis-Maddox, Angela K., editor.
Title: Disrupting political science : Black women reimagining the
 discipline / edited by Angela K. Lewis-Maddox.
Description: Albany : State University of New York Press, [2025] | Series:
 SUNY series in Black women's wellness | Includes bibliographical
 references and index.
Identifiers: LCCN 2024022299 | ISBN 9798855800869 (hardcover : alk. paper) |
 ISBN 9798855800883 (ebook) | ISBN 9798855800876 (pbk. : alk. paper)
Subjects: LCSH: African American political scientists—Biography. | Women
 political scientists—Biography. | Minorities in higher education—United States. |
 African American women in higher education—Social aspects. | Ethnology—
 Biographical methods. | Political science—Research.
Classification: LCC JA92 .D58 2025 | DDC 320.092/52—dc23/eng/20241023
LC record available at https://lccn.loc.gov/2024022299

Now to Him who is able to [carry out His purpose and] do superabundantly more than all that we dare ask or think [infinitely beyond our greatest prayers, hopes, or dreams], according to His power that is at work within us.

—Ephesians 3:20 AMP

Dedicated to Dad, Mom, Regina, Aiden, and my life partner, Rob

*In Loving Memory of Joshua Fitzgerald Warren
and Mrs. Vernon Maddox*

Contents

Foreword   xi
   Nikol G. Alexander-Floyd

Acknowledgments   xv

1. Introduction   1
   Angela K. Lewis-Maddox

2. She's Not a REAL Political Scientist   19
   Terri R. Jett

3. That's Not Political Science: Disrupting "Traditional" Political Science Inquiries   29
   Lakeyta M. Bonnette-Bailey

4. Setting Political Science to a Different Tune: Reflections on the Role of Black Women as Rhythm Disrupters   41
   Desireé R. Melonas

5. The Absence of Rational Resources: How a Black Woman's Presence Redefines the Discipline's Norms   55
   Sherice Janaye Nelson

6. Cultivating Joy in Academia   65
   Adaugo Pamela Nwakanma

7. The Impact of Active and Passive Representation in the Field of Public Administration: Lessons Learned and Best Practices 79
   Stephanie A. Pink-Harper

8. When the Discipline Disciplines: Stories of a Black Female Political Scientist 91
   Julia S. Jordan-Zachery

9. Transforming Political Science: Founding the Transnational Black Womxn Scholars of African Politics Research Network 109
   Tiffany Willoughby-Herard, T. D. Harper-Shipman, Kira Tait, Robin L. Turner, and Tara Jones

10. The Duality of Disruption: Black Women in Midwestern White Liberal Arts Institutions 147
    Clarissa Peterson

11. Truth Telling: The Limits of Institutional Liberalism, Neutrality, Objectivity, and Meritocracy 163
    Angela K. Lewis-Maddox

12. On Becoming a Black Woman Political Scientist: Rising to the Rank of Full Professor at a Major R1 Institution 187
    Evelyn M. Simien

13. Racial Discrimination and the Harassment of African American Women in Academia 213
    Sharon D. Wright Austin

14. A Black Unicorn in the Academe: A Testimonial of a Black Feminist Scholar in the Field of Political Science 225
    Caroline Shenaz Hossein

15. Journey of a Young Black Woman Political Scientist 251
    Lauhren Olivia McCoy

16. A Word of Advice to the Doctoral Sisters Who Just Graduated: Leave Hungry, Not Starving 261
    Ashley C. J. Daniels

| Contributors | 267 |
| Index | 277 |

Foreword

NIKOL G. ALEXANDER-FLOYD

Anyone concerned about the practice of and hope for democracy in the twenty-first century should seriously engage this work, *Disrupting Political Science: Black Women Re-Imagining the Discipline*, edited by Angela K. Lewis-Maddox. As the discipline most closely linked to formal political institutions on various levels of scale and dedicated to understanding the operation of power, political science not only deciphers but, indeed, reflects and aids in constructing, the US political system as we know it. This book, a stellar collection of essays written by Black women in political science, exposes how systemic forces, such as racism and sexism, have shaped political science as a discipline and reveals the paths, strategies, and organizing Black women have undertaken to diversify who can teach political science, challenge and reshape the organizations that uphold and direct the discipline, and expand our means of knowledge production and the very definition of what constitutes the political.

In her introduction, Lewis-Maddox recounts the critical features of political science as an intellectual and professional space, organizationally and within departments in the United States and beyond. From its inception, political science and its progenitors supported ideologies that were directly linked to white supremacy. As a relatively new discipline, compared to history and sociology, for instance, political science has lagged behind in terms of the entrance of white women and racial minorities into its ranks, a deficit that has lingered for more than a century. As Lewis-Maddox explains, despite some progress, the number of white women and racial minorities in political science continues to be out of step with their number relative to the US population, which is increasingly diverse, a point underscored by Diane Pinderhughes and Paula McClain, the only two Black women who have led the American Political Science Association, widely seen as the field's flagship organization.

Disrupting Political Science invites several points of inquiry. As Pinderhughes and McClain ask in the reports from the American Political Science Association task forces they led, what does it mean that a discipline dedicated to studying politics fails to represent the rich diversity found in the United States and globally in terms of race, gender, sexuality, class, and other markers of difference and bases for inequality (*Political Science in the Twenty-First Century*, 2011; *Systemic Inequalities in the Discipline*, 2021, respectively)? How has the introduction and advancement of Black women in particular revealed the fissures within democratic practice in the United States and elsewhere as reflected in the experiences and treatment of Black women? How have Black women, through their very presence in traditionally white male spaces and through their scholarly concerns, efforts at institutional change, and community engagement, challenged and changed political science as a discipline? What lessons are there to be learned from the stories of persistence, genius, and ingenuity represented in these pages, lessons that can aid not only those who walk in their footsteps in political science but all those concerned about the operation of power as it impacts knowledge production, institutions of higher learning, and society more broadly? The answers to these and other vital questions are generously and cogently provided by the Black women political scientists in this book.

All of these scholars, in essence, have been disruptive to the business as usual of academia in general and political science in particular. They have, in the words of civil rights icon and senator John Lewis, made "good trouble." Hailing from a variety of backgrounds, geographical locations, subfields, professional trajectories, and institutions, these disruptors, or good trouble makers, give us insight into our social and political lives, how our ideals of democracy, education, and social and political progress play out in the day-to-day lives of Black women as they interact with students, colleagues, administrators, and community members, and other public stakeholders. Although feminists and scholars of color, including Black women, have written about their journeys in academia (Linda Alcoff's *Singing in the Fire* [2003] and Deborah Gray White's *Telling Histories* [2008] come readily to mind for philosophy and history, respectively), the contributions of this volume are unique. Although there are sure to be parallels, unlike most of these other works, the majority of these Black women in *Disrupting Political Science* have come of age and/or developed professionally, not with the undergirding of active social movements but, rather, in the post-civil rights, postfeminist era, a time when many optimistically believed that racism and sexism were largely things of the past, marked by episodic occurrences of individual-level attitudes and actions. They have lived and labored in a time where they understand the difference between the rhetoric and reality of diversity, equity, and inclusion, and, building on the work done by previous generations of political scientists, such a Jewel Prestage, Mae King, Melanie Njeri Jackson, Diane Pinderhughes, Paula McClain, Kathie Stromile-Golden, Linda Williams, among others, have fashioned journeys that have exposed the ongoing institutional dimensions of oppression and made a way out of no way. These disruptors are examples of Black women political scientists who have built lifelines for themselves and others, nurturing networks and institutions for sustaining community, as they publish, teach, challenge and direct departments and campuses, and engage politically for themselves and their communities. If, as Angela Davis (*A Turbulent Voyage*, 2000, 87) states, survival is a "form of resistance . . . [and] a prerequisite for all higher levels of struggle," then these disruptors provide real-life examples of how to not only survive but thrive, not only with an eye toward oneself but also that of others, both now and for future generations.

To be sure, as a seasoned disruptor herself, Angela K. Lewis-Maddox was well situated to produce this work. Like many featured in this volume, Lewis-Maddox has been an advocate for diversifying the profession and promoting equity, bringing insight and ingenuity to the institutional spaces in which she has labored. Research-wise, she was prescient in understanding the significance of Black conservatives and Black conservatism. Although political scientists are now paying greater attention to Black conservatives in politics and the implications for Black conservatism ideologically, more generally, she was among a handful of people, such as Mack Jones and Tasha Philpot, who decades ago committed to an in-depth investigation of the aforementioned research agenda. Following on this important stream of research on Black conservatives, with *Disrupting Political Science*, Lewis-Maddox has produced a milestone in research on women and racial minorities in higher education. In addition to the aforementioned ways in which it is set apart, its use of autoethnography is unique and broadens and affirms a range of methods deemed a valid means of producing knowledge. In both its form and substance, thus,

Disrupting Political Science is a powerful gift, intellectually and politically, one that can fertilize and provide a model for more work on Black women and other minoritized groups in political science and beyond.

Acknowledgments

I affirm that each contributor to this project is worthy of every good thing life offers: rest, peace, joy, love, play, prosperity, and good health. I acknowledge that these honest and heart-wrenching accounts of their journey as students and then professors were not the most pleasant memories to recount. Some invited contributors could not bear the burden of telling their stories, while some authors had concerns about the legalities of their contributions and had to have them reviewed by legal counsel. I do not take it lightly that they shared their stories with me in this project. I express my deepest gratitude. The stories and views presented in this volume represent the respective authors, not the editor or the publisher.

This volume was born from an experience[1] that ultimately brought joy, transformation, and community. In May 2020, during the height of the COVID-19 pandemic, Donna Murch, PhD, associate professor of history at Rutgers University, and Crystal Hayes, PhD, postdoctoral scholar at the University of North Carolina Center of Excellence in Maternal and Child Health Education, Science and Practice, decided to send out a call for Black womxn in higher education to meet and write in community on Zoom. Thank you, Donna and Crystal. We met daily and shared trials, tribulations, and triumphs in our careers and personal lives. In this community, I discovered scholarship on my terms, and Julia Jordan-Zachery was instrumental in guiding me on that journey; thank you, Julia. Years after that initial meeting in May of 2020, we continue to write in community. Courtney Buggs, Danielle Cooper, Zophia Edwards, Deidre B. Flowers, Leta Hooper, and Julia Jordan-Zachery, there are no words to thank you all for what you mean to me.

I remember my initial meeting with the SUNY Black Women's Wellness Series Editor Stephanie Y. Evans. It was Stephanie's enthusiastic support and guidance that assured me that SUNY was the right home for this work. I also thank colleagues who participated in the Southern Political Science Association's annual meeting in Puerto Rico in 2020, Sharon Wright Austin, and Sherice Nelson, Linda Trautman, Duchess Harris, LaDella Levy, and Lisa Scott, who assisted in the early stages of this project before I knew this book would happen. Although we never met, Deborah Gray White, editor of *Telling Histories: Black Women Historians in the Ivory Tower*, provided a blueprint for this work for Black women in political science.

I would also like to thank numerous friends, including the moms of the Birmingham chapter of Jack and Jill of America, my sorority sisters of Delta Sigma Theta Sorority, Inc., and colleagues for their support. To Cedric and Lady Pollard, thank you for stepping in and providing meals, carpools, a warm bed, and much-needed joy during basketball season. To Coach Christopher Blanding, thank you for answering the call at a pivotal time. I would also like to mention the following individuals who made life a bit easier for me during this project: Shayvonne Prichett, Nancy Thomas, Haley Wilson, and Kendan Maddox. A special thank you is extended to my church family, Faith Chapel Christian Center in Birmingham, Alabama, the lead pastor, Michael K. Moore, and the founding pastor, Dr. Mike Moore.

I pay homage to numerous Black women scholars: bell hooks, Audrey Lorde, Brittney Cooper, Julia Jordan-Zachery, Nikol G. Alexander-Floyd, Diane Pinderhughes, Paula McClain, Mae King, Jewel Prestage, and Valeria Sinclair Chapman. I also mourn the loss of too many Black women in higher education: Joanne A. Epps of Temple University, Dr. Orinthia T. Montague of Volunteer State Community College, and Dr. Antoinette "Bonnie" Candia-Bailey of Lincoln University.

Compiling this volume came with the assistance of many individuals, some of whom I am sure I forgot to mention. Please know that I thank you for your love, support, care, meals, carpools, and everything. Wendy Gunther-Canada, thank you for being the best colleague, who is also a friend and my sister. Thank you to my sister, Regina Warren, for being my chef. Mom and Dad, thank you for your unwavering support and love. Finally, to my son, Aiden Lewis Wilson, who has grown up to be a fine young man, your mom is proud of you. Being your mother has taught me balance. You are a wise young man, and I am so glad God chose you to be my son. And my husband, friend, life partner, and biggest fan, Keith "Rob" Maddox, thank you!

Note

1. For more information, see A. K. Lewis-Maddox, "Black Women, Just BREATHE . . . : Personal Healing during 'the Rona,'" in *Lavender Fields: Black Women Experiencing Fear, Agency, and Hope in the Time of COVID-19*, ed. Julia S. Jordan-Zachery (Tucson: University of Arizona Press, 2023), 174–89.

1

Introduction

Angela K. Lewis-Maddox

Space invaders, individuals who occupy spaces where they do not belong, composed this book. They do not appear to belong in the space they occupy, so they are treated differently from those who seem to belong. Can someone exist in a space they invaded? If so, how and for how long? Black women political scientists are space invaders because they fall outside political science norms (Alexander-Floyd 2015). In an academic discipline that is overwhelmingly white and male, Black women's presence disrupts the field's homogeneity. If you ask a Black woman political scientist about her experiences inside and outside the classroom, you will discover that she is beset by acts of bias against what she teaches, how she teaches, what she chooses to research, and how she conducts research. Ultimately, a Black woman's ability to be successful as a political science professor is influenced by the hegemonic demands of the discipline. These demands often do not include the study of Black women as political subjects (Alexander-Floyd 2018) or the use of pedagogical styles of Black women professors.

Despite this positioning as space invaders, Black women professors create spaces that challenge the status quo within political science by exposing truths about the discipline's origin, politics, and government. Black women political scientists bring an alternative perspective to the discipline by doing political science differently, thereby adding to the relevance of political science as an academic discipline. This volume examines Black women's unique experiences and contributions to the discipline and acts as a catalyst to help transform and reimagine the discipline by centering Black women as political subjects. It also shares success stories of Black women political scientists who practice creative resistance and self-care while navigating the hegemonic demands of the academic discipline.

What is political science? What is the nature of the work of political science professors? "Political science is about the scientific study of political phenomena" (Kellstedt and Whitten 2018, 1) or the study of politics. Inherent to politics is power, an ambiguous and difficult concept to define. However, scholars agree that power means that A has influence over B to get B to do something they would otherwise not do (Walton and Smith 2000). In short, political scientists study power within government and society. The heart and soul of political science is "the study of who wins and who loses in public policy" (APSA 2011, 38). Thus, political science professors teach about politics, power, governments, and public policy. Traditionally, as an academic discipline, political science has been divided into several subfields, including American government, political theory, international politics, comparative politics, research methodology, and public administration. More recently, there have been variations to the subdivision of the academic discipline, but most of the work of political scientists falls into these categories.

Marginalization in the Discipline

Professional associations support the development of the discipline and individuals within the field by disseminating research, networking, and serving to recruit new faculty. The oldest political science association in America, the American Political Science Association (APSA), was set up in 1903. The International Political Science Association (IPSA) was formed in 1949, seeking to connect scholars globally. The National Conference of Black Political Scientists (NCOBPS) started in 1969 as an organization to address problems faced by Black political scientists in the United States. The Association for the Study of Black Women in Politics (ASBWP), formed in 2008, promotes research in the United States and across the globe. There are also other regional political science associations in the United States, such as the Southern Political Science Association and the Midwest Political Science Association. Political scientists worldwide support associations where, in most, a president and a council govern.

White men led as president for the first fifty years of APSA's existence. In 1953, Ralphe Bunche was the first Black American elected president. The first woman, Judith Shklar, was elected president in 1989. It would take over 100 years before APSA elected Dianne Pinderhughes from the University of Notre Dame—the first Black woman political scientist—as president, in 2007. Since then, only one Black woman, Paula McClain, has led the association, from 2019 to 2020. As for IPSA, in 1991, forty-two years after its founding, the international association elected a woman, Carole Pateman, as president. No Black men have led IPSA. Pinderhughes would go on to lead IPSA in 2021 as the first Black woman president, seventy-two years after the association was founded.

Pinderhughes's presidential address to APSA occurred the same night as the Democratic nominee for president, then-senator Barack Obama, the first Black American nominee (and later the first Black president), spoke at the Democratic National Convention in Denver, Colorado. She said that she struggled with the extent to which race would be discussed in her address, considering the historic moment. Pinderhughes notes that only three APSA presidents mentioned race in their official address to the association. In her analysis of presidential addresses, using a broad definition of race, which would include slavery, abolition, or race, only 27.6 percent of the presidents mentioned race. The discussions were not complex, and they only touched on race in passing. Moreover, of the 103 addresses, only 5 percent had complex or deep discussions of race. Pinderhughes also pointed out that political science as an academic field has failed to adequately discuss and infuse its study with fundamental questions about race and American democracy (Pinderhughes 2009).

Political science as an academic discipline "has never viewed the study of race as important"

In 2019, the second Black woman, Paula McClain, would lead the APSA as president at the association's first virtual meeting. Her presidency coincided with several historical events that highlighted race in America: the COVID-19 pandemic and the murders of George Floyd in Minneapolis, Ahmad Arbery in Georgia, and Breonna Taylor in Louisville. McClain tackled the race topic head on in her address to the association, eloquently laying out how racial and ethnic minorities have been convenient scapegoats for US society, which blames Black Americans and other racial and ethnic minorities for crises. Most remarkably, African Americans were blamed for slavery instead of questioning the moral responsibility of those who enslaved them. And in the 1980s several US agencies scapegoated Haitians for HIV and, more recently, blamed the COVID-19 pandemic on Asians and Asian Americans.

McClain detailed how John W. Burgess considered the founder of political science as a field of study and, as former president of APSA (1921–1922), viewed Blacks as an inferior race and saw slavery as a positive institution. The first political science journal, *Political Science Quarterly*, helped to perpetuate this view, as Burgess served as an editor. McClain showed that the negative view of Blacks and the justification of slavery and segregation continued in the journal until at least 1907. Although W. E. B. DuBois and other scholars critiqued Burgess's views and the overall direction of political science, the tone of the discipline had already been established.

The APSA presidential addresses are not representative of the entire work of the discipline. They represent one point in time, influenced by the area of expertise of the scholar elected as president. However, the lack of discussions about race in presidential addresses is demonstrative of McClain's claim in her address that political science as a discipline "has never viewed the study of race as important" (McClain 2021, 12).

If the discipline does not view the study of race as important, how do professors address race in political science classrooms? Is race mentioned, or is it swept under the rug? Or a better question, in an academic field that ignores, minimizes, and marginalizes discussions of race, is how do those who have been scapegoated face the challenges of teaching race and ethnicity?

Although McClain (2021) does not mention how America scapegoats Black women specifically, Mae King (1975), in her seminal work on Black women in the American political system, analyzes how the United States does this to Black women using caste systems, stereotypes, and myths. Of particular interest to this collection are two assertions by King. The first is that race in America is based on a caste system that places people classified as white in a position of power, with opportunities for status and privilege, and those who are not white in a less powerful position with much less opportunity for status and privilege. She extends her assertion by stating that Black female stereotypes are "indispensable to the maintenance" of the caste system (King 1973, 2). These stereotypes are based on exaggerated beliefs and are utilized to rationalize and justify oppression.

King suggests three stereotypes of Black women: "the nonfeminist," "the loser image," and the "depreciated sex object." The nonfeminist is demonstrative of the matriarchal head of the household—hardworking, tough, and strong. This image is antithetical to the traditional "American femininity" or a "delicate" image of white women (King 1975, 121). There are numerous implications of this stereotype of Black women, including the demasculation of Black men, the exploitation of Black women in the workforce, and the defeminization of Black women. As such, violence against Black women usually fails to generate public outcry. The loser image serves to stifle the "self-esteem, respect and aspirations of the [B]lack woman" (King 1973, 19). This image is designed to reduce the possibility of Black women aspiring to move beyond what society deems is her place. King provides examples of Black women "in their place" as happy, but when they attempt to transcend their place, they have tragic endings. There is also an "invisible orientation" toward Black women, an intentional disregard for discrimination against them. This invisibility leads to a lack of laws protecting Black women and a failure of society to notice violence against Black women. Finally, the depreciated sex object stereotype King asserts is tied to interracial marriage, which President Abraham Lincoln relates to power. This stereotype frees white males from any emotional ties due to sexual contact with Black women such that marriage to the Black woman and thus the conferring of "respect, dignity, and responsibilities" that come with marriage becomes unlikely. In short, stereotypes work in conjunction with caste systems to limit the social mobility of Black women.

Scapegoating and stereotypes are integral to the US political system and to political science. The primary goal of political science is to maintain both a power and a caste system that excludes Black women (Alexander-Floyd 2018; Jones 1977; King 1973, 1975). In short, if one considers the history of political science as an academic discipline along with the lack of Black women as political subjects, Alexander-Floyd (2018) argues that political science is seen as the discipline for white males. Considering McClain's (2021), King's (1973, 1975), and Alexander-Floyd's (2018) work, I believe that the foundation of the academic discipline of political science is also set up as a caste system. This caste system places white men and how they obtain and disseminate knowledge at the top. The discipline has attempted, albeit somewhat unsuccessfully, to freeze everyone else at the bottom or at least in a position of less importance. This freezing out could be through admission to political science graduate programs, departmental funding for graduate students, job placements, publications, the granting of tenure, promotion to full professor, and leadership in associations, programs, and departments. As a result, political science has been and continues to be a white male-dominated field.

Despite scapegoating, stereotypes, and caste systems within the discipline, it is essential to note the impact Black women have had on political science, even though that influence is often marginalized. For both APSA and IPSA, over a century passed before a Black woman was elected to lead the organizations. Unlike mainstream political science associations, however, not only was a Black woman integral to establishing the path that led to the formation of the NCOBPS, but less than a decade after its founding, the same Black woman political scientist, the late Jewel Prestage, became president. Prestage convened the historic meeting of Black political scientists from historically Black colleges and universities on the campus of Southern University in Baton Rouge, Louisiana, in 1969. The conference, funded by both APSA and the Ford Foundation, produced a report, referred to as the *Prestage Report*, concluding that "the discipline simply had failed to illuminate adequately those aspects of politics that are of most interest to America's out-groups" (Alexander-Floyd et al. 2015, 319). Attendees at the meeting would later form a Black caucus, separate from APSA, and present their demands to APSA. Among the demands from the *Prestage Report* is "the need for the discipline to consider the study of Black politics as a legitimate subfield" (Alexander-Floyd et al. 2015, 319). The report also recommended that APSA provide funding support for Black faculty research and that the association end relationships with entities that discriminate against Blacks (McCormick 2011).

Despite efforts to present the demands to APSA, there were differences among the political scientists who met in Baton Rouge. While some wanted to make demands, others were uneasy with the possible confrontation. And yet others did not believe the Black caucus should prioritize "making 'demands' on white folks" (McCormick 2011, 176). Ultimately, caucus members founded NCOBPS "on the belief that Black scholars face unique challenges that require a dedicated space to engage with those who share their lived experiences and their scholarly commitments" (Alexander-Floyd et al. 2015, 320). Inherent in NCOBPS's founding is the "dominant emphasis on race," which, although appropriate at the time, did not give serious attention to intraracial differences such as gender, class, and location (McCormick 2011, 169). Thus, in 2004, two Black women political scientists, Nikol G. Alexander-Floyd and Rose M. Harris, laid the groundwork to establish the ASBWP, established to encourage and professionally develop Black women political scientists, and to promote the development of scholarship on Black women within political science.

APSA Task Force Reports Addressing Race and Gender

Pinderhughes and McClain both commissioned task force reports to discuss the academic discipline of political science regarding race, ethnicity, and diversity. "Political Science in the 21st Century," commissioned by President Dianne Pinderhughes, deals with the diversity of society and whether political science is positioned to embrace that diversity in its research, teaching, and professional development. The report commissioned by Paula McClain, "Systemic Inequalities in the Discipline," discusses how systems within the discipline impact career trajectories, especially those of marginalized groups. Both reports made a list of recommendations, some of which are related to this volume.

"Political Science in the 21st Century" (2011) provided recommendations in the areas of research, teaching and pedagogy, and access and inclusion. An abbreviated list of the most important recommendations related to this volume are included below:

- Political scientists need to be more intentional and systematic in using APSA to develop training programs to encourage and support students from a broader range of backgrounds to consider political science as a profession and to complete graduate training in political science. (2)

- Departments should be more inclusive of the types of journals valued in the assessment of scholarly productivity. (2)

- Diversity, inclusiveness, and inequality should be incorporated as categories of analysis that inform each unit of study rather than be seen as a separate or supplementary unit in the curriculum. (3)

- Political science faculty should be encouraged to actively engage in the process of deliberation/self-reflection by questioning their own assumptions and exploring their own views regarding diversity, inclusiveness, and inequality. Such self-assessment can serve as a model for students to follow. (3)

- Baseline demographic longitudinal data of all political scientists in the profession should be maintained to track changes in faculty by race, ethnicity, and gender. A specific number of workshops on best practices for recruitment and retention strategies of diverse faculty that are targeted specifically to department chairs need to be developed. (4)

"Systemic Inequalities in the Discipline" (2021) focused on tenure and promotion, citation practices, graduate training and experiences, and climate issues:

- APSA should develop and launch a major quantitative and qualitative longitudinal data project that will track the development of differently positioned and structurally marginalized faculty over at least a ten-year period to record who exits the discipline and academy, who is promoted with tenure or to full [sic], whose promotion is denied, and the degree to which other factors enhance one's chances for promotion. (6)
- Departments should engage in an equity evaluation of the components of their tenure process and criteria, with a focus on identifying any explicit or imbedded biases that systemically disadvantage some faculty over others. The results of the equity evaluation should be posted on departmental websites so all in the department have access to the results. (6)
- Departments should regularly conduct a climate evaluation to monitor and track resource allocation, perceived hostility and collegiality, and who is being invited for lectures and workshops through the department and subfields. Departments should establish an equity and inclusion committee, including representatives of all subfields and ranks in the department, to review and make public recommendations based on the data from the climate evaluation. (6)
- While women researchers have received the majority of attention with regard to examining citation biases, such examinations should also dedicate more attention to other researchers such as persons of color and LGBTQ scholars, and conduct more detailed examination as to the extent and nature of biases. (6)

"Political Science in the 21st Century" reports that political science as an academic field continues to be demographically homogenous. While the population of college students has reached some level of diversification, the demographics of political science faculty have only slowly changed. For example, in 1980, 96.4 percent of political scientists were white, and in 2010, 88.9 percent were white. An overwhelming majority of professors, nearly 90 percent of all political science professors, are white and 71.4 percent are men. Less than a third of political science faculty, only 28.6 percent, are women. Suffice it to say, most students who enter a political science course will have a white male professor. When reviewing the data by gender, the numbers are nearly the same. In 1980, 93.4 percent of all women political science professors were white. By 2010, the number of whites had only decreased to 86.6 percent.

Reviewing the number of Black women political scientists who are members of APSA, we find the numbers steady but low between 2016 and 2021. In 2016, Black women comprised 1.93 percent of all association members. By 2022, that number had only increased to 1.98 percent. Considering the homogenous nature of the professoriate in 2010, the report stated that political science "may not be sufficiently prepared for the future, as political scientists work in increasingly multicultural and interdependent nation-states" (APSA 2011, 6). The lack of diversity in the political science professoriate and in the approaches to teaching the discipline severely limit political scientists' ability to be truthful about politics and government or the legacies of the discipline. Alexander-Floyd (2015) notes that a survey of departments completed in her study from Alexander-Floyd (2008) found fifty-eight Black women at the associate level and nineteen at the level of full professor in political science departments in the United States.

In addition, I suspect that the institutional violence that occurs in other predominantly male-dominated fields is probably much the same in political science. Cueva states that "Institutional violence is a type of microaggression relating to the effects of racism and race-based trauma that produces psychological and physiological consequences particularly to women's bodies, minds, health, and quality of life in the academy" (2014, 144). The very nature of the field of political science, one that explains the dynamics of power and often the practice of the area, lends itself to a particular kind of power play that perpetuates the subjugation of Black women. For example, Richards (2019) discusses how student evaluations of teaching are used as a form of gendered racial oppression and how students and colleagues serve as "coconspirators" in an oppressive system that privileges whiteness (137). Evaluations are used as "mechanisms of racialized social control" in a situation in which "student evaluations may influence whether we are (re)hired, tenured, or promoted" (138). When Black women professors do not meet the stereotypical expectations of students or when their communication style is direct and straightforward, students label and evaluate the Black woman professor as "mean," "uncaring," or rude. Wallace, Lewis, and Allen (2019) confirm that student evaluations of teaching within political science suggest gender and racial bias. Their research shows that students made comments about professors' competence and professionalism that contained elements of retaliation. Specifically, for faculty women of color, students made more connections to personality, style, and cultural habits than they did with other faculty. They conclude that "comments, assigned to women and faculty of color, tend to suggest overt or stereotypical connotations and tend to be more derogatory and damaging" (Wallace, Lewis, and Allen 2019, 9).

Academic violence is occurring in political science against the historic all-woman editorial board of the *American Political Science Review* (APSR), one of the top-ranking journals in the academic discipline. In July 2019, the journal released the names of its new editorial team (APSA 2019). For the first time in the association's history, the editorial team comprises all women editors. Several are from underrepresented groups; two are Black women. The press release provides a statement from the editors, followed by comments from then-APSA president Rogers Smith and Executive Director Steven Rathgeb Smith. The press release encourages comments.

It took less than a week for the comments to be closed. After the first three comments, the remaining eight were negative, questioning the team's diversity and asking where the men were. The last comment stated simply, "Pathetic." A political science blog addressed the announcement of the all-women editorial team, further demonstrating the existence of a caste system in political science. The blog contains numerous attacks, from individuals with female names questioning the new editorial team's competence and their approach to leading the journal. Although the comments are from individuals with female names, there is no way to know if the individuals commenting are actually women. An overarching theme on the blog site is that the journal's rigor and ranking will suffer. One comment even goes so far as to urge others to discontinue their membership in APSA. Another states, "I was skeptical when the board was announced. But never imagined it would go down so fast" a comment from someone labeled as Annmarie (Political Science Rumors).

Here are some other comments on the blog site:

Wow. APSR to toilet. What can be done? How can intelligent people retake control? Maggie (Political Science Rumors)

I will be interested to seeing the impact factor of APSR in a year or so. If it goes down, they will probably drop the team. Isn't that what happened at the JOP? Mary (Political Science Rumors)

The process of selecting journal editors is not rocket science. I have served on a handful of journal editor selection committees, and there are usually professional teams comprised of scholars with strong scholarly credentials and reputations for good scholarly judgment for search committee members to consider. If a search committee is lucky, you might have two (or maybe three) highly qualified editorial teams that you could reasonably see as editing the journal in question. In such a case it is a matter of selecting from among two or three competitive editorial teams. One can't go wrong in such cases.

This was not the case with the most recent APSR editorial search. There was one editorial team that was a no-brainer choice—this was the Gerring team. No reasonable committee members applying widely accepted scholarly standards could have come up with any other choice. The only way that the current team could have been selected is if the search committee set aside rigorous scholarly criteria and substituted nonscholarly (political, diversity) criteria instead. This is what happened in this case, and the APSR is making a good run at losing its reputation for publishing top-notch scholarly research. I now look elsewhere for the best research in political science. Darrin (Political Science Rumors)

Ugh my life. I h8te the REP crowd for inflicting this upon us. Alysha (Political Science Rumors)

The last comment refers to the APSA Race, Ethnicity, and Politics (REP) section, founded in 1995. REP members, those interested in studying or teaching race or ethnicity, make up one of the largest subfields in the association. The blog site's overarching theme, however, was focused on the all-woman editorial board. For women political scientists, there is the Women, Gender and Politics section, founded in 1986. Organized sections of the Association provide groups of APSA members with a common interest "to organize meetings and coordinate communications under Association auspices" (APSA website). These sections offer opportunities for networking and publications and recognition for members.

Space Invaders

For Black women political scientists, there are no groups affiliated with APSA. Alexander-Floyd (2015) refers to Black women as "space invaders" because they are outside the "somatic norms" of political science. Although her reference to Black women focused on Black women political science professors, those who study Black women as research subjects would also be outside the norms of the discipline. Reviewing how political science journals treated Black women as research subjects from 2006 to 2010, Jordan-Zachary finds a scarcity of articles centering Black women, or those manuscripts where "Black women are the singular focus" (2018, 37). Two journals included in the analysis were *APSR* and the *Journal of Politics* (*JOP*), top-ranking journals within the discipline. Both journals were "apt not to publish research on Black women as singular research" and "tended not to include articles within which Black women are treated as singular research subjects" (39). Thus, for Black women researching Black women, "the omission of Black women among published articles sends the message that such research is not valued and, as such, should not be pursued" (39).

Furthermore, because Black women political scientists are "space invaders," they are evaluated more harshly than those who fit the traditional gender and race norms of the field. Utilizing critical race Black feminism—which understands that social characteristics like race and gender are not separate and hierarchical factors impacting oppression but rather work in tandem—Alexander-Floyd argues that while descriptive forms of representation are essential in the political science profession, "if taken as a point of closure, [they] can leave institutional patterns and practices of discrimination insufficiently challenged" (2015, 464). In other words, formal equality or descriptive representation gets a faculty member into the institution. What happens once they are present is substantive equality or how underrepresented groups experience institutions. Although they may appear to be treated fairly, when Black women enter political science departments, they are outside the norm and are thus unsettling to the environment, particularly for white men. They are invisible but also hypervisible because they are flaunted as being representative of the diversity within the department or the institution. They are invisible to the extent that the normative structures in place would have them believe and would judge their work as not ever being good enough. And they may internalize this perception and "overfunction" (Rockquemore and Laszloffy 2009). Even those who have climbed the ranks in the professoriate and have become full professors or leaders may remain stifled by these burdens of doubt and representation. The result of these experiences leads to suffering and an impact on health, and it saps time and creativity that could be used for further advancing Black women.

Despite the difficult positioning of Black women political science professors as space invaders, there are attempts to create space in professional associations and research outlets. Most political science associations have groups that focus on race, gender, and ethnicity; they also have journals devoted to publishing research on these topics. Moreover, several associations have status committees for Blacks and women within their governing structure, such as the REP and Women Gender and Politics Research section in APSA. However, a cursory review of political science associations' websites found no groups, caucuses, or spaces designated specifically for Black women political scientists. For this reason, Wendy Smooth, former NCOBPS president, set up the Black Women's Initiative in 2013, which formally affiliated the ASBWP with NCOBPS between 2014 and 2015. In addition to the work of Black women political scientists and trailblazers such as Jewell Prestage (1991, 1977) and Mae King (1973), there are resources available to Black women in political science. Among them are several edited volumes, special journal symposiums, and spaces created by the ABSWP and NCOBPS at annual meetings (see Jordan-Zachery and Alexander-Floyd 2018). Most notably, NCOBPS president Tiffany Willoughby-Herard set up the first space exclusive to Black women political scientists at the first national conference of the ASBWP, "Scandal in Real Time," in 2016.

Notwithstanding these developments, we have yet to see work that addresses the experiences of Black women academics in political science. Although the demographics in the political science professoriate are slowly changing, it is imperative that the experiences of Black women be documented and shared. The impact of Black women's invisibility and hypervisibility has been written about in academia generally and in history, business, law, and medicine (White 1985). It is time to document their experiences in political science. Although political science has a steady pace of work centering Black women, this volume captures the experiences of those who teach and do research in political science.

The Conceptualization of this Volume

This work is meant to be disruptive and transformative and has allowed me to reimagine political science as a profession. Yes, it explores diverse voices within political science by sharing narratives from Black women professors and scholars in political science at different institutions, but it does so much more. After twenty years as a political science professor, I was at a crossroads where I was forced to choose a different career path than I had intended. I write about this in *Lavender Fields*, because it happened during the early stages of the COVID-19 pandemic (Lewis-Maddox 2023). I mention this here because the idea of this volume came during my time with a Black feminist writing group that introduced me to the works of Black feminists like Audrey Lorde and bell hooks. Their works sent me to the works of contemporary Black female political scientists like Alexander-Floyd, Simien, and Jordan-Zachery. They helped me find a renewed interest in academic scholarship within political science. I was also introduced to the work of Black women historians who wrote a volume about their personal stories in institutionalizing African American women's history (White 2008). These experiences provided me with a unique perspective of scholarly activity that led to my desire to bring this volume together and think about how to contribute to Black women's academic work within political science.

This volume centers on Black women political science professors using autoethnography, which is described by Durham as "a spiritual act of political self-determination, of reclamation" (2017, 23). It is divided into two sections. The first section provides information from a holistic perspective of the discipline, while the second has more individualized stories of Black women professors. These stories document Black women's experiences across institutions, regions, age, and identities. The contributors to this volume have faced both hypervisibility and invisibility as space invaders. Yet despite our positioning as space invaders, we work diligently to transform the discipline.

Several contributors discuss how they were doubted/distrusted as political scientists because of what they chose to study. Now a full professor, the author in Chapter 2 says that she was accused of not being a "real" political scientist. Jett has been in the field for over two decades. Bonnette-Bailey, who received her degree many years later, notes that her choice to study hip-hop and politics was queried by numerous professors while she was writing her dissertation. Melonas's contribution suggests that political science has a certain rhythm and that Black women working in the field have a different and more nuanced way of teaching and researching and conceptualizing the community. Nelson complements Melonas' chapter by discussing how the lack of resources among Black women causes others to question their work. However, despite how the field may or may not accept our work, author Nwakanma is on a quest to find joy. Pink-Harper discusses the nationwide conversation over how the current first lady of the United States, Dr. Jill Biden, was asked to remove the title "Doctor" from her name. She proceeds to explore best practices for institutions to support Black women public administration scholars. The first section of the volume is closed out by two authors providing a clear pathway for Black women scholars. Jordan-Zachary produces a stream of knowledge that grounds her resistance to race-gendered violence in political science, while simultaneously creating a Black Girl Blueprint to exist, heal, and be whole as a political science professor. At the same time, Willoughby-Herard and coauthors Harper-Shipman, Tait, Turner, and Jones, discuss the successful formation of a research network for Black women scholars studying African politics.

In the second section of the book, Peterson, Lewis-Maddox, Hossein, Simien, and Wright-Austin discuss their distinct experiences. Peterson invokes the angry Black woman mantra imposed upon her by colleagues, and explores how she continues to overcome the disruption her presence brought to the department and the institution. Lewis-Maddox echoes the sentiments of Nelson in her discussion of becoming a full professor and having her work as a Black scholar minimized. Hossein, a tenured professor, discusses how her nontraditional pathway led to her success in the field, despite having to endure anti-Blackness in Canada. Simien details her experience of rising to full professor in political science while highlighting how a father-daughter relationship influenced her trajectory in a predominantly white male profession. Wright-Austin describes her experience of isolation, discrimination, harassment, and bullying at various institutions. Despite these obstacles, Peterson, Lewis-Maddox, Simien, and Wright-Austin have become full professors, along with contributors Jordan-Zachary and Jett.

We close the book with contributions from recent graduates in political science. One, Daniels, graduated from a doctoral program, and the other, McCoy, from an undergraduate program. Closing with the recent graduates provides insight into Black women students' challenges as they choose to study political science on both the graduate and undergraduate levels. McCoy's perspective considers how professors use instruction to disrupt and reimagine the discipline, depending on where they are in their careers and what impact that decision has on students. Daniels offers a letter to Black women political science graduate students who are wondering what steps to take after graduation, considering the many options before them.

It was important to close the book with the two contributors most affected by the presence or lack of Black women political scientists. As space invaders, we know that what we do and how we do it changes the narrative, disrupts the status quo, and brings truth that is long overdue in the discipline. Moreover, the inclusion of Black women as political subjects serves to expand discussions of power, politics, and policy in ways to forever change the trajectory of political science. We do not offer recommendations for the discipline here because both Black women APSA presidents have provided important recommendations. We do, however, endorse these recommendations and urge political scientists to consider their policy's impact on the well-being of space invaders.

References

Alexander-Floyd, N. G. 2008. "Written, Published . . . Cross-Indexed, and Footnoted." *PS: Political Science and Politics* 41, no. 4: 819–29.

———. 2015. "Women of Color, Space Invaders, and Political Science: Practical Strategies for Transforming Institutional Practices." *PS: Political Science and Politics* 48, no. 3: 464–68.

———. 2018. "Why Political Scientists Don't Study Black Women, but Historians and Sociologists Do: On Intersectionality and the Remapping of the

Study of Black Political Women." In *Black Women in Politics: Demanding Citizenship, Challenging Power*, edited by J. S. Jordan-Zachery and N. G. Alexander-Floyd, 5–26. New York: State University of New York.

American Political Science Association [APSA]. 2011. "Political Science in the 21st Century," Report of the Task Force on Political Science in the 21st Century. https://www.apsanet.org/portals/54/Files/Task%20Force%20Reports/TF_21st%20Century_AllPgs_webres90.pdf.

———. 2019. APSA Announces the New Editorial Team for the *American Political Science Review*. July 26. https://politicalsciencenow.com/apsa-announces-the-new-editorial-team-for-the-american-political-science-review/#comments.

———. 2021. APSA Presidential Task Force on Systemic Inequalities in the Discipline Executive Summary. https://www.apsanet.org/Portals/54/APSA%20Presidential%20Task%20Force%20Executive%20Summary%202021[26043].pdf?ver=4Ytshg9N8KK2KWfpu4QSlg%3d%3d.

———. APSA Section on Race, Ethnicity, and Politics about Us. https://www.apsanet.org/section33

———. Organized Sections. https://www.apsanet.org/sections.

Association for the Study of Black Women in Politics. http://www.asbwp.org/index.html.

Cueva, B. M. 2014. "Institutional Academic Violence: Racial and Gendered Microaggressions in Higher Education." *Chicana/Latina Studies* 13, no. 2: 142–168. http://www.jstor.org/stable/43941436

Durham, A. 2017. "On Collards." *International Review of Qualitative Research* 10, no. 1: 22–23. https://www.jstor.org/stable/26372232.

Githens, M. and Prestage, J. 1977. *A Portrait of Marginality: the Political Behavior of the American Woman*. New York: McKay.

Jordan-Zachery, J. S. 2018. " 'I ain't your darn help': Black Women as the Help in Intersectionality Research in Political Science." In *Black Women in Politics: Demanding Citizenship, Challenging Power*, edited by J. S. Jordan-Zachery and N. G. Alexander-Floyd, 27–43. New York: State University of New York.

Jordan-Zachery, J. S., and N. G. Alexander-Floyd. 2018. "Black Women's Political Labor: An Introduction." In *Black Women in Politics: Demanding Citizenship, Challenging Power*, edited by J. S. Jordan-Zachery and N. G. Alexander-Floyd, 27–43. Albany: State University of New York.

Kellstedt, P. M., and G. D. Whitten. 2018. *The Fundamentals of Political Science Research*. 3rd ed. Cambridge, UK: Cambridge University Press.

King, M. C. 1973. "The Politics of Sexual Stereotypes." *Black Scholar* 46, no. 7: 12–23. http://www.jstor.org/stable/41163792.

———. 1975. "Oppression and Power: The Unique Status of the Black Woman in the American Political System." *Social Science Quarterly* 56, no. 1: 116–28. http://www.jstor.org/stable/42859475.

Lewis-Maddox, A. K. 2023. "Black Women, Just BREATHE . . . Personal Healing During 'The Rona.'" In *Lavender Fields: Black Women Experiencing Fear, Agency, and Hope in the Time of COVID-19,* edited by J. Jordan-Zachery, 174–89. Tucson: University of Arizona Press.

McClain. 2021. "Crises, Race, Acknowledgement: The Centrality of Race, Ethnicity, and Politics to the Future of Political Science." *Perspectives on Politics* 19, no. 1: 7–18. https://doi.org/10.1017/S1537592720004478.

McCormick, J. 2011. "Beyond Tactical Withdrawal: An Early History of the National Conference of Black Political Scientists." *National Political Science Review* 13: 158–79.

Pinderhughes, D. 2009. "Presidential Address: The Challenge of Democracy: Explorations in American Racial Politics." *Perspectives on Politics* 7, no. 1: 3–11. www.jstor.org/stable/40407208.

Political Science Rumors. https://www.poliscirumors.com/topic/another-doozy-in-the-apsr.

Prestage, J. L. 1991. "In Quest of African American Political Woman." *ANNALS of the American Academy of Political and Social Science* 515, no. 1: 88–103. https://doi.org/10.1177/0002716291515001008.

Richards, B. 2019. "Faculty Assessments as Tools of Oppression: A Black Woman's Reflections on Color-Blind Racism in the Academy." In *Intersectionality and Higher Education: Identity and Inequality on College Campuses,* edited by W. C. Byrd, R. J. Brunn-Bevel, and S. M. Ovink, 136–52. New Brunswick, NJ: Rutgers University Press.

Rockquemore, K. and T. Laszloffy. 2008. *The Black Academic's Guide to Winning Tenure—without Losing Your Soul.* Boulder, CO: Lynne Rienner Publishers.

Wallace, S. L., A. K. Lewis, and M. D. Allen. 2019. "The State of the Literature on Student Evaluations of Teaching and an Exploratory Analysis of Written Comments: Who Benefits Most?" *College Teaching* 67, no. 1: 1–14. https://doi-org.ezproxy3.lhl.uab.edu/10.1080/87567555.2018.1483317.

Walton, H., and R. C. Smith. 2000. *American Politics and the African American Quest for Universal Freedom.* New York: Longman.

White, D. G. 2008. *Telling Histories: Black Women Historians in the Ivory Tower.* Chapel Hill: University of North Carolina Press.

2

She's Not a REAL Political Scientist

Terri R. Jett

My relationship to the discipline of political science is personal in the same manner that my pursuit of a career in academia was situated in my personal needs alongside my professional aspirations. I pursued a PhD to secure a career that would allow me flexibility and provide conditions where I could still have a real presence in the life of my children. At the time I was a divorcing mother of two young children; however, the idea of a flexible career that allowed a degree of freedom was something I thought about before I became a mother. The discipline of political science and more so the specialty areas of public policy and policy implementation fit a curiosity that I carried from a childhood experience of catching a big yellow bus to elementary school every day. Being bused created a nagging desire to understand the decision-making process of federal legislation and court decisions that directly affected people of color, specifically a young Black girl. Even though I was forging my place in this particular discipline because I was approaching it from a more intersectional lens, I did not think about the idea that I would be called a "political scientist." I was simply embracing the vision of myself as a scholar-activist, and the discipline of choice was more about the tools and the approach to my work. I had so many other factors shaping my identity that the notion of someone labeling me in that way was not that critical until I heard someone say that I had been discussed as not being a "real political scientist." It wasn't the first time I heard something to that effect, but I found it a bit humorous since at the time I was a tenured associate professor and had even served as a political science department chair. Considering my work both within and outside of the institutional structure of academia, I would argue that I am very much a "political scientist" in theory and in practice.

I was encouraged to pursue a PhD by a group of faculty members in the Ethnic Studies Department, especially Dr. Barbara Paige-Pointer, who modeled for me what it meant to be an intellectual or scholar-activist. Working in the department allowed me to view an environment of which I did not receive a lot of information about from my own family. My mother went to Kaiser Nursing School after high school and pursued her bachelor's and master's degrees while she was well into her career as a nurse and my father went to a community college and worked for the US Postal Service and then as an accountant, so they did not pass on much information about four-year colleges and universities. I was encouraged to pursue higher education as the path of liberation through financial stability so my experience as an undergraduate was actually shaped by profound struggle learning to navigate the institution, but it was ultimately rewarding. And having the fullness of understanding of the sacrifices that my maternal and paternal grandparents had made as they had migrated from the South to the West in search of better economic opportunities and to escape the overt racist hostility that they faced was also my motivation to do better. I think many people forget that we are not that many generations descended from the Great Migration of thousands of Black families, including my own, and successive generations carry an obligation to build upon the pain, loss, and sacrifices that were at the heart of that disruption of roots.

As a child growing up in Richmond, California, I was bused to school, and that left a deep mark on my psyche because even as a child I knew that there was a political decision behind my not being able to attend the elementary school that was around the corner from my house. That school was named Martin Luther King Jr. Elementary School. It was a curiosity for me that I had to go to a school some distance away from my neighborhood to a very wealthy predominantly white neighborhood in the hills in order to get a decent education, Kensington Elementary School. I remember asking my mother why I couldn't go to the school in my neighborhood with my friends and she said that I had "tested out" of the school. I don't recall taking a test, but what I do recall is thinking that if that was supposed to be a good thing, "testing out" of one's neighborhood school, it didn't feel very good. The sting of the whiteness I was surrounded by in school was only tempered by the fact that a significant majority of the white students attending that school were also Jewish, and those families carried with them a traumatic past that somewhat mirrored that of my own Black identity cast in the shadow of a history of slavery—but not quite. Because I had not stepped foot in any of the classrooms at Martin Luther King Jr. Elementary School in my neighborhood, I did not understand why this white school was deemed so much better, superior, other than the fact that there were white kids attending it rather than the Black ones in my neighborhood. And there were no Black teachers.

The travel time was tiring, and I felt a certain level of shame steeped in blatant race and class disparities that I had to face on a daily basis, recognizing that I was on the short end due to no fault of my own or my parents, as I witnessed them working very hard. In fact, I was a latchkey kid, so I understood firsthand how their days were long and arduous. I loved my neighborhood in Richmond, California, so it was not that I desired to live in a wealthier, white area, I just desired a close proximity to my school. I longed to be able to just walk to school, rather than walk to a bus stop and wait for a big yellow bus. I wanted to go to school with my neighborhood friends.

While I was curious about the political aspects of this busing policy implemented to effect a positive change in my life, I knew that it was created by someone who knew nothing about me as a Black child from a working-class Black neighborhood. A busing policy was put in place that carried dynamics of a racialized agenda that shaped my life in particular ways that would define my subsequent educational opportunities for the rest of my life. At some point I knew that once I had some control over what I wanted to learn as far as education was concerned, which was not until college, the education had to help me make sense of what it means to be a Black person in the United States.

A degree in ethnic studies seemed like a logical starting point. Ethnic studies is interdisciplinary and allows insight into the historical, political, economic, and societal issues that shape the collective lives of people of color in the US context. It also is a discipline created out of an activist interrogation of the academic arena, broadly defined, its lack of relevance to people other than white people, and the resistance to the validity of neutrality; and it has afforded me a sense of validation. In her article "Citizenship and Silence: Speaking the Stories Aloud," Pandit offers, "Our very humanity is tied up in our ability to be seen as human beings, first and foremost. As we know, this is a country founded [on] and sustained by the logic of slavery. This logic, infused in all American institutions from judicial to economic, creates a world in which Black people are seen as property, capitalism thrives, colonization is civilization, the prisons boom and teem with Black bodies at once disenfranchised and working for free" (Pandit 2015).

I took a couple of political science classes as an undergraduate ethnic studies major, and while I learned a lot about government policies and institutional structures, what was missing for me was a familiar voice, other than one that was white and authoritative. In my ethnic studies courses, there was an emphasis on the narrative, storytelling—the lived experiences of collective groups of people of color. The faculty that made up the department, all faculty of color, taught history, politics, and culture from a passionate standpoint that felt personal for them. It appeared that the emphasis in the political science courses was an assumption of neutrality—dispassionate—practically the opposite of what I witnessed in ethnic studies. And yet there was something compelling about understanding government structures and processes that I learned from my political science courses. I felt so comfortable at my undergraduate institution that I pursued a master's in public administration with a focus on program evaluation, and then life happened. I got married, had two children back-to-back, and then unfortunately divorced. I decided to keep following my dreams and to pursue a PhD.

It was my busing experience that moved me to apply to Auburn University in Alabama, where I was accepted into their public policy and public administration program. I knew I wanted an understanding of the rural, predominantly Black communities where the fight for civil and voting rights movements took place, and so the location of my graduate studies was important. And I wanted to learn how the Black people in those communities benefited from all of their sacrifices that led to legislation toward opening up democratic participation for Black people in the United States. And there was that ongoing "nag" that a policy consequence that resulted in busing policies was related to passage of the Civil Rights Act. I actually lived off and on during my graduate studies in Wilcox County through a program established by the first Black vice-president at Auburn, Dr. David Wilson, to place Black graduate students in Black Belt communities to be of service. That incredible opportunity allowed me access to Black county-level political officials, all of whom I interviewed for my dissertation.

And I met and developed a lifelong friendship with Sheryl Threadgill, daughter of Reverend Thomas L. Threadgill, a Presbyterian minister who started the first Black high school in that community. Sheryl helped create a highly successful youth-focused organization called BAMA-Kids, Inc., which is one of the most recognized and successful youth organizations in the Black Belt region of Alabama and beyond. Many times during the course of my studies, I thought about the idea of remaining in the Wilcox County community, but I also remained open to other possibilities in the academic environment that might be available to me.

During the time period when I completed my PhD, the late 1990s, the process for securing a tenure-track faculty position included participating in an intimidating initial interview at the American Political Science Association (APSA) annual meeting. It was there that I would meet my fate as I interviewed with two faculty members of the current institution where I am now a full professor, twenty years later. I interviewed with sixteen colleges and universities at that conference in Boston, and I remember my immediate reaction and impression of those places based on the conversations I had with their faculty representatives. Even then I was seeking a political science department that allowed some level of interdisciplinarity, given my ethnic studies background and the tenure-track position that I secured specifically focused on African American and urban politics. But it wasn't just about the department and the institution: I was looking for a good place to raise my children where the cost of living wasn't exorbitant. I landed firmly at this liberal arts-based master's-level private institution in Indianapolis, founded by an abolitionist, in a political science department that was intentionally left-leaning in identity and situated in a very diverse, though economically and racially stratified, neighborhood. It was apparent that community engagement, which I saw as central to my life as a Black intellectual, was available within relatively close reach.

I was not the first Black faculty member in that political science department, but I was the first Black female faculty member, and I was replacing the previous Black faculty member, unbeknownst to me at the time of my interview. One thing that I value at my institution is the emphasis on masterful teaching, as evidenced by the extensive core curriculum that is required by every undergraduate. This core curriculum is defined by its interdisciplinary core, which is actually a second iteration that we now operate under. The initial core curriculum that I experienced was a little more tied to traditional discipline boundaries like arts, humanities, sciences, and social sciences and was controlled by the associated departments.

Because there is an expectation in our political science department that every member will contribute to the core curriculum, it allowed me to blur the infusion of my ethnic studies foundation in both the core courses, as well as the political science courses, in a manner that seemed natural to the students that I teach at our predominantly white university. My classes do tend to draw more students of color than the average course, but the climate of the institution is still steeped in whiteness. All of my course offerings are distinctly political and infused with my womanist lens (Phillips 2006), such as my first-year seminar course Assessing the American Dream through the Lens of Black Women; my text and ideas course, the Politics of Alice Walker; and my political science course, Black Political Thought. Where there have been challenges with regard to teaching, it has been with our incoming students who have a traditional notion of how American government and US politics should be presented. Layli Phillips writes, "Indeed, womanism seeks to enable people to transcend the relations of domination and oppression altogether" (2006). When presented with a critique of our governmental institutions, they initially find this lens to be challenging to absorb. Many if not most of these white students have been politically socialized to see this critique as antipatriotic, anti-American, and therefore problematic. They also have been taught to expect a false notion of "neutrality" from the professor, being particularly hypersensitive in this expectation if the professor is not a white male, and so my evaluations often contain accusatory remarks of bias—something I know to not be uncommon in the experiences of Black women in the political science discipline (Dionne 2019; Lazos 2012; Sampaio 2006).

I was able to shake this expectation up a little when I unexpectedly became the chair of my department, just a year after becoming tenured. Within a year, a new dean for our College of Liberal Arts and Sciences was hired, and I found him to have a leadership style that was difficult for me to relate to and understand. A few years into what was to become six years as serving in the capacity of chair when I had the benefit of attending a department chair training at an APSA teaching and learning conference, I recall mentioning to other, more seasoned chairs in attendance that I was really struggling under the leadership of that dean. They collectively remarked, "Don't worry about it; he won't last very long." I found their collective responses comforting, and in fact within a year or two, he was gone—let go by the provost, which was a search committee that I had served on at the request of the then president of the university.

Another benefit of attending that department chair training was that the only other Black person there was the president of the APSA at the time, Diane Pinderhughes. Her presence, particularly as the president of APSA and even more importantly to me as an accomplished Black political scientist, was one of the most special moments in my academic career. We were the only two Black people in that training, but with her presence I felt that I belonged, and she has continued to be an important role model for me.

The role of the department chair is not something that you are trained for in graduate school, and I found it to be both a very difficult position and yet also one where I could make some changes that affected me very directly but also shaped the department in new and interesting ways. There are tasks such as annual faculty evaluations, departmental assessment and external reviews, faculty searches, recruitment of incoming students and marketing tasks, and interactions with other department chairs within the college that present unique and insightful opportunities. In this middle-management position of department chair, I also thought about how best to represent a social justice and equity lens in the work—using a more collective decision-making approach for my department and taking a more holistic approach to the evaluation process. Interweaving narratives of the teaching, scholarship, and service of my colleagues was a way of my acknowledging that I fully understood why and how they work as academics. It was how I wanted to be understood. However, taking advantage of these opportunities to effect real changes is not without sacrifice, and in fact, there have been many well-documented studies regarding the service of Black women to make transformational institutional changes that can become burdensome and somewhat disruptive to their upward trajectory. While I was busy asking questions and being a disruptive department chair, the old boys network of the college was busy revising the standards of what was required to become a full professor.

When I became the fourteenth department chair, it was the first time in the history of that college that the majority of department chairs were women; there were nine of us, though I was the only one who was Black. So right up under us at this teaching-focused institution, the standards for promotion, particularly in our college, shifted to more scholarship demands—right when women were assuming these heavy middle-management department chair positions. We were busy servicing, doing assessment, looking more closely at racial and gender disparities, and making changes, and so were the old guard white men and women—in the opposite direction of more entrenched standards that even they couldn't meet, but they were already full professors. Sara Ahmed points out, "When we are trying to intervene in the reproduction of power, we have to think differently; we have to think on our feet" (2017).

One of the tasks that came to us from the new dean was to consider how the college as a whole could be more "marketable." A few faculty members created a liberal arts values statement for the college (https://www.butler.edu/las/core-values), and then the "new" dean tasked each department with coming up with their own statement of how the discipline was connected to the pursuit of a liberal arts education. As department chair, this afforded me the opportunity to write the draft statement and then seek input from my colleagues, and to my surprise, they adopted most of what I wrote, with some minor and creative additions. It is here:

> The faculty members of the Political Science Department at Butler University see our discipline as connected to Liberal Arts which are about studying and understanding ourselves, other peoples, different ways of being and knowing, of developing tolerance and empathy, and learning to use evidence and think critically. As political scientists we seek to understand the causes of wars, social injustices, economic disparities and uneven technological growth for the purpose of alleviating suffering. Because a liberal arts education encourages an activist disposition we look for ways to address problems such as world poverty, inadequate health care, educational disparities between neighboring communities and environmental degradation and seek nonviolent solutions to human rights violations worldwide. The Political Science Department at Butler University deliberately challenges systems, institutions and leaders that dehumanize, marginalize and oppress any persons and other living beings. We seek to engage in intellectual practices that provide sustainable solutions for the betterment of all.
>
> The department is committed to teaching students how to effect positive social change. In practicing citizenship skills that include empathetic listening, moral reasoning, personal responsibility and a greater awareness of one's responsibility to the human polity, our students develop as active and engaged citizens at the local, national and international levels. We offer

courses that include service-learning and community-based research and that encourage students to accept responsibility for their learning and to recognize that knowledge may be obtained from a variety of different people and situations.

This statement provided a platform to shift the expectations of prospective and incoming students, as it provided a clear understanding of how we go about the business of teaching political science that is not aligned with what most of them experienced in their high school government courses. It also provided a more liberating and interdisciplinary avenue for job descriptions when we were authorized to conduct two new faculty searches with the retirement of one of our faculty members and the allowance to expand our small department from five to six faculty members. Further, I eschewed the style of evaluating my colleagues pushed by the dean as bullet pointing them into the hard-lined categories of teaching, research, and service and instead wrote narratives of my colleagues that showed how all of their work was interconnected (Moscowitz et al. 2014).

While I served as the department chair, some changes that arose based on the retirement of a colleague and the support of our department by a new provost led to the hiring of two new colleagues. We were a small department with a significant student base that demonstrated we needed an additional line. Being in a position where I was able to not only help shape the job description but also be on the forefront of our recruitment efforts ultimately led, through our regular search processes, to the hiring of two faculty women of color. Today, though we are small we are an unusual political science department, where three of the five tenured faculty members are women of color, including two Black women, both tenured. Soon after my term as the department chair, I was tapped to serve the provost in her diversity, equity, and inclusion efforts, which led to the creation of an Inclusion advocate program that shapes all faculty searches at our institution.

As I am now a full professor and the newly appointed faculty director of the Hub for Black Affairs and Community Engagement, what I can honestly state is that my experiences coming up the ranks in the Political Science Department and then serving in a leadership capacity allowed me to be involved as the institution has transformed and responded to societal changes. The discipline of political science allows a unique advantage of being able to anticipate and respond to societal changes that affect the academic environment as a whole. As a Black woman, because these societal changes are often steeped in racial and gendered intersectional dynamics, your intellectual life is simultaneously personal. I say I am a political scientist based on my education, training, knowledge, and work as spelled out in this chapter, and I don't feel compelled to prove it any further.

References

Ahmed, Sara. 2017. *Living a Feminist Life.* Durham, NC: Duke University Press.

Berry, Daina Ramey, and Kali Nicole Gross. 2020. *A Black Women's History of the United States.* Boston: Beacon Press.

Cooper, Brittney C., Susana M. Morris, and Robin M. Boylorn. 2017. *The Crunk Feminist Collective.* New York: Feminist Press at City University of New York.

Dionne, Kim Yi. 2019. "There's a Gender Gap in Political Science. Our Series Examines the Problem—and Looks at Some Solutions." *The Monkey Cage*, August 19. https://www.washingtonpost.com/politics/2019/08/19/theres-gender-gap-political-science-our-series-examines-problem-looks-some-solutions/.

Lazos, Syvia R. 2012. "Are Student Teaching Evaluations Holding Back Women and Minorities? The Perils of 'Doing' Gender and Race in the Classroom." In *Presumed Incompetent: The Intersections of Race and Class for Women in Academia*, edited by Gabriella Guitierez y Muhs, Yolanda Flores Niemann, Carmen G Gonzalez, and Angela P. Harris, 164–85. Boulder: University Press of Colorado.

Moscowitz, David, Terri Jett, Terri Carney, Tamara Leech, and Ann Savage. 2014. "Diversity in the Times of Austerity: Documenting Resistance in the Academy." *Journal of Gender Studies* 23, no. 3: 233–46.

Pandit, Eesha. "Citizenship and Silence: Speaking the Stories Aloud." Crunk Feminist Collective. January 1, 2015. https://www.crunkfeministcollective.com/2015/01/01/citizenship-and-silence-speaking-the-stories-aloud/.

Phillips, Layli, ed. 2006. *The Womanist Reader.* New York: Routledge.

Sampaio, Anna. 2006. "Women of Color Teaching Political Science: Examining the Intersections of Race, Gender and Course Material in the Classroom." *PS: Political Science and Politics* 39, no. 4: 917–22.

3

That's Not Political Science

Disrupting "Traditional" Political Science Inquiries

LAKEYTA M. BONNETTE-BAILEY

When I entered graduate school, I was a young, idealistic, Afrocentric, nerdy rebel. I thought I knew what I wanted to study, women in prison, and I thought that I was extremely smart. I mean, I did get accepted to The Ohio State University's (OSU's) Political Science Department, which boasted in their welcome letter that they were ranked fourth in the *world* in political science research at the time. I was uberconfident, having been nurtured at a small liberal arts college in Rock Hill, South Carolina, Winthrop University. Additionally, my selection as one of twenty participants as a Bunche scholar in the illustrious Ralph Bunche Summer Research Program at Duke University, under the guidance of famed political scientist Paula D. McClain, further cemented my confidence in my academic prowess. From these nurturing and supportive experiences, I was supported in asserting my voice and was provided a platform to have a more expansive reach. In fact, this reach was realized while at Winthrop. On campus I was known for my knowledge on topics that related to Black people and music as well as my leadership (serving as president of the Black club, Taking Integrity Back), as I was called upon by the Delta Sigma Theta Sorority (before I became a member) to speak on two of their panels about the diaspora and Jill Scott's music as well as other campus speaking engagements. However, none of my speaking engagements were as prominent as the one with the Miles to Go panel. I was the only student invited to speak on a panel with scholars and activists about education in South Carolina, and the panel included famed Harvard professor Gary Orfield and South Carolina Senator Maggie Glover. By participating on this panel, not only were students and faculty at Winthrop University able to witness my intellectual abilities but also scholars from other universities, state congressional leaders, and many others from Charlotte and the surrounding areas who came to Winthrop to hear this panel. Thus, because of these experiences as an undergraduate, I was very idealistic and confident about my potential and ability to complete a doctorate program.

I entered OSU with a nontraditional research agenda. While women in prison as a general topic was very political, it was not the "typical" political science topic of research. As I was told by numerous professors, my research didn't succinctly align with political science; in fact, it was asserted that my research was more aligned with sociology or criminal justice. Observing the latest version of the *Oxford Handbook on Political Science* (Goodin 2011), there are ten areas of political science research. According to the index these ten areas are divided into parts labeled, Political Theory, Political Institutions, Law and Politics, Political Behavior, Contextual Political Analysis, Comparative Politics, International Relations, Political Economy, Public Policy, and Political Methodology (Goodin, 2011). Of these ten sections, only one has a subsection that addresses some aspect of identity politics, and that is the law and politics section, which has a chapter titled "Feminist Theory and the Law" (Goodin, 2011). Even the section on political economy does not address the socioeconomic status of individuals and their political engagement. Thus, besides feminist theory, no other aspect of identity politics is addressed in this handbook of political science research. Still, as a young scholar I was not aware of the status of the discipline in this regard. Therefore, I was not deterred in my interests or education and continued to pursue research on the relationships between women and imprisonment. However, I quickly found that my research interests were not articulated in any of the documents I read for my courses and that there were no courses on the relationship between mandatory minimum sentences and the increase of women of color in prison in political science. In order to understand more and in preparation of beginning my research, I enrolled in undergraduate criminal justice courses as a grad student. I was determined to continue the research that interested me. My alternative approach to my research, taking classes outside of my discipline, was an option I utilized throughout my graduate career because the majority of the political science courses at OSU did not provide "adequate graduate training in the study and teaching of issues related to identity, difference, gender, class, race, and ethnicity" (Fraga, Givens, and Pinderhughes 2011, 9). This lack of training was a major critique of many top programs in the discipline. They were simply not preparing scholars to understand the intricate intersections within and between identities as they related to politics. While a lack of relevant courses was a problem I overcame, there were other incendiary experiences that had more of an impact on my confidence and psyche.

Being an Outsider Within

In graduate school, I was consistently reminded that I was the "outsider within" (Collins 1986). I was an outsider as a first-generation, Black, southern, woman, PhD student within a predominately white institution in the Midwest. While there is an increasing number of faculty of color, we are still underrepresented in academia, and those that are first-generation college students are also extremely underrepresented. Here I was, an outsider, with no guidance or history of a graduate education or undergraduate education. I did not have the privilege of receiving guidance from my parents of their experiences in college and advice on how to study, what to pursue, or how to engage with my peers. I was definitely an outsider, and at OSU I experienced both micro- and macroaggressions that reinforced my outsider status. In turn these aggressions made me feel like an outsider, an impostor, especially among my peers and my professors. Data confirmed my outsider status as well.

According to the task force report in 2010, a year after I completed my doctorate program, only 5 percent of political science faculty were Black and only 6 percent of all women faculty were Black women (Fraga, Givens, and Pinderhughes 2011, 39–42). Considering these startling statistics, I recall several occasions when comments were made about my race, ethnicity, gender, or culture both directly and indirectly. These aggressions definitely didn't make me feel wanted or accepted and led to the development of a very strong impostor syndrome. Impostor syndrome is a mentality that is developed from being an outsider within any prestigious institution or organization. Specifically, impostor syndrome is a feeling or belief that you are not an insider, that you do not have the knowledge, ability, and skills equivalent to those of your peers. Impostor syndrome' is not developed internally but instead is developed from external micro- and macroaggressions that point to your outsider status. For instance, at the end of one semester in political science at OSU, one of my professors informed me that I "brought color to the class, in more ways than one." I was shocked and confused and was unsure of how to respond. Do I take the comment literally? Was he commenting on my "color," or did that mean that my comments were colorful, or was he insinuating that I brought race into the conversation? Even today, reflecting on that comment I am still unsure of how I should have responded, but in the moment, I simply said thank you.

Years later, I found out that this same white male professor confided in my lighter complexioned peer that my skin tone and dialect meant I would not be successful in the program, reinforcing his idea that I did not belong, a sentiment I felt even when it was never explicitly stated. It is precisely this type of thinking and implicit alienation that makes graduate school difficult for underrepresented students. When I am asked about my graduate experience, I often say that it was akin to five years of hazing: racialized and intellectual hazing. It severely impacted my confidence and had me doubting myself and my ability to continue in the program.

Yet, these comments were not the only ways in which my marginalized status was demonstrated to me. There were also examples of lack of inclusion in study groups, not being informed of potential fellowship opportunities, and a lack of engagement at social events. However, fortunately, I had several great mentors and participated in numerous supportive and encouraging programs that informed me of these types of microaggressions and prepared me to finish my program by advising me to develop a strong support system, a supportive dissertation committee, and, most importantly, a strong dissertation chair.

Changing My Research Agenda

After two years of coursework, I was very concerned if my research topic was a viable topic for political science. I was dismayed and disheartened by the comments I received when I spoke of my research interests. Therefore, I begin thinking of other possible research questions I could pursue that were still within the realm of criminal justice but aligned better with political science research. It wasn't until after viewing Dave Chapelle's film *Block Party* that I knew what I wanted to study and how it was political.

Immediately after watching *Block Party*,[1] I begin to think about which professors would be supportive and willing to serve on my committee as I examined the political impact of rap music. I immediately went to the professor in the program that I felt provided me the safest space during my matriculation at OSU, Dr. William "Nick" Nelson. While Dr. Nelson joked with me about the "hippity-hoppity," he was my biggest advocate and consistently brought me articles and informed me of his knowledge of the role of music in the Black community. In fact, one day we met for lunch and Dr. Nelson handed me a *New York Times* article that exclaimed "Hip-Hop Is Dead" discussing New York rapper Nas's album of that same title. We joked about it and what that could mean for my research, but Dr. Nelson never discouraged my interests or the pursuit of this topic. He made me believe that I could truly conduct research on the political impact of rap music. Having secured Dr. Nelson as my chair, I chose three other faculty members that I felt provided a safe space for me while at OSU and whose research aligned with aspects of my dissertation research.

As an idealistic young graduate student I thought my idea was brilliant! Most importantly, it came to me in the organic way I was told dissertation ideas come to young scholars: unexpectantly while participating in a normal activity. What I learned those first two years in graduate school, among other things, is that research interests and dissertation ideas often changed. Many people that entered graduate school with ideas about what they were going to research often changed their minds, and I was no different. Still, what I soon became aware of as I excitedly informed other professors in the department about my topic is that it too was not in the realm of "typical" political science research. In fact, many questioned how it was political science at all, although examining culture and music among political scientists was not new.

There are numerous political scientists who examined some aspect of culture or music and their relationships with politics (Lusane 2004; Meier 2004; Street 2003; Iton 2008). For instance, in 1990, acclaimed political scientist Charles P. Henry released his book *Culture and American Politics*. In this book Henry examined Black folklore, blues music, and Black churches to understand how Black attitudes and beliefs about politics are maintained within Black communities. Specifically, Henry states, "The search for Black ideology must begin with the oral tradition" (1990, 7). Moreover, not only had scholars observed and examined culture, including music, before my interest in Hip-Hop music and political attitudes, a number of political scientists also examined the idea that rap music impacted political attitudes and was asserting political beliefs of marginalized communities in the United States (Dawson 2001; Henderson 1996; Walton and Smith 2000; Harris-Lacewell 2004; Lusane 2004; Cohen 2010; Spence 2011). Specifically, Clarence Lusane stated, "Rap is the voice of the alienated, frustrated and rebellious Black youth who recognize their vulnerability and marginality in post-industrial America" (2004, 351), while Michael Dawson contended that "both exposure to rap music and the belief that it constitutes an important resource of the Black community play substantial roles in shaping Black political opinion both directly and indirectly" (2001, 78). Yet, at the time that I was developing my research topic, it was the work of political scientists Michael Dawson (2001), Errol Henderson (1996), Melissa Harris-Lacewell (2004), and Clarence Lusane (2004) that provided the evidence that my interests were indeed political science and lie in a scholarly cannon that had been established within the discipline. Yet, even with this established scholarly tradition, maintaining a research agenda of culture and politics and specifically rap music and politics has not been an easy sale within the discipline. After successfully defending my dissertation and obtaining a tenure-track position, I transitioned from defending my research to attempting to publish my research.

Getting Published in Political Science

During the onset of my career, I found it incredibly difficult to get published in flagship political science journals. Yet, I was told by colleagues at my institution that the way to get tenure was to get a couple of publications in one or more of the flagship journals. However, after perusing those journals, I did not see much research that was related to my specific research interests, and the research that was related to my general interests was very limited. This observation was confirmed with the task force on Political Science in the 21st Century, where it was stated that "issues related to marginalization including race, gender, and inequality are not well represented in articles published in the discipline's flagship journals" (Fraga, Givens, and Pinderhughes 2011, 1).

Most of the research we have within the discipline on rap music was published outside of those flagship political science journals (Henderson 1996; Bohn, 2011) In fact, research addressing race, gender, culture, and marginalization in general found a home in selected political science journals, which often were not the flagships, or in interdisciplinary journals outside of the discipline. As stated in the task force report, "Claims are made about the infrequent presence of articles examining multiculturalism in its various forms in top-tier journals and major presses" (Fraga, Givens, and Pinderhughes 2011, 9).

What I had to learn quickly at the onset of my career was what many others knew before me: the type of research I did was going to need outlets outside of these flagship journals. Therefore, through guidance and mentorship, I sought out more diverse, inclusive, and interdisciplinary journals and other avenues for getting my research published. Fortunately, I found journals that were interested in my topic, even political science journals, and have successfully published several articles, primarily in interdisciplinary journals. Of course, with changes in leadership and the release of Political Science in the 21st Century task force results, we have observed changes within political science journals, including the expansion, accessibility, and change of direction of journals, including the *Journal of New Political Science*, which is the only political science journal that has published my research thus far. However, journals were not the most important source of publishing for me. Many people are able to negotiate journal publishing and build their career on it. I found that book publishing was more amenable to my topic and style of writing.

So, I turned my efforts to book publishing, an area where research on marginalized communities in political science finds success. My first book was published within the political science series American Governance: Politics, Policy and Public Law with the University of Pennsylvania Press. This book, *Pulse of the People: Political Rap Music and Black Politics* (2015), explored the impact of political rap music on Black political attitudes and behavior and examined the ways in which Hip-Hop artists and subscribers have pushed for democratic inclusion. In this book, I found that those exposed to political rap express stronger beliefs in Black nationalism and feminism in comparison to those exposed to nonpolitical rap or no music. I also observe the numerous ways in which the Hip-Hop community is involved in democratic inclusion through voter mobilization and registration campaigns (e.g., P. Diddy's Vote or Die and T. I.'s Respect My Vote Campaign), campaigning with political candidates (e.g., Jay-Z and Barack Obama, Cardi B and Bernie Sanders, Killer Mike and Bernie Sanders), running for and securing political office (e.g., Representative Antonio Delgado, D, NY), organizing and participating in nonelectoral politics (e.g., J. Cole and Big Boi), providing commentary on political issues, and impacting policy change. Therefore, I argued that the study of rap music assists in the understanding and the development of political attitudes, thoughts, ideologies, and behavior among those who listen to rap. This research expands the knowledge of rap music and other cultural forms as resistance mechanisms, as methods to ensure political inclusion, and as a voice for marginalized communities.

Later, I found success with a second book, coedited with Adolphus Belk Jr. and titled *For the Culture: Hip-Hop and the Fight for Social Justice* (2022). This edited volume explores the relationships between Hip-Hop culture and social justice, including education, feminism, the Black Lives Matter movement, the global utilization of Hip-Hop, and mass incarceration. This book is a contemporary examination of the numerous ways Hip-Hop culture is involved in social justice efforts globally. Similarly, I have also been able to publish several book chapters in other volumes, including one of the Oxford handbooks, this time on protest music. However, even with my publishing successes I don't think I would be classified as a "successful" political scientist because I do not have a slew of political science publications. Within the field, when political scientists are evaluated for tenure and promotion, most handbooks use measures of prominence. For many departments across the country, this measure of prominence is determined by the number of publications one has in top-tier or flagship political science journals. Thus, the measure of success among many political scientists within the field is publications in political science journals. Because of this biased measure of success, I may not be classified as a "successful" political scientist. However, while I am not as published as some of my peers in flagship political science journals, I am published, and more importantly to me, my work is forward facing and leads to specific information about society and the impact of culture on politics within the Black community, which is observable through my media engagement.

Media Engagement

Beyond obtaining my doctorate, there are three significant highlights of my career. My first highlight was gaining tenure at the institution of my first job within six years and after having three children. Another highlight was presenting my research at a TedX talk at Georgia State University. The final highlight of my career, thus far, was being selected as a Nasir Jones Hiphop Fellow at Harvard University. These opportunities provided recognition of my research, hard work, perseverance, and the importance of my research in society. However, while these opportunities have been the highlights of my career, they are not the only markers that allowed me to recognize the reach of my research and its importance.

Considering my research, I have been contacted by numerous print and broadcast media sites to discuss Hip-Hop and its relationship with politics. For instance, I have been interviewed by both domestic (*Washington Post, Associated Press, Atlanta Magazine, Vox, PBS, Salon, Atlanta Journal-Constitution, W.A.B.E.*, etc.) and international (*CGTN America, BBC news, Diario de Noticias,* and *DH LES Sports*) news outlets to discuss Black popular culture, Hip-Hop, and Black politics. With these news outlets I have discussed topics as varied as Kanye West's political bid for the presidency, the political meaning of Beyonce's Superbowl performance, the political relevance of Beyonce's *Black Is King* visual album, and rappers campaigning for politicians, including Barack Obama, Stacy Abrams, Bernie Sanders, and Keisha Lance Bottoms. I have been invited to countries as far away as Germany and Iran (virtually) to discuss social justice and culture and racial unrest in the United States. Additionally, I have presented numerous lectures and sat on many panels to discuss the role and political power of Hip-Hop music and the Hip-Hop community. In fact, my research has always had a public face, even when I was in grad school, where I raised funds to host the first-ever Hip-Hop and Politics conference at OSU. I went on to host a Hip-Hop and Social Justice Conference and Beyond the Culture: Black Popular Culture and Social Justice. I raised over 14,000 dollars to host both of these free, public conferences.

Finally, I have been able to parlay my research interest, training, and knowledge into a podcast that is public facing and relevant. My podcast, *The Intersection Where Black Popular Culture Meets Social Justice*, examines numerous Black popular culture productions, including in music, film, television, and art, and their relationships with efforts of social justice. Because of the experiences I have had in the discipline, I have learned to chart my own path and navigate my career outside the margins.

Conclusion

Within academia, there are a number of ways in which a person can define success for themselves. For instance, one person might point to obtaining tenure as a marker of success or publishing a certain number of books or articles. Some may measure success by the prestige of the institution where they work, teaching evaluations, leadership roles, or media engagement. Considering all of these different ways to define success, I have had a very successful career thus far. However, when I first began as that young, idealistic rebel, I would not have imagined that my career would progress in the way that it did. It was difficult navigating graduate school and dealing with numerous microaggressions. Yet, I had a strong support system that was there to tell me I could finish and that supported my research. The problems that are addressed in the task force on Political Science in the 21st Century point out the lack of minority faculty, the lack of minority-oriented courses, and the lack of inclusion of identity politics within flagship political science journals. Despite all of these obstacles I was able to finish my degree and have a flourishing career, but it wasn't easy. There are numerous times I felt discouraged and wanted to quit. These obstacles and lack of inclusion make political science a very difficult place to navigate. I have heard numerous times from peer and senior colleagues that my research is not "real" research or that it is not important. The problems that the task force identified are still plaguing our discipline today and may even be exacerbated currently, as we live in an era when racism is overt and prominent. Similarly, it may be as, if not more, difficult for minority graduate students and faculty who feel like they do not have a safe place in their department or within the field.

When I entered the profession as a graduate student, I knew there were certain schools where I could go to focus on racial and ethnic politics, specifically Black politics. The number of PhD-granting institutions that have that focus within political science has dwindled, with a small percentage of departments having two or more scholars that study racial politics within their department. In most departments, there is only one faculty member that studies Black politics. Thus, while I was able to navigate the discipline, the issues that were discussed in the task force's report still rang true and the action items detailed still need to be carried out. There is still much work to do in political science to ensure that all perspectives are heard, acknowledged, and provided the opportunity to thrive.

Note

1. *Block Party* was a film that was a recording of a block party that took place in a New York neighborhood featuring rap and neosoul artists that have been classified as socially and politically conscious artists because of their lyrical

content. It was during the viewing of this film that I personally and powerfully felt the impact of exposure to political rap music on one's beliefs and behaviors. After this experience, I decided that I wanted to study Hip-Hop music and its impact politically and psychologically on behavior and attitudes.

References

Bohn, Lauren E. 2011. "Rapping the Revolution." *Foreign Policy*, July 22. Middle East Channel. http://mideast.foreignpolicy.com/posts/2011/07/22/rapping_the_revolution.

Cohen, Cathy. 2010. *Democracy Remixed: Black Youth and the Future of American Politics*. New York: Oxford University Press.

Collins, A. C. 2001. "Black Women in the Academy: An Historical Overview." In *Sisters of the Academy: Emergent Black Women Scholars in Higher Education*, edited by R. O. Mabokela and A. L. Green, 29–42. Sterling, VA: Stylus.

Cook, Elizabeth A. 1989. "Measuring Feminist Consciousness." *Women and Politics* 9, no. 3: 71–88.

Dawson, Michael C. 2001. *Black Visions*. Chicago: University of Chicago Press.

Fraga, Luis, Terri E. Givens, and Dianne M. Pinderhughes. 2011. "Report of the Task Force on Political Science for the 21st Century." Washington, DC: American Political Science Association. www.apsanet.org/portals/54/Files/Task%20Force%20Reports/TF_21st%20Century_AllPgs_webres90.pdf.

Gooding, Robert E., ed. 2011. *The Oxford Handbook of Political Science*. Oxford, UK: Oxford University Press.

Harris-Lacewell, Melissa. 2004. *Barbershops, Bibles and BET*. Princeton, NJ: Princeton University Press.

Henderson, Errol. 1996. "Black Nationalism and Rap Music." *Journal of Black Studies* 26, no. 3: 308–39.

Henry, Charles. 1990. *Culture and African American Politics*. Bloomington: Indiana University Press.

Iton, Richard. 2008. *In Search of the Black Fantastic: Politics and Popular Culture in the Post-Civil Rights Era*. Oxford, UK: Oxford University Press.

Lusane, Clarence. 2004. "Rap, Race and Politics." In *That's the Joint: The Hip-Hop Studies Reader*, edited by Murray Forman and Mark Anthony Neal, 403–16. New York: Routledge.

Meier, Kenneth J. 2004. "Get Your Tongue out My Mouth 'Cause I'm Kissing You Goodbye: The Politics of Ideas." *Policy Studies Journal* 32, no. 2: 225–33.

Spence, Lester. 2011. *Stare in the Darkness: The Limits of Hip-Hop and Black Politics*. Minneapolis: University of Minnesota Press.

Street, John. 1986. *Rebel Rock: The Politics of Popular Music*. New York: Basil Blackwell.

———. 2003. "'Fight the Power': The Politics of Music and the Music of Politics." *Government and Opposition* 38, no. 1: 113–30. doi:10.1111/1477-7053.00007.

Street, John, Seth Hague, and Heather Savigny. 2008. "Playing to the Crowd: The Role of Music and Musicians in Political Participation." *British Journal of Politics and International Relations* 10, no. 2: 269–85. https://doi.org/10.1111/j.1467-856x.2007.00299.x.

Walton, Hanes, and Robert Smith. 2000. *African American and the African American Quest for Universal Freedom*. New York: Addison-Wesley Longman.

4

Setting Political Science to a Different Tune

Reflections on the Role of
Black Women as Rhythm Disrupters

Desireé R. Melonas

The title of this essay is somewhat ironic, isn't it? Black women are often—and sometimes mistakenly—presumed to possess an innate fitness for locating the rhythm of a song and consonantly moving the lines of their bodies against it in a way that does not appear forced or unnatural. On that point, I have had folks in the past, while at events where dancing was involved, more or less demand that I take part in the collective improvisation on the dance floor, because, you know, I just looked to them like a person who had some good rhythm. They *are* right, by the way, but they had no basis on which to form such a judgment other than the cultural belief of an insoluble tie between the image of the Black woman and the concept of rhythm. I begin in this way to signal the rhetorical and conceptual dissonance we might experience when encountering this coupling: "Black woman" and "rhythm disruptor."

This essay puts forward a counternarrative to a prevailing supposition concerning the relationship between Black women and the concept of rhythm. Against a more prosaic rendering of "rhythm," considered rigidly in terms of its relation to music, the idea of the Black woman as a rhythm disrupter might register as a mismatched conceptual pairing. This work, however, dwells on the etymological understanding of the concept, where to be in possession of a rhythm connotes forming oneself around or aligning something in accordance with a distinct pattern, a discrete arrangement of sorts. My analysis is therefore rooted against this stripped down, attenuated perspective onto what constitutes a rhythm.

I propose that in the context of the academy, and specifically political science—spaces organized around the continued enactment of a distinct rhythm, a specific way of cohering its institutional and disciplinary elements—Black women political scientists have the capacity and often *do* enter in these spaces and impart different and nuanced ways of researching, teaching, and conceptualizing community and its relation to the academy. That is, we sometimes clear the way for our departments/units to be moved by the static of a different rhythm, which requires a break with—*a disruption* of—the existing one(s). It is in this sense that I want to inspire some reflection about Black women political scientists' roles as "rhythm disruptors," as those individuals who have the ability to unhinge departments from modes of conducting political science research and engaging students in inquiry work that reinforce a homogeneity of thought and values that continue to shape the discipline. I am speaking specifically of the set of rather durable trends along lines of research, pedagogical practices, and faculty and student representation that persist in contouring political science in ways that can signal a general noninclusiveness.

I briefly outline what I mean when referring to political science as having an operant rhythm and how that has been given specific historical expression in my previous department.[1] From there, I reflect on how my arrival into my former institution's political science department constituted a break[2] with a now old rhythmic order, not only at the level of representation but also at the levels of curriculum mapping, pedagogy, and student recruitment into the discipline. I pay particular attention, for instance, to the genealogical current of curriculum development and how through a simple, cursory content analysis of the department's course catalogs over the past fifteen years, one is able to observe a clear shift in what types of knowledge the department judges as valuable and therefore necessary to include in an undergraduate political science curriculum. It is important to note that this deviation occurred coevally with my hiring. Finally, in a concluding turn, I detail the work I have done to disrupt the rhythm of my department in ways that represent a response to some of the challenges to the discipline as laid out in the Political Science in the 21st Century 2011 taskforce report commissioned by Dianne Pinderhughes, then president of the American Political Science Association.

Ultimately, this work is intended to energize the claim that Black women have engaged and continue to engage in the work necessary to shape the discipline in ways that are reflective of a multifaceted, heterogenous reality. On this point, Patricia Hill Collins's insights are instructive. She urges that spaces of knowledge production are substantively transformed only when those who are considered outside the boundaries of dominant paradigms and epistemologies contest their limits (Collins 2000). I therefore stress the virtue of thinking about those undertakings as rhythm-breaking practices and Black women, in the context of political science, as potential disruptors. For that, I offer my experience as a window into viewing the specifics of being a rhythm-disrupting Black woman political scientist.

In that sense, I don't so much mind being offbeat.

"Feel the Beat of the Rhythm": Detecting What Moves Us and How

When I decided to write an essay on rhythm looked at through the lens of Black women's experience as political scientists, I was instantly reminded of "The Rhythm of the Night,"[3] a 1980s song performed by the DeBarge family I enjoyed listening and dancing to as a child (and, well, in my adult years, too). The song is captivating; it immediately ushers the listener into a vortex of notes pinging back and forth off the other, activated by the layering of a cluster of musical instruments. The choreography of tones and percussive beats conjoined create the sense of being swept up in a swell of energy so intense that it would often leave me feeling as though I had no choice but to move my body in response.

The lyrics then put into words the somatic experience that the rhythmic components of the song intend to stimulate. For instance, the chorus tempts the listener to "Feel the beat of the rhythm of the night, / dance until the morning light. / Forget about the worries of your mind, / you can leave them all behind. / Feel the beat of the rhythm of the night." Here, the listener is being persuaded into becoming possessed by the rhythm's vibrations to the point that aspects of one's reality to which they would otherwise be present get obscured, deprioritized, and subsumed beneath the rhythm's waves, for example, "Forget about the worries of your mind." In other words, what the song purports to make available to the listener is a context in which they can permit the rhythm of the song to do the work of circumscribing their field of action and delimiting their immediate sphere of interests, that is, doing away with distractions that might impede their ability to move in agreement with the rhythm. In that sense, the rhythm becomes the central agent governing one's corporeal schema. The point of the rhythm, then, as tacitly expressed through the song's lyrics, is for the individual to allow it to penetrate one's body to the degree where they become impervious to the fact of *being* moved. The rhythm, in that sense, begins to condition the individual into an embodied belief around what one ought to consider a natural and necessary mode of comportment. We might say that rhythms *gather*; they pull toward the pattern, insisting that you huddle around the beat.

This is what rhythms do. They organize movement in accordance to a distinct pattern, a specific coordination of elements. Consider for a moment the etymology of *rhythm*. Derived from the Latin *rhythmus* meaning "movement in time," from the Greek *rhythmos* "measured flow or movement, symmetry, arrangement," to have a rhythm assumes a specific choreography of elements in order to maintain movement in accordance with a given end. Against this view, highlighting the rhythm of something or someone then is intended to make visible the way they are able to repeatedly carry out, with fluidity, a discrete arrangement of things, be they associated with music or related to something else. For instance, we may employ the language of rhythm to describe the kind of workflow where everything seems to come together in a manner that promotes ease of performance and production. Thus, those things that contradict or disrupt the rhythm's measured arrangement is considered cacophonic and must therefore be ignored or removed beyond the range of one's hearing.

We see this sentiment, for instance, expressed throughout Frantz Fanon's writings, notably in *La Damnés de la terre* (1963), where he makes visible the rhythm that underwrites the colonial project and annunciates therefore the urgent need for the colonized to engage in concrete, collective actions that throw it into chaos. In the opening chapter, Fanon references the existence of a colonial rhythmic order consisting of interminable episodes of violence, cleavage-deepening antagonisms, and noxious economic practices that drum colonialism along. The constancy of the pattern—that is, the repeated enactment of this discrete rhythm—gives the appearance of permanence, subsequently summoning individuals into participating in actions and developing a consciousness that enable the rhythm to carry on without much impediment. Fanon demonstrates, though, that through the work of collective action, rhythms *can* be disturbed and muted over by the induction of a new rhythmic order, one that compels individuals into different, fundamentally humanizing relationships with one another (Fanon 2004, 80). It is in that sense that he calls repeatedly for the colonized to infuse their environment with a "new rhythm, specific to a new generation of men" (2). In other words, a new generation of men can spring forth only when done so alongside the creation of a fresh constellation of patterned values, ideas, and movements around which to organize. *A new rhythm.*

James Cone, too, writing on the resiliency of the enslaved and the role of the spirituals in helping to sustain the human spirit, invokes the language of "rhythm" to describe that experience. In *The Spirituals and the Blues*, he argues, "The spirituals enabled blacks to retain a measure of African identity while living in the midst of American slavery, provided both the substance and the rhythm to cope with human servitude" (Cone 1972, 30). Here, Cone indicates how the spirituals granted the enslaved a portal into accessing alternative ways of negotiating reality; they allowed them to *pattern* their lives according to a dignity and a commitment to live and compelled them pulsate with the belief of the possibility of a different future. In other words, the spirituals called the enslaved toward a new rhythm, one that would militate against slavery's harsh rhythms bearing down upon them.

This preceding discussion is intended to demonstrate that systems and institutions operate according to distinct rhythms whose continued enactment functions as evidence of the purported need for the rhythm to persist. But rhythms *can* change, they can be disrupted and replaced with something new.

To that end, I urge us to consider political science's rhythms, to locate its characteristic components that, when gathered together, produce a specificity of direction, which is to say a certain tempo that guides the discipline, its aims, values, and reinforces a commitment to keeping intact a dominant vision depicting the embodiment of what constitutes "good" political science. Namely, I am interested in calling attention to the practices that reproduce the false sense that, in terms of research, teaching, and representation, political science is more provincial than it actually is or ought to be. The acknowledgment therefore of Black women political scientists as rhythm disruptors can only occur if we first make legible the rhythm that is to be disrupted. In other words, I want to know what these patterns are around which political science continues to orient itself.

46 | Desireé R. Melonas

I use my former department as a limited case study for discerning just what these rhythms are and how they materialize in content and in form. For the sake of space, I restrict the scope of my examination to two rhythmic components: faculty representation and curriculum development, with a focused attention on its slate of course offerings over the last fifteen years.

Detecting a Rhythm, Exhibit A: Where Are All the Black People?

Oh. It's just me here.

I mean "here" in the present sense but also in a transtemporal sense. In other words, at the time of writing this, I was the only Black woman employed in my (albeit very small) political science department, and I was the only Black woman, in the department's fifty-year history, to have ever received a tenure-track appointment.[4] The department's track record along lines of faculty representation is consistent with the broader trends among political science departments across the country. For instance, according to the 2011 task force report on Political Science in the 21st Century, of the 28.6 percent of women political science faculty,[5] the overwhelming majority of those are white women, while, as of 2010, only 4.3 percent of the total number of women faculty are Black (American Political Science Association 2011). That is a staggering figure.

So, on a rather objective level, my arrival to my department indeed entailed a divergence from the former faculty representation pattern that had concretely shaped their hiring practices since its inception. I disrupted a rhythm that had rapped on for fifty years. *Fifty years.*

Detecting a Rhythm, Exhibit B: the Course Catalog

After being hired, one of the projects I sought to immediately take on was introducing into the course inventory classes that better reflect the broad range of perspectives implicated in political science inquiry. Up to the point of my appointment in 2017, no courses had been offered in my department, for instance, that center Black politics and political thought. Nor were there courses that expressed a serious engagement with non-Western scholars, feminist thinkers, or indigenous and LGBTQ+ scholarship. Between the years spanning 2001 to 2017,[6] the only courses on record that nominally appear to have exposed students to a partial perspective onto the expansiveness of the discipline are Civil Rights and Justice, Introduction to Latin American Politics, Politics in China and Japan, and Politics of Central Mexico and America. This suite of "diverse" classes remained relatively undisturbed until 2017, which is the year I was hired as an assistant professor. Thus, a distinct feature of my department's rhythm—an element that shows quite clearly its patterned commitments to prioritizing and disseminating certain kinds of knowledge—was a course catalog anemic on classes that presented openings for students to come into contact with the sort of diverse perspectives that inhabit political science and the world.

Course catalogs are statements of value, expressed both through what is included in them and what gets omitted. In relation to a body of undergraduate course offerings, one is to assume that the classes that make the list represent an adequate introduction to the field. This especially appears to be the case in the context of small departments, whose faculty are likely overextended, a reality that places limits on the number and assortment of classes made available to its students. Faculty in these positions, then, are often constrained when deciding which courses to offer that will provide students graduating from these programs a strong basis for identifying the boundaries that circumscribe the field, as well as the requisite skills necessary to go on and do work in political science-related domains. In my department's case, limited resources translated into the development and reproduction of a rather monochromatic curriculum that partitioned off engagement with thinkers and ideas situated at the margins. From the standpoint of value, what this suggests is that these perspectives are not worth engaging in or are not legible as political science. To that point, I can recall while an undergraduate having a conversation with a senior scholar in political science during which I asked why their curriculum stopped short of seriously engaging women or Black thinkers. They looked at me and said, quite assuredly, "This is all there is. Anything beyond this, you need to know, is not political science." There was no equivocating in that moment. For them, the absence of Black thinkers, women, and those writing from the Global South signified their value relative to the discipline, which I suppose I was to infer is nothing at all.

That moment was a critical juncture for me. Years later, and after some deep reflection, I recognized that that scholar had perhaps unwittingly allowed me to peer behind the veil, so to speak, to behold the meaning contained in the choice for departments to include some perspectives and not others among its list of courses. In his view, the curriculum's ambits took the form they did because political science is ostensibly exclusive and therefore necessarily hostile to the imposition of voices, ideas, and approaches to conducting political science research and teaching that appear to threaten a hegemonic standard that both defines what political science is and powers claims regarding who best embodies its principles and aims. Even now, I am astonished at their ability to look into the face of a student who is both Black and female and declare that political science has no room for her, that Black women could spectate but not participate in a production of knowledge that would advance the field.

It was that moment that cemented my commitment to take on roles that would place me in the position to shape curriculum content and do so in such a way that enables a more diverse set of students to see their interests and experiences reflected in the collection of course offerings. I understand at the level of experience what it means to read into a curriculum's interstices and silences problematic presumptions about the relationship between one's identity and the field against which the curriculum is organized. I understand how those gaps in knowledge might lead one to draw the conclusion that political science is a space open to some and fundamentally foreclosed to others. It has therefore remained critical that I disrupt what I perceived to be part of political science's rhythm, which is a general pull toward producing course registers that present a distilled, myopic version of reality.

To that end, in my previous academic appointment, my rhythm-disrupting work took the form of injecting into the institution's course catalog a raft of classes that might assist in orienting the department to the direction of a new rhythm, one marked by an express desire to make political science welcoming to all students. One of the ways we are able telegraph this is through the courses we elect to offer. On that note, and at the time of writing this, I had developed six new courses (a few in collaboration with colleagues with whom I cotaught) and radically amended other inherited courses to address a previous deficit. The list of new courses included

- Black Political Thought;
- The Politics of Identity;
- Introduction to Black Studies (cross-listed with political science);

- The Notorious Angie D: Angela Davis and the Project of Freedom (cross-listed with history);
- Three Pillars of Africana Thought: Douglass, Du Bois, and Fanon; and
- Race Antiquity and Its Legacies (cross-listed with classics).

In addition, I am the architect of and was program coordinator for the institution's new Black Studies program inaugurated in the 2019–2020 academic year. The idea for this emerged out of my commitment, once again, to ensuring that education be reflective of a very complex, multifaceted, heterogenous human reality. Also, it is important to note that the institution is at the geographic center of Birmingham, Alabama, a majority Black city, situated blocks away from the neighborhood infamously dubbed "dynamite hill" during the civil rights era; and yet, the school's Black student population is hovering at just around 12%. Financial inaccessibility is a part of this story, sure, but the problem lies also in the fact that students need to see their interests and perspectives meaningfully reflected in the content of their study. As one of my former students put it, "I need material by which I can feel touched, content that moves me and incites in me a desire to implicate myself meaningfully into the world. Black Political Thought has been that for me." Another student of color remarked that political science had not registered as a viable course study option until they saw on the class roster courses that seemed to speak more directly to their lived experience. We need to be aware that an education that does not account for marginalized perspectives places underrepresented students at a distance, for they are presented with a partial view of reality masqueraded as reality itself. In this way, substantively integrating Black perspectives into a political science curriculum sends a signal to students of color that the department—and by extension, the institution—is trying to more accurately reflect the heterogeneity of the world, its people, and its values.

So, you see, my students had intuitively recognized the need to be swayed by a different rhythm. The old one did not move them; it left them feeling out of step with the department and, by extension, political science, more generally. With the addition of these classes, my intent was to create a space whereby more students of color, in particular, feel welcomed to participate in political science. If I have anything to do with it,

I do not want them to leave my classes wondering—as I did when I was an undergraduate—if political science can be home to Black students and faculty. The inclusion of these courses, then, was meant to convey the idea that my former department was making a genuine effort to establish a new pattern around how we inhabit political science. This is only possible by creating a rift in the old pattern, that is, through disruption.

[Don't] "Let me See that One-Two Step"[7]:
The Virtue of Getting Out of Step with Political Science's Dominant Rhythms and Other Concluding Ruminations

> At least I had smashed their rhythm of inevitability.
>
> —Angela Yvonne Davis

The above passage is taken from Angela Davis's biography at a moment in her narrative when she is being surreptitiously extradited from New York to be surrendered into California jurisdiction in the dead of night and without warning. She describes how the entire scene "had a choreographed air about it," from the way the extradition cars lined up inside the jail's courtyard to how they forcefully maneuvered her about. On an impulse, the only thing she could think to do was to come to an abrupt stop just shy of entering the car that was there to take her to the airport and openly protest the tightness of her handcuffs. She expressed that her point in acting in this way was to disrupt the performance of what was occurring and therefore compel the guards into an awareness of what exactly it was they were doing; they seemed to have been somnambulantly executing orders, that is, following a rhythm they were not entirely aware had been guiding them. Davis's disruptive act, then, jolted the guards out of a trance which subsequently inhibited their ability to carry on according to the rhythm in the kind of unbroken, fluid manner that had previously characterized their movements. In other words, her disruption created space for the possibility for something new, something different to emerge in that moment. She had "smashed their rhythm of inevitability" (1974, 71). And on the other side of that smashing, the guards loosened her cuffs, something that would not have happened otherwise.

Davis's words raise the idea that different futures become available when we persist in disrupting the rhythms of institutions and structures, those animated by alienating patterns that will continue to reproduce unless something/someone intervenes to throw them off. Against this view, this work is a very small window into the ways in which Black women political scientists smash the discipline's rhythm of inevitability and how, through forcing disruptions in the field's sometimes outmoded and alienating rhythms, we are critically involved in forging a future in which political science is more inclusive. I deploy my experience to illustrate how I have attempted to help set my former department along a different path, specifically through showing up as a Black woman political scientist faculty member in a space where no Black women had previously occupied that role and in altering the composition of a course catalog in a way that signals inclusiveness.

On the practice of rhythm disruption, I will conclude with some considerations to bear in mind[8]; we might call these "brief disclaimers on rhythm disrupting":

Rhythm-disrupting work can be hard to stay engaged in and not become enervated in the process. This is especially relevant for Black women academics, folks whose energies are often splintered in different directions because of a prevailing presumption baked into higher education (and other) spaces that Black women are there to labor incessantly for others and in extreme excess of their formal obligations (Collins 2000; hooks 1994 [1982]; Walker 1994). The wearing down might also emerge out of an eagerness and a sense of urgency to participate in as many projects that could lead to the eventual disruption of as many problematic rhythms as possible. My message to you, sister colleagues, is to take your time and be deliberate with how you allocate your energy. I must admit that this is something I am still working on, but I better recognize now that my capacity to continue in this work is contingent on resisting the abrasion that can come as a result of taking on too much and too soon. That said, rhythm-breaking work takes time and this is because we are attempting to unsettle patterns that have characterized the discipline and perhaps our departments for quite some time. It will take time to unfix these rhythms and to set the conditions for the establishment of new ones.

On that note, I am reminded of Cornel West's beautiful foreword to Angela Davis's *Freedom Is a Constant Struggle* (2016), specifically his remarks capturing how Davis's deep impact on liberation struggles across the globe is a function of her being what he calls a "long-distance" activist. This designation alludes to Davis's shaping her commitments around the recognition that the conditions having led to the dehumanization of so many took time to become that way, meaning then that undoing them will also take time. These insights are useful for thinking about the work needed to transform political science into becoming more inclusive to faculty and students. The patterns, the rhythms that have made political science into a discipline that appears to lack room for scholars and students of color and lagging on introducing pedagogical practices/assessment strategies that promote a richness and diversity of thought have been reinforced over the years. Thus, we need to be aware that rhythm-disrupting work, in this context and in others, is long-distance work.

Rhythm disrupting will awaken countervailing forces. I grew up in the Pentecostal church, and while I have several memories of those times, the scenes that I can recall with much clarity are moments when a choir member would appear visibly offbeat with the rest of the choir. In the case of someone swaying in the opposite direction, for instance, it was quite common to see the adjacent choir members use the force of their bodies to bind the out-of-line singer back into the rhythm of things. The opposing force of the offbeat choir member incited an alarm (perhaps involuntarily) among the nearby choir members to wrestle the aberrant individual back into place, that is, back to moving in concert with the flow of things.[9] This is metaphor for what can occur when Black women political scientists operate in a rhythm-disrupting role and attempt to move things in a direction other than that which appears normal, contrary to a "how things have been done" pattern. One can expect resistance, forces that amount to getting hip checked, as it were, back to a choreographed way of doing things. What I am saying here is that disruption is not always a welcomed event. And, recall that rhythms continuously pull one back to their pattern so as to continually reproduce the rhythm. Thus, people whose very presence and actions represent a threat to that will likely be challenged in some form. *Prepare for this.*

Finally, rhythm-disrupting work is not meant to be done alone! This disclaimer follows from the previous two. To draw this out, I return briefly to Fanon's (1963) discussion of the rhythm of the colonial world. When calling on the colonized to bring about the destruction of the colonial regime, he argues that one of the things that must be immediately jettisoned is the spirit of individualism. For Fanon, this is so not only because of its being a Western value antagonistic to the values that structure many African communities but also because it impedes on the colonized's ability to withstand the shocks that inevitably come as a result of the colonized's attempts at destroying the rhythm of the colonial world. Likewise, when Black women scholars attempt to disrupt some of political science's rhythms, we need others to stand with us to help absorb the shock of resistance that may arise. We need others also to affirm that we indeed feel and hear, so to speak, the rhythms at work in our departments and that we are not crazy. To that end, rhythm-disrupting work is fundamentally community work.

I hope this work elucidates not only the virtue of disruptive, rhythm-breaking practices but also their necessity, emphasizing that many Black women political scientists have been and continue to be engaged in this important work across different dimensions.

Notes

1. In the period between the manuscript's original submission and publication, I accepted a position at a different institution. All reflections here are based on my time and experience at my former institution.

2. Though not necessarily a clean break.

3. Song found at: https://www.youtube.com/watch?v=eFs8FeXXW-k.

4. I hope to soon be the first Black women in the school's history to be tenured in political science!

5. This figure has increased significantly since 1980, with female faculty then numbering 769, or about 10.3 percent (American Political Science Association 2011, 42).

6. I have not been able to locate the course catalog for the 2002–2003 academic year.

7. This is taken from the chorus of a song called "1, 2 Step" sung by R&B artist Ciara.

8. I hope to elaborate on these in a longer version of this work.

9. Sara Ahmed (2017) conveys a similar idea, arguing that when folks attempt to do work that resists dominant attitudes and ideologies, they can expect to encounter resistance. She uses the example of traffic, noting that traffic generates a self-reinforcing current, making it difficult to move in a contravening direction.

References

Ahmed, S. 2017. *Living a Feminist Life*. Durham: Duke University Press.
American Political Science Association. 2011. *Report of the Task Force on Political Science in the 21st Century*. https://www.apsanet.org/portals/54/Files/Task%20Force%20Reports/TF_21st%20Century_AllPgs_webres90.pdf.

Collins, P. H. 2000. *Black Feminist Thought: Knowledge, Consciousness, and the Politics of Empowerment*. New York: Routledge.
Cone, J. 1972. *The Spirituals and the Blues: An Interpretation*. New York: Orbis Books.
Davis, A. Y. 1974. *Angela Davis: An Autobiography*. New York: International.
———. 2016. *Freedom Is a Constant Struggle: Ferguson, Palestine, and the Foundations of a Movement*. Chicago: Haymarket Books.
Fanon, F. O. 1963. *La Damnés de la terre*. Translated by Constance Farrington. New York: Grove Press.
———. 2004. *La Damnés de la terre*. Translated by Richard Philcox. New York: Grove Press.
hooks, b. 1994 (1982). *Ain't I a Woman: Black Women and Feminism*. London: Pluto Press.
Walker, A. M. 1994. "In Search of Our Mother's Gardens." In *Within the Circle: An Anthology of African-American Literary Criticism from the Harlem Renaissance to the Present*, edited by A. Mitchell, 401–9. Durham, NC: Duke University Press.

5

The Absence of Rational Resources

How a Black Woman's Presence Redefines the Discipline's Norms

Sherice Janaye Nelson

A life in academia chose me. I did not choose it! Being a lawyer was the goal, with pushing the judicial system to be just to those in my community, and eventually becoming a judge was the dream. Had I understood how racist academia was at its outset, I would have chosen another profession. In many ways, there was a conscious avoidance of corporate America because of its known racism despite its financial benefits. This was preached in my household and easy to detect in my social surroundings. I am the first in all four lines of my familial heritage to become a doctor of philosophy; although my relatives are extremely proud of me, they do not have the slightest understanding of what I do as a professor and an academic. This is often realized when they refer to me as a teacher instead of a professor and if corrected are resentful. Yet, they understand my passion for service and understand that the work I do is less about scholastic pursuits and far more about the service of others.

There is an affinity for service in my family due to my paternal grandfather's service in WWII as well as the Korean War. This translated into my father's military experiences and the commitment by my mother to serve the citizens of California for thirty years. As a professor, it is my responsibility to serve students, fellow faculty, and the institution. As a Black woman who teaches in the political science discipline, the ability to serve others with my scholarship is my driver and definition of success. However, in academia my definition of success is an afterthought, as prominence is awarded based upon books published and journal articles written.

It was not until I was pushed into the world of academia as an adjunct professor that I realized collegiate education was the last breeding ground for social and political acculturation and indoctrination. In the political science discipline, students are introduced to Eurocentric philosophers like Aristotle, Rawls, Hobbes, Rousseau, Plato, and Kant. They are taught that these philosophers and their work matter, and non-Eurocentric philosophers are not taken into consideration in the fundamental courses. The exploration of ethnic philosophers are reserved for separate courses that are used as an elective, which does not guarantee students' exposure to other political thought. This solidifies the thoughts of white superiority, which are foundational in the composition of Western society (Goldberg 2002). Therefore, my mere presence as a Black woman makes the objective of subtly teaching white superiority at predominately white institutions difficult. My presence naturally raises questions about my belonging, my worthiness, and my intellectual capacity.

This phenomenon is quite different at predominately white institutions in comparison to historically Black colleges and universities (HBCUs). Being only HBCU educated, I was shielded from much of the racial anxiety that students that look like me experience in college. At a HBCU, your race or ethnic makeup is not consistently being leveraged by those who find your presence to be a benefit or a detriment. For this insulation I am grateful; I am confident that I would not be a professor today if I were required to navigate my worthiness and belonging while simultaneously navigating the realms of scholarship.

As a Black woman my presence demands a shift in the meaning of scholarship, especially in the discipline of political science. Political science was designed to mimic the racial overtones that constituted this country (Smith 2004). The study of race in the discipline's founding was not even a consideration and thus produces a bias that is prevalent in the discipline today. Such a bias has been discussed by Jennifer Hochschild the H. L. Jayne Professor of Government, professor of African and African American studies, and a presidential professor at Harvard University. She states:

> The discipline of political science tends to have a split personality on the issue of whether the underlying driving force behind political action is material or ideational. Put too crudely, mainstream (disproportionately White) scholars tend to focus on structural conditions such as laws or the economy, the self-interest of leaders or activists, political incentives, or even geography in order to explain ethnic identification and conflict. Conversely, scholars who study racial politics (disproportionately people of color), tend to start from racial or ethnic identity and conflict in order to explain structural conditions, understandings of self-interest, or political incentives. (Hochschild 2005)

Hochschild's proclamation is accurate, yet it required the narration of a well-decorated and respected white woman at an Ivy League institution in 2005 before it was truly taken into consideration by the discipline. Although white women have gained more standing in the discipline over time, the minority status they have occupied resulted in their scholarship being disregard as inconsequential. Subsequently, white women are more apt to see the quality of scholarship and the impact other minority groups bring to the discipline. Therefore, Black women are saddled with a double minority status that deems us unworthy to participate, robbing us from the space needed to pontificate, which is provided to other scholars; tempers us from espousing our ideas with our colleagues and our students; and ultimately deems us misfits that must be duly terrorized to ensure failure because we do not fit the norm.

A Black woman's worthiness or deservedness is always being questioned in political science because we are not viewed as rational actors and are thus presumed incompetent. *Presumed Incompetent: The Intersections of Race and Class for Women in Academia* was published by a compilation of women across disciplines that discussed the idea that in academic spaces women have to prove their competence (Muhs 2012). The constant need to prove is due to the lack of rational resources available to Black women. The foundation of rational choice theory is that individuals, known as rational actors, will anticipate the outcomes of known alternative courses of action and calculate which will be the best strategy (Goldthorpe 1998). Such strategies need resources, and in rational choice theory there are four resources: time, information, approval, and prestige.

These resources help develop alternative choices known as *rational action*. A *rational actor* is defined as a conscious social actor engaging in deliberate calculative strategies (Goldthorpe 1998). Men are societally viewed as rational individuals because they choose the alternative that is likely to give them the greatest satisfaction. This in turn creates social order, which champions a particular set or system of linked social structures needed for relating and behaving.

Such behaviors are defined by white men in the discipline of political science who are being faced with the loss of scholastic primacy. A shift is underway in the discipline whereby ideational research is no longer seen as the only valuable research framework. This is best exemplified in the new journals that have provided a respected place to publish about politics from a racial or ethnic lens. *Politics, Groups, and Identities* is an official journal of the Western Political Science Association that published its first journal in 2013, making the journal less than ten years old. The journal's current chief editor is a Black woman who has achieved tenure. This is a structural sign that the ideational framework consistently generalized in the discipline to be the standard is being challenged by many who long to center the scholarship of non-Eurocentric scholars. This exemplifies how Black women push the discipline outside of their departments using different tactics to actualize change. Such ideological influences result in the lessening of superiority of one theoretical framework over another, leveling the playing field for all scholarship.

To prevent the collapse of Eurocentric dominance in the discipline, generalizations are created and used. These generalizations are critical in the maintenance of the discipline's norms because they nullify the need and creation of research performed through a different ideational lens. Simply put, generalizations questioning Blacks scholastic ability serve as a distraction for the root cause plaguing the discipline. This is far more true with the double minority status of Black women, as the academic attacks are often far more tailored and precise.

Black women lack access to the rational resources of approval and prestige. Our choice of research topics, focused on the driving force of political action wrought with racism, sexism, or homophobia, are seen to be in abstention to the discipline's assumed norms and thus unworthy of prestige. Our decision to inject the lived experiences of those affected by the policy decisions of others is deemed trite and incapable of approval. Our decision to take a position at a community college, a HBCU, or a liberal arts teaching institution is seen to be foolhardy, lacking prestige.

Why? Because approval is only provided to those who secure positions at research one institutions with a plethora of human and financial resources. The discipline never takes into consideration that Black educated women are typically the breadwinners in their families and must balance work (after all this is still a job) and home life. Nor does the discipline take into consideration that Black women may not have the freedom to move across the country to take that coveted job at a research one institution. Nor does the discipline consider the desire of many Black women to serve students who are often forgotten in the educational system and get lackluster instruction and halfhearted commitment at the community colleges.

Without access to the rational resources of prestige and approval, Black women must still engage in the discipline's norms, despite their relatively low status, to be considered rational actors and preserve their careers. The racial hierarchy established alongside the gender hierarchy in this country, and subsequently in political science, has shaped its norms and simultaneously made it impossible for Black women to interact with morality, cooperation, and trust the way a white man can. Simply, approval and subsequent prestige is only ascribed to chief executive decision-makers who are white men. This is reflected in the discipline's editorial boards for premier journals and the number of white men serving as the chair of political science departments across the country. A review of the top twenty-five political science programs ranked by *U.S. News & World Report*, shows that not one political science department is led by a Black woman (Best Political Science Schools 2021). Access to the full cadre of rational resources, which include time, information, approval, and prestige, is reserved for white men as a preservation of order in the discipline. Therefore, the presence of a Black woman in the academy, especially in political science, places stress on these structures and challenges the discipline to rethink the lens through which power exercised by the state is studied and taught.

The study of political science is often expressed to students as the study of power. The study is designed to answer who used the power, when and how much power was used, why such power was used at that juncture, and what was the outcome. Subsequently, Black women are going to see the power paradigm differently than other scholars in the field. This results in different pedagogy, different scholarship focuses, and different positions on the meaning of success in the field as well as in academia overall. If those in power have stripped Black women of being seen as rational actors, Black women have co-opted the discipline's norms with moral authority, commitment to scholarship, and exemplary service to our students. Black women consistently decide to become even more committed instead of bending to the established norms. They have accepted the challenge to prove themselves due to their perceived incompetence but not in ways that will result in the regaining of the rational resources lost in approval or prestige. Instead, Black women have decided to create space in the discipline by refusing to integrate into norms that are inherently bigoted and have been willing to pay with career-stifling consequences. This is with the hope that their stance will provide opportunity for other Black women behind them.

As a junior scholar, I have most evidently seen this in meeting Black women political scientist throughout the country at academic conferences. A review of the American Political Science Association (APSA) membership shows that Blacks constitute only 3.59 percent of membership while Whites constitute 61.51 percent of the membership (Mealy 2018). Although these data are not aggregated to display these ethnic breakdowns by gender, the data do show that women compose only 35.6 percent of the APSA membership (Mealy 2018). These data substantiate Black women as double minorities. Therefore, the stories heard at such conferences about the racism and sexism Black women face from their colleagues and how this results in only a handful of us achieving tenure is not surprising. Our double minority status highlights the fact that chasing approval and prestige inside the discipline is both dubious and elusive, which often will result in disappointment.

I remember when I graduated from my PhD program at Howard University, where many of the scholars there tried to shield me from such disappointment. I was the only Black woman political scientist in the world studying leadership through a multidisciplinary lens. The multidisciplinary lens of the dissertation received pushback at Howard, yet I was ignorant about exactly why. Many of the scholars who trained me were guarding a well-kept secret that multidisciplinary scholarship was frowned upon in political science. Many were nervous that my use of multidisciplinary theoretical frameworks alongside my double minority status in the discipline would make landing a tenure-track job nearly impossible. In many ways they were correct, as I was an adjunct professor for four years before landing a tenure-track position. Although no one had the heart to just tell me the secret, they eventually supported my use of different frameworks. They undoubtedly did not want me to become discouraged and leave academia altogether. Yet, I understood that to study the political phenomenon of women's participation in government at the senior level, other theories must be examined. The lives of women are not neatly categorized, and this is exponentially true for Black women. Therefore, the study of women in governmental leadership required integrated scholarship, which did not receive broad approval in the discipline.

Due to Black women's commitment to scholarship that disrupts political science norms, many of us must secure tenure outside of political science departments. Instead, Black women secure tenure in ethnic studies departments, women's studies departments, or African American studies departments. There is nothing fallacious about such appointments except that those departments receive far less funding and support by academic institutions indiscriminate of size. Now there are always exceptions, but Black women's lack of rational resources and the choices they make in response to the lack results in them pushing the discipline outside of the departments at their given institutions. This is done with joint appointments where Black women are still committed to producing excellent scholarship that challenges the discipline's constant need to encourage the study of structural conditions to understand political phenomenon above all else.

This is primarily done with overreliance on quantitative methods. The top ten journals in political science read like mathematical journals, as dependent variables, independent variables, linear regressions, and interactive models are the norm. This is in part due to the study of political interaction in the frame of structural conditions, which lend themselves to interactions that draw causal ties. However, the study of political interaction in the frame of ethnic or racial conflict does not allow for the same clean use of variables. Often these variables provide conflict that results in correlative relationships that are not as statistically strong. Subsequently, Black women draw attention to these inequities by organizing diversity initiatives and smaller conferences within larger conferences (SPSA 2018). These efforts enhance Black women's quantitative and qualitative skill sets and provide a space for decompression while simultaneously taking the discipline to task for years of neglect.

Black women also use their moral authority to push the discipline to change. Instead of griping and complaining about the lack of access to premier journals, the lack of financial resources to perform case study experiments, or the lack of information purposefully not disseminated to reduce competition, they went to other departments and took them by storm. This often requires the learning of different methodologies so that the scholars in the departments do not view Black women as impostures who are undervaluing their work. This broader methodological knowledge is infused into Black women's scholarship and teaching. This in turn broadens the methodological reach of students in political science. Black women consistently participate in scholarship that is meaningful to them despite what prestige or approval they receive from the political science discipline at large. These instances are the use of moral authority that makes others in the discipline question their actions.

In a profession and in a discipline that champions egalitarianism and is strict about objectivity, a Black woman's fight to study what she deems important is revolutionary. It forces the discipline to see its hypocritical nature and acknowledge the split personality highlighted by Hochschild. Black women use the racial conflict seen in political systems, which account for governments behaviors around the globe, as a signal for political scientists to see that same behavior in the discipline. They commit themselves to tenure and review processes that they know have a racialized history yet refuse to be deterred (Rucks-Ahidiana 2019). They teach students who have been subconsciously taught to question their authority, due to their double minority status, with pride (Lilienfeld 2016). They work with colleagues whose constant use of microaggressions make them second-guess their competence.

Yet with all of this, Black women are still pushing the discipline to reimagine itself in a way that not only tolerates but welcomes a broader perspective. That scholarship is truly evaluated based upon its rigor and innovative genius rather than by the institution from which the scholarship hails. They continue to believe that although we lack the rational resources of others, that lack is nothing that should stop us from producing scholarship, teaching our students, and serving our communities with our knowledge about the study of power. For we know that "If there is no struggle there is no progress. . . . Power is not conceded without a demand. It never did and it never will" (Douglass 2023). Black women's presence in the discipline of political science, our scholarship, our teaching pedagogies, and our service form our demand that the power inside the discipline change.

References

Best Political Science Schools. 2021. https://www.usnews.com/best-graduate-schools/top-humanities-schools/political-science-rankings.

Douglass, Frederick. 2023. Voices of a People's History. August 3, 1857. https://www.peopleshistory.us/about.
Goldberg, David Theo. 2002. *The Racial State*. Malden, MA: Blackwell.
Goldthorpe, John H. 1998. "Rational Action Theory for Sociology." *British Journal of Sociology* 49, no. 2: 167–92.
Hochschild Jennifer, L. 2005. "Race and Class in Political Science." *Michigan Journal of Race and Law* 11, no. 1: 99–114.
Lilienfeld, Eva. 2016. "How Student Evaluations Are Skewed against Women and Minority Professors." Century Foundation. June 10. https://tcf.org/content/commentary/student-evaluations-skewed-women-minority-professors/?agreed=1.
Mealy, Kimberly A. 2018. Diversity and Inclusion Report: American Political Science Association. https://www.apsanet.org/Portals/54/diversity%20and%20inclusion%20prgms/DIV%20reports/Diversity%20Report%20Executive%20-%20Final%20Draft%20-%20Web%20version.pdf?ver=2018-03-29-134427-467.
Muhs, G. G. 2012. *Presumed Incompetent: The Intersections of Race and Class for Women in Academia*. Boulder: University Press of Colorado.
Rucks-Ahidiana, Zawadi. 2019. "The Inequities of the Tenure-Track System." Inside Higher Education. June 7. https://www.insidehighered.com/advice/2019/06/07/nonwhite-faculty-face-significant-disadvantages-tenure-track-opinion.
Smith, Rogers M. 2004. "The Puzzling Place of Race in American Political Science." *PS: Political Science and Politics* 37, no. 1: 41–45.
Southern Political Science Association (SPSA). Preliminary Program. 2018. https://spsa.net/wp-content/uploads/2018/10/2019-SPSA-Prelim-Program1.pdf.

6

Cultivating Joy in Academia

Adaugo Pamela Nwakanma

The Quest for Joy

> . . . i found god in myself
> & i loved her/i loved her fiercely.
>
> —*A Laying on of Hands* (Shange 1989)

While joy does not have a single definition, psychologists, theologians, and philosophers have developed an expansive understanding of joy as either an emotion, disposition, mood, or spiritual fruit that "can happen in response to some desire being fulfilled, or in anticipation of the desire being fulfilled. . . . [It] involves physical and cognitive freedom to 'broaden and build', which involves exploring and creating new motor, behavioral and cognitive schemas and new social relationships and resources" (Johnson 2020). Joy involves liberation, and our liberation is embedded in our commitment to authenticity. Creative resistance, self-care, and authenticity are fundamental to our cultivation of joy. Black feminist philosophers highlight the importance of self-care in the fight for social justice. This politics of care often deviates from individualistic notions of self-indulgence and instead focuses on the necessity of our well-being as significant subjects worthy of respect and as members of political communities. As

Audre Lorde teaches us, "Caring for [ourselves] is not self-indulgence, it is self-preservation, and that is an act of political warfare" (1988).

Joy is truly an emblematic fruit in that it needs to be planted and cared for before it can be harvested. Cultivating joy is an intentional process rooted in gratitude and a decision to commit to said process. When I was admitted into my PhD program at twenty-one, I knew that I did not want to spend most of my twenties being miserable. This decision to pursue joy in my twenties and onward stemmed from a desire to diverge from the pain that I experienced as a child. I had a turbulent childhood growing up between Los Angeles, California, and Aba, Southeast Nigeria, in a home environment where my parents underwent a messy divorce and an even messier trans-Atlantic custody battle that culminated in the death of my immediate younger sister. The trauma that I experienced in my childhood through domestic violence at home, abusive floggings at school in Nigeria, negligence on the part of my father, and the failure of our community to adequately intervene left a deep wound in my spirit. As a teenager, I grew to be distrustful, depressed, and exceedingly high achieving in academics to escape the realities of my home life. When I went to college at the University of California, San Diego, at sixteen years old, I was enthusiastic about the possibility of starting afresh in a new environment but did not realize how much my exposure to genuinely kind humans and diverse perspectives would affect me personally and draw me closer to God.

My college years provided the time and space that I needed to slowly unlearn the normalized violence of my childhood and embrace healing. The seed of joy was slowly germinating in my spirit, and so were faith and courage. After graduating from college, I took a leap of faith to move to New York City from California. I lived in Brooklyn and worked as an educator at a charter school in Manhattan. I also got involved with a Seventh-Day Adventist church in the city, where I deepened my learning about Christianity from a multicultural lens. Diverse people's life stories influenced my imagination of what is possible and helped me see the threads of God's hands in my life despite the turbulence of my childhood. From that limitless imagination, I started to think about how I could make sense of my life's trajectory thus far and receive the training and the language that I needed to answer larger questions on identity, migration, and development in all its complex forms. Pursuing a PhD opened up those possibilities. In addition to investigating complex issues, I wanted to lean into the possibility of succeeding in school while enjoying the journey.

While working toward my doctoral degree, I have engaged in self-care and creative resistance by prioritizing joy cultivation. Within this process, I had to decide to stay true to my authentic, multidimensional self for the seeds of joy to continue to germinate within my soul. In order for these seeds to blossom sustainably, I had to ensure that my commitment to this process was deeply rooted in an unwavering foundation. My understanding of joy, drawn from my Christian faith, "grounds the goal of life—including one's career—in a higher purpose of serving God and humanity" (Cramer, Alexander-Floyd, and Means 2019). This meant allowing my faith background to shape how I approach my professional and personal life. My joy is rooted in gratitude toward the one I believe loves me infinitely despite my circumstances. From this belief, I understand that faith is about where we put our trust. Where we put our trust ultimately shapes our identity. I choose to identify myself in such a way that my work is not what defines me. Rather, my relationship with God defines me. I am a child of God, and who I am shapes what I do. My doing therefore flows from my being and not the other way around.

Academia and even the world cannot take away a joy that it did not give me. I would rather not pay the cost of my integrity to fulfill other people's ideas of success for an institution and global economy that does not care about my well-being. I choose to spend my time and energy being wise and strategic about making the most of what privileges academia affords me. Black women in the United States are more susceptible to the early onset of chronic diseases, particularly hypertension and diabetes, due to the "weathering" effects of prolonged stress brought on by racism and sexism (Geronimus et al. 2010). Similarly, we are faced with "the reality of a lethally disciplinary state and a political economy that proscribes, devalues, and excludes [us] from prosperity" (Woodly 2019, 219). With this in mind, my approach to my professional and personal life is rooted in a commitment to self-care and radical Black joy as these commitments are necessary for survival in a world constantly trying to kill us.

Navigating the Ivory Tower

Historically and contemporaneously, Black women have been underrepresented in political science. While the presence of historically underrepresented groups in the discipline has augmented over the decades, progress has been slow and limited. In 1980, African American women composed about 4.3 percent of women political science faculty (APSA 2011). The American Political Science Association's (APSA's) most recent diversity and inclusion report reveals that only about 3.2 percent of members are Black, Afro-Caribbean, or African American (Brown and Lajevardi 2020). Interdisciplinary data reveal that Black women make up about 3 percent of the professoriate in the United States, and out of 1.5 million faculty positions, only 2 percent are Black women full professors (Williams and Hardaway 2018). These numbers are dismal and paint a broad picture of the gaps that exist within the discipline and in academia more broadly.

Moving beyond the numbers, rich narratives of Black women's experiences within the academy demonstrate how this lack of representation translates into marginalizing learning environments. Structural as well as interpersonal racialized and gendered inequities intersect to affect Black women in unique ways. Interpersonally, given the intersecting legacy of racism, sexism, classism, and other forms of human prejudice, Black women disproportionally face discrimination in their daily lives (Lewis and Neville 2015; Spates et al. 2020). This often shows up as anti-Black misogyny, otherwise known as misogynoir (Bailey and Trudy 2018). Misogynoir presents itself in and outside of the classroom in the form of everyday microaggressions, prejudiced teaching evaluations, the stymying of research on Black women, and the undervaluation of diverse scholarship in favor of research that is "reflective of a more accepted, White-normed [epistemic] paradigm" (Jones, Hwang, and Bustamante 2015).

Structurally, Black women and other women of color have detailed their challenges in finding mentors that can effectively support their career objectives. Conversely, due to the low representation of Black faculty and the power of role model effects (Papageorge et al. 2018),[1] Black women faculty often face higher demands on their time and energy from students seeking guidance and expertise from professors of similar racial or cultural backgrounds. For women of color faculty, this increased mentorship load contributes to a perception of women of color as serving as nurturing maternal figures instead of rigorous academics (APSA 2011; Constantine et al. 2008).

Similarly, Black women faculty and administrators often face higher service responsibilities. In addition to taking on more teaching and advising, research suggests that Black faculty are more likely to be asked to serve on committees, particularly those related to equity, diversity, and inclusion initiatives, than their white counterparts (Allen et al. 2000; Constantine et al. 2008). Coined by Padilla (1994), this "cultural taxation" can affect Black academics' scholarship productivity, which has detrimental effects on their success and retention in academia (Louis et al. 2016). This is especially pertinent in spaces where administrators and other faculty undervalue these service roles, as is the case in many R1 universities.

These structural inequities have unique impacts on Black women's experiences navigating the ivory tower. Faculty from underrepresented backgrounds are more likely to report feelings of isolation, stress, marginalization, and a chillier institutional climate (Hesli and Burrell 1995; Rockquemore and Laszloffy 2008). These experiences contribute to a leaky pipeline that perpetuates racial and gender gaps in salaries, promotion rates, retention, and job satisfaction. Nevertheless, even in the face of institutional and interpersonal misogynoir, Black women create opportunities for creativity, rigor, and enrichment.

Engaged Scholarship

As institutions wrestle with legacies of exclusionary policies and practices, Black women have and continue to create magic out of close to nothing. Dr. Melissa Harris-Perry highlights that even from positions on the margin, Black women political scientists have and continue to "[contest] the field, [challenge] the academy, and [contribute] to the development of more just communities" (Harris-Lacewell 2005, 342). Many Black women entering political science doctorate programs are prompted by interests in intellectual development and a commitment to engaged scholarship (Harris-Lacewell 2005). Through engaged scholarship, Black women and other people of color from underrepresented backgrounds often pursue research agendas that not only meet the rigorous demands of the discipline but also produce knowledge and praxis relevant for the communities they partner with. In doing this work, Black women often employ intersectional, emancipatory, and multicultural frameworks to their research and teaching that challenge and transform hegemonic epistemologies and pedagogical approaches.

Building on this legacy of engaged scholarship, my dissatisfaction with the essentialist portrayal of African women in political science and development economics fueled my unique and interdisciplinary research and teaching agenda. I study women's empowerment in business and politics. More specifically, I employ a transnational Africana feminist lens in my interrogation of how social power influences the relationship between economic and political power in spaces of patriarchal politicking

(Nwakanma 2022a, 2022b). The lens I use to approach my research agenda treats African women "as producers of knowledge and makers of theory" (Nnaemeka 2004).

In my doctoral research, I focus on traders operating in traditional open-air markets and women engaged in Nigeria's rising digital technology sector. The motivation for my pursuit of this research agenda stemmed from my desire to engage in scholarship that had real-world implications for women's experiences in the entrepreneurial ecosystem. As a Black, Nigerian American woman, my interest was also fueled by the desire to challenge deficit teachings of African women that essentialized us as populations in need of saving and push for a more comprehensive and critical standard of intellectual inquiry that centered African women in political economy discourse.

In this pursuit, I have questioned the essence of political science. As has been modeled by the Black women political scientists who continue to transform the discipline and the world through their engaged scholarship, I reify and center knowledge produced by the communities I research. I seek to infuse this knowledge in pedagogy and praxis given the understanding that the academy and the world of ideas serve as catalysts for policy and institutional change (Mukand and Rodrik 2018). As I invest my time and energy in pursuing rigorous scholarship that is also culturally relevant, I have learned the significance of authenticity for sustaining excellent scholarship. To successfully navigate the discipline's research, teaching, and service demands while staying true to my convictions, I have focused more on who I am becoming in the process of what I am doing. This prioritization, as informed by Black feminist philosophies of self-care, has aided me in cultivating joy along my academic journey.

Confronting Challenges

As I think about what it takes to live intentionally—to live on purpose—I constantly ask myself how I want to define my work. It is truly a privilege (and a rarity) for me to say that even amid all the ups and downs of the PhD journey, I am enjoying the process. During my PhD studies, I faced structural and interpersonal marginalization that materialized itself through the lack of faculty advisers of color, nonexistent departmental course offerings or support in my core subfields—African and gender politics—

the sidelining of Black voices in course syllabi, having to self-advocate for equitable teaching compensation, and dealing with stylized pushback from white faculty who engage in performative allyship.

Relatedly, I was told "life is not fair" by a white adviser after elucidating the variety of ways in which the lack of courses in African politics in my department was affecting my education. This same adviser undervalued my work with Black students as well as my commitment to studying African languages and engaging in learning opportunities outside of the predominantly white workshop spaces. In essence, the metaphorical ivory tower has not been welcoming or particularly kind to me. Though disheartening, I know who I am and did not seek validation from institutions I know were not built for me. Self-care and creative resistance for me in this climate meant deepening the roots of my joy, leaning on the wisdom of my faith, defining success for myself, and intentionally seeking and engaging with communities committed to the work I ultimately care about. I proceeded to expand my intellectual circle by pursuing a secondary field in the African and African American studies department at my university and taking up teaching and research initiatives through diverse programs and centers. Making this decision felt empowering, especially given the fact that it was self-motivated.

Although I am indeed grateful for how my extradepartmental involvements enriched my experience and shaped me into the phenomenal interdisciplinary scholar that I strive to be, it would be myopic to overlook the systemic and interpersonal failures that created a hostile environment for someone with my intersecting identities to begin with. Academia upholds norms of professional performance that are rooted in the neoliberal myth of the ideal worker and privileges an institutional environment devoid of responsibility (Cramer, Alexander-Floyd, and Means 2019). I experience cognitive dissonance when I think of how my doctoral journey demonstrates resilience, intentionality, and personal liberation in the face of institutional failures. As modeled by many Black women who came before me, I created magic even amid nonsense. I cultivated a rich doctoral life out of less than favorable circumstances. I was committed to not only surviving the PhD but thriving. Thriving for me means truly enjoying who I am becoming in the process. To thrive, I had to ensure that my quest for joy was deeply rooted in faith: in the belief that God is the shaper of my destiny and not humans, and most definitely not institutions.

Transforming the Discipline: The Way Forward

> ... When you learn, teach.
> When you get, give.
> As for me,
> I shall not be moved ...
> She searched God's face.
> Assured,
> ... No one, no, nor no one million
> ones dare deny me God, I go forth
> along, and stand as ten thousand.
> The Divine upon my right
> impels me to pull forever
> at the latch on Freedom's gate.
> ... She stands ...
>
> —*Our Grandmothers* (Angelou 1991)

We come from a rich legacy of people who have come before us to show us the way: Black women who have cultivated joy where possible while transforming the world around them. When I show up in academia as my authentic self, I go forth along and stand on the strength, wisdom, and guidance of tens of thousands of Back women who have lighted the way to joyful resistance. My commitment to cultivating joy in and around me stems from the wisdom of the Black women who come before me. Learning is a communal process, and my intellectual community is not bound by time or space. To cultivate joy effectively, we need to care for ourselves physically, spiritually, mentally, emotionally, and socially. I practice self-care by being mindful of how I value and treat my body, being cautious of what worldviews I allow into my spirit, creating space and time for intentional reflection in nature, letting go of disempowering relationships, and ultimately investing in relationships and activities that serve to empower my purpose on this earth. To protect the temple of my mind, body, and spirit, I engage in frequent self-reflection through journaling, talk therapy, prayer, and meditation on scripture. Through this practice, I am better at discerning which worldviews are profitable and which are not.

Likewise, to care for myself as an embodied scholar, I invest in and sustain meaningful relationships and communities within and outside of the academy. In my journey thus far, I have engaged with scholars across disciplines and at different institutions through workshops, trainings, mixers, and symposia. Beyond academic connections, I recognize the value of creative, artistic, spiritual, and cultural communities, as these spaces of nourishment are not disconnected from intellectual pursuits. The work of cultivating joy in academia takes conscious effort and requires an investment in the self outside of academia. To embody joy as a scholar, I invested in communities such as the Kuumba Singers of Harvard College, which celebrate Black spirituality and creativity via dance, poetry, music, theater, and other mediums taught and passed down through diverse African traditions. When I show up in academia in my primary roles as researcher and educator, the work I do consistently to care for myself and community members improves my scholarship.

Success is intimately linked with inner well-being. bell hook's extensive work on education as a practice of freedom highlights the significance of embodied scholarship in research and pedagogy. On this, she narrates:

> a holistic approach to learning and spiritual practice enabled me to overcome years of socialization that had taught me to believe a classroom was diminished if students and professors regarded one another as "whole" human beings, striving not just for knowledge in books but knowledge about how to live in the world. . . . Indeed, the objectification of the teacher within bourgeois educational structures seemed to denigrate notions of wholeness and uphold the idea of a mind/body split, one that promotes and supports compartmentalization. (hooks 1994, 14, 16)

Despite the bourgeois educational structures that work to strip us of our full humanity, Black women's presence in political science disrupts the homogeneity of the field in ways that are expanding and transforming the intellectual ecosystem to be more inclusive, equitable, and valuable to the world around us. The work that many Black women do to decolonize academia, democratize knowledge, and foster self-actualization has exponential impacts on other Black women and the world at large. Various organizations amplify work on and by Black women and other underrepresented groups such as the Black Women's Studies Association, the National Conference for Black Political Scientists, the Black Doctoral

Network, the National Center for Faculty Development and Diversity, and many others.

In addition to these organizations, several Black women in recent times have spearheaded initiatives that enrich the academic ecosystem by creating supportive and productive environments specifically for women scholars of color. Amid a global pandemic, Dr. Nadia E. Brown, professor of political science and African American studies, created the PS Sistah Scholar virtual community for women of color in political science to serve as a place for professional development, community building, and authentic dialogue on the unwritten rules of academia. In the same vein, Dr. Ijeoma Kola, public health historian, lifestyle blogger, and entrepreneur, created Cohort Sistas, a fast-growing online network that empowers Black women at different stages of the doctoral journey through resources, mentorship, and community building across disciplines and geographic locations. Alongside institutionalized programming, both initiatives demonstrate the power of Black women in adopting creativity during a global crisis to transform the academic ecosystem by providing empowering spaces for Black women's success.

As I continue to define success for myself in a way that is true to my soul, I am reminded of the mission of one of my creative homes in graduate school, the Kuumba Singers of Harvard College. Celebrating Blackness through art and community service, members and alumni of the organization are committed to "doing what we can with what we have to leave a space better than we found it" (Kuumba 2020). Whether through the power of representation or through modeling what it means to be an engaged scholar, the presence of Black women in the discipline serves as a catalyst for transformation that has multigenerational ripple effects.

Black women often leave spaces they enter better than they found them, but academia has yet to foster a holistic space for Black women to thrive. Narratives such as that of historian Thea Hunter, who died after many years of navigating the deficiencies of the perennial adjunct professorship system, illustrate how academia can exploit people's labor while undervaluing their humanity. Black women are often most affected by these exploits, given that Black women are disproportionately hired as contingent faculty (Nzinga 2020). Highlighting some of the statistics on the positions of underrepresented scholars such as Thea Hunter, Harris (2019) notes, "From 1993 to 2013, the percentage of underrepresented minorities in non–tenure-track part-time faculty positions in higher education grew by 230 percent. By contrast, the percentage of underrepresented minorities in full-time tenure-track positions grew by just 30 percent. . . . [Thea Hunter] was a black woman in academia, and she was flying against a current. Some professors soar; adjuncts flap and dive and flap again—until they can't flap anymore." Academia has a long way to go in terms of making itself more conducive for Black women not just to survive but to thrive by having rich personal and professional lives without having to combat misogynoir continually. But we, too, are academia, and by constantly showing up in our womanhood and Blackness, we are pushing our fields to improve. As much as political science and other disciplines have toxic elements, we also enjoy certain privileges as creators of knowledge, teachers, and scholar-activists. Perspective determines how we experience life, and to joyfully thrive in institutions that were not built for us, we must be wise in our pursuit of success.

As I continue to stay true to who I was created to be by focusing my time and energy on spaces, activities, and relationships that serve to enable my purpose on this earth, success is inevitable. This commitment is not easy; however, I do not approach this mission alone. I do not come as one but as many. I stand on the shoulders of all the Black women before me, known and unknown, named and unnamed, seen and unseen, who by virtue of them being Black and women in this world paved the way for me. When we, as Black women, enter these spaces, we do so as many and not only navigate the demands of our various disciplines but transform the very roots of these spaces. With this empowering perspective, it is only natural for me to desire to cultivate joy in my life and contribute to the garden of Black women coming after me.

Note

1. Papageorge et al. (2018) provide empirical evidence that suggests that role model effects help explain increased educational attainment among Black students mentored and taught by Black teachers.

References

Allen, W. R., E. G. Epps, E. A. Guillory, S. A. Suh, and M. Bonous-Hammarth. 2000. "The Black Academic: Faculty Status among African Americans in U.S. Higher Education." *Journal of Negro Education* 69: 112–27.

American Political Science Association (APSA). 2011. "Political Science in the 21st Century: Task Force Report." *American Political Science Association*. https://www.apsanet.org/portals/54/Files/Task%20Force%20Reports/TF_21st%20Century_AllPgs_webres90.pdf.

Bailey, Moya, and Trudy. 2018. "On Misogynoir: Citation, Erasure, and Plagiarism." *Feminist Media Studies* 18, no. 4: 762–68. https://doi.org/10.1080/14680777.2018.1447395.

Angelou, M. 1991. "Our Grandmothers." *Drumvoices Revue* 1, no. 1: 119.

Brown, Nadia E., and Nazita Lajevardi. 2020. "Introduction: Building, Sustaining, and Supporting the Race, Ethnicity, and Politics Community." *PS, Political Science & Politics* 53, no. 1: 137.

Constantine, M. G., L. Smith, R. M. Redington, and D. Owens. 2008. "Racial Microaggressions against Black Counseling and Counseling Psychology Faculty: A Central Challenge in the Multicultural Counseling Movement." *Journal of Counseling & Development* 86: 348–55.

Cramer, R., N. Alexander-Floyd, and T. Means. 2019. "Balance Is a Fallacy: Striving for and Supporting a Life with Integrity." *PS: Political Science & Politics* 52, no. 1: 35–38. doi:10.1017/S1049096518001154.

Geronimus, Arline T., Margaret T. Hicken, Jay A. Pearson, Sarah J. Seashols, Kelly L. Brown, and Tracey Dawson Cruz. 2010. "Do US Black Women Experience Stress-Related Accelerated Biological Aging? A Novel Theory and First Population-Based Test of Black-White Differences in Telomere Length." *Human Nature (Hawthorne, N.Y.)* 21, no. 1: 19–38.

Harris, A. 2019. "The Death of an Adjunct." *Atlantic*. https://www.theatlantic.com/education/archive/2019/04/adjunct-professors-higher-education-thea-hunter/586168/.

Harris-Lacewell, M. 2005. "Contributions of Black Women in Political Science to a More Just World." *Politics & Gender* 1, no. 2: 341–50.

Hesli, V., and Barbara Burrell. 1995. "Faculty Rank among Political Scientists and Reports on the Academic Environment: The Differential Impact of Gender on Observed Patters." *PS: Political Science and Politics* 28, no. 1: 101–11.

hooks, b. 1994. *Teaching to Transgress: Education as the Practice of Freedom*. New York: Routledge.

Johnson, M. K. 2020. Joy: A Review of the Literature and Suggestions for Future Directions. *Journal of Positive Psychology* 15, no. 1: 5–24.

Jones, B., E. Hwang, and R. M. Bustamante. 2015. "African American Female Professors' Strategies for Successful Attainment of Tenure and Promotion at predominately White Institutions: It Can Happen." *Education, Citizenship and Social Justice* 10, no. 2: 133–51.

Kuumba Singers of Harvard College. 2020. "President's Letter." https://kuumbasingers.org/.

Lewis, J. A., and H. A. Neville. 2015. "Construction and Initial Validation of the Gendered Racial Microaggressions Scale for Black Women." *Journal of Counseling Psychology* 62: 289–302. https://doi.org/10.1037/cou0000062.

Lorde, A. 1988. *A Burst of Light: Essays (Black Women Writers)*. Ithaca, NY: Firebrand Books.

Louis, D. A., G. J. Rawls, D. Jackson-Smith, G. A. Chambers, L. L. Phillips, and S. L. Louis. 2016. "Listening to Our Voices: Experiences of Black Faculty at Predominantly White Research Universities with Microaggression." *Journal of Black Studies* 47, no. 5: 454–74.

Mukand, S., and D. Rodrik. 2018. "The Political Economy of Ideas: On Ideas versus Interests in Policymaking." *NBER Working Paper*. https://doi.org/10.3386/w24467.

Nnaemeka, Obioma. 2004. "Nego-Feminism: Theorizing, Practicing, and Pruning Africa's Way." *Signs: Journal of Women in Culture and Society* 29, no. 2: 357–85.

Nwakanma, Adaugo Pamela. 2022a. "From Black Lives Matter to EndSARS: Women's Socio-Political Power and the Transnational Movement for Black Lives." *Perspectives on Politics* 20, no. 4: 1246–59. https://doi.org/10.1017/S1537592722000019.

———. 2022b. "Theorizing Justice from the Margins: Black Feminist Insights on Political (Protest) Behavior." *Politics, Groups, and Identities* 11, no. 5: 1190–1202. https://doi.org/10.1080/21565503.2022.2086470.

Nzinga, Sekile M. 2020. *Lean Semesters*. Baltimore, MD: Johns Hopkins University Press.

Padilla, A. M. 1994. "Ethnic Minority Scholars, Research, and Mentoring: Current and Future Issues." *Educational Researcher* 23: 24–27.

Papageorge, N., C. Lindsay, J. Hyman, S. Gershenson, and C. Hart. 2018. "The Long-Run Impacts of Same-Race Teachers." *NBER Working Paper* 25254. https://doi.org/10.3386/w25254.

Rockquemore, K., and T. Laszloffy. 2008. *The Black Academic's Guide to Winning Tenure—without Losing Your Soul*. Boulder, CO: Lynne Rienner.

Shange, N. 1989. *For Colored Girls Who Have Considered Suicide When the Rainbow Is Enuf: A Choreopoem*. New York: Collier Books.

Spates, K., N. Evans, M. Watts, B. Clarvon, N. Abubakar, and T. James. 2020. "Keeping Ourselves Sane: A Qualitative Exploration of Black Women's Coping Strategies for Gendered Racism." *Sex Roles* 82, nos. 9–10: 513–24.

Williams, J., and A. Hardaway. 2018. "The Metaphysical Dilemma: Academic Black Women. Diverse Education." https://diverseeducation.com/article/127139/.

Woodly, D. 2019. "Black Feminist Visions and the Politics of Healing in the Movement for Black Lives." In *Women Mobilizing Memory*, 219–37. New York: Columbia University Press.

7

The Impact of Active and Passive Representation in the Field of Public Administration

Lessons Learned and Best Practices

Stephanie A. Pink-Harper

On December 11, 2020, Joseph Epstein wrote a highly publicized yet criticized opinion piece in the *Wall Street Journal*. The article was titled, "Is There a Doctor in the White House? Not if You Need an M.D.: Jill Biden Should Think about Dropping the Honorific, Which Feels Fraudulent, Even Comic." In this article, Epstein requests first lady elect Jill Biden to remove the "Dr." handle from her name while serving in the upcoming role she will assume in January 2021.

This opinion piece by Epstein drew much national attention to the discussion regarding respect in the academic profession. Attention in particular was cast on women and the challenges and obstacles that they face in the academia realm. Many questioned if Epstein's arguments should be a relevant point of consideration. Drezner (2020) acknowledged this disregard as sexist and demeaning. Russell (2020) acknowledges that in the academic field such behavior has become the expected "norm" by men. In response to Epstein's op-ed, Tonya Russell (2020) acknowledges such behavior as "degrading working women." In response to Epstein's piece women across Twitter (now X) urged others in academia with a doctorate to show that women in academia exist in large numbers (Kindelan 2020).

Interestingly, Epstein's (2020) op-ed piece highlights only a few of the challenges that women in academia face. Unfortunately, his article only skims the surface of the unique challenges and obstacles that women in academia face in their career paths to success. Acknowledging these growing concerns recently highlighted by the media, this chapter explores the best practices learned for navigating this environment particularly at research-intensive higher education institutions. The aim is to shed light on the challenges and obstacles that Black women specifically face in the academic profession, particularly in the field of public administration.

The chapter is outlined as follows. First, it begins by exploring the role of women in the field of public administration in general. It examines this connection through the theoretical lens of representative bureaucracy. Then the chapter highlights the best practices learned from personal experience in the field. It concludes by offering suggestions for future research to consider to help promote the inclusion and advancement of Black women in the field of public administration.

Women in Public Administration via the Theory of Representative Bureaucracy

The field of public administration once was only recognized as a subfield of political science (Kettl 1999). However, today it is noted as a distinct field of study. Public administration shapes almost every aspect of our lives.

Public administration explores the administrative side of government. One aim of the field is to enhance the delivery of public goods and services to citizens. Practitioners in the field work at the city, county, state, and federal levels of government. Research in this field explores a myriad of questions regarding how to improve performance of governmental functions. For example, public administration students and scholars examine such issues as local policing, issuing unemployment payments, ensuring the safety of vaccines during a pandemic, and the implications of anti-discrimination policies on the public sector workforce.

Exploring these questions helps us to recognize the injustices faced by citizens receiving these services. In turn, identifying answers to these questions helps public administration scholars determine ways to improve the overall functions of government at all levels. Importantly this chapter seeks to aid us in understanding how current and future public administrators can develop the skills needed to effectively manage and thus enhance the operations of government.

According to Kennedy (2012), the theory of representative bureaucracy suggests that a diverse bureaucratic workforce will lead to the development of more representative public policies. The theory suggests that the diversity promoted through this system will help in the policy formulation and implementation process (Selden 1997). When applying this theory to the academic workplace, it is suggested that more diversity across a field of study will help to ensure that the interest of all students and faculty are best represented in the development of university policies and curriculum decisions for both faculty and staff. Furthermore, more representation and inclusion of marginalized groups in the classroom will help in the creation and implementation of public policies by representative bureaucrats.

So what does the makeup of the field look like? In 2000, Marilyn Rubin conducted a study of women in the field of public administration. In this study Rubin (2000) examines trends for women in the American Society for Public Administration (ASPA). ASPA serves as the bridge between "scholarship and practitioner in the field."

In Rubin's (2000) research, she notes that women in ASPA have progressed over the then sixty years the organization has been in existence. Rubin acknowledges that women in ASPA had progressed from "virtual invisibility, to token representation, to major participation" (61). At the time of ASPA's inception, Rubin noted that only 28 percent of women in the field of public administration were a part of the national workforce. Also, interestingly, women were only employed in "helping" professions. However, sixty years later women have progressed to working in positions previously held only by men. She also found women serving as executive directors of nonprofit organizations and as university presidents. However, no details are provided that disaggregate these numbers by race or gender.

According to the most recent ASPA (2020) membership statistics, ASPA membership includes and informs "civil servants, city managers, elected officials, appointed officials, researchers, scholars, thought leaders, nonprofit managers and more." Interestingly, the membership is 53 percent men and 47 percent women. Also, these statistics from ASPA show that only 15 percent of the membership is African American. However, unknown are these statistics specifically by gender for African Americans.

A more recent work, by Rauhaus and Schuchs Carr (2020), explores the challenges that women faculty experience in higher education. The authors note that men's domination in higher education has caused women faculty to experience differences in their pursuit to advancement in the academic profession. Also interesting, they note that women traditionally serve in additional, "invisible capacities" as mentors and advisers that take time from their research or other advancement pursuits. They also found that serving in these additional capacities has caused women to be less likely to advance up the career ladder into leadership positions across campus. Supporting findings from Scutelnicu, Knepper, and Tekula (2018) note that almost half of all public administration doctoral degrees are earned by women. However, only 36 percent of these women take on academic careers.

These trends have implications for not just women in academia. Rauhaus and Schuchs Carr (2020) also note that students may be impacted by these trends. For example, the lack of gender representation in public administration faculty may hinder the progress of the students we are training to be the public administrators of the future.

Noting the differences among women and men in public administration faculty, Rauhaus and Schuchs Carr (2020) recognize that there are several "invisible challenges" hindering women's progress in the field. The first is the glass ceiling. This challenge recognizes that women experience barriers in their professional advancement pursuits. The next invisible challenge they recognize is referred to as *gender consciousness*. This idea is similar to Naff's (1995) interpretation of subjective discrimination. This idea suggests that in fields where women perceive their opportunities for advancement as limited (i.e., women faculty in academia) and are aware of the challenges that they may face in their professional pursuits, this may lead to a sense of inferiority. In other words, women in these areas perceive there to be discrimination that may thus hinder their success or career potential.

These comparative trends from ASPA in 2000 and 2020 illustrate that women have progressed in the field of public administration. However, there is still room to grow. African American women are still perceived to be lacking in comparison to the numbers for their peers in the field.

In an effort to help bridge this gap, the next section of this chapter provides insight on the best practices learned over the course of my career. These challenges are recognized as invisible career work.

Women and minorities are typically assigned to service positions working in various capacities acting as mentors to others who look like them. This is problematic because although women and minorities spend a large amount of time devoted to such assignments, they typically only represent a minimal level of their official workload assignments. These assignments cause many women and minority members to have unequal service obligations in comparison to their men counterparts. The final challenge they note is related to issues of discrimination and harassment in the workplace. Although this can impact all workers, it disproportionately impacts women faculty members in academia (Rauhaus and Schuchs Carr 2020).

Noting the work of Rauhaus and Schuls Carr (2020) and others in this section, I can personally attest that each of these challenges has either directly or indirectly impacted me in my career pursuits in higher education. In the next section I share my personal experiences of best practices that have aided me in my career.

Best Practices

NATIONAL CENTER FOR FACULTY DEVELOPMENT AND DIVERSITY

In the summer of 2020, in the midst of the greatest pandemic known to our generation, I received a grant from the dean of the college and the university's DEI (diversity, equity, and inclusion) office[1] funding my participation in the National Center for Faculty Development and Diversity's (NCFDD) Faculty Success Program. This has been a great experience for me. This online program focuses on faculty identifying strategies to meet the research, writing, and service demands of the profession while simultaneously maintaining a supportive work-life balance (NCFDD nd). More specifically, the program sheds light on the importance of time management, finding a suitable work-life balance, and the necessity for self-care while juggling the demands of an academic career.

The NCFDD was created in 2010 by Kerry Ann Rockquemore, PhD, an African American women in higher education. The program offers professional development, networking, training, coaching, and mentoring opportunities for academics at various stages of their career (NCFDD 2020). One of the most transformative takeaways I gained from this program is the importance of developing strong and sustainable writing habits.

More specifically this was achieved in the program through the "WriteNow" (NCFDD nd) component. This aspect of the program encouraged participants to establish weekly personal writing goals. The program also encouraged the creation of a "weekly planning meeting." This was a great way for me to make plans according to the goals that I had outlined for weekly task completion. This would require me to, first, reflect upon my commitments for the week regarding my personal, research, teaching, and service responsibilities. Then, I would take time to determine how much time I could commit to each area during the week. Once the goal setting had taken place, I would use the "WriteNow" timer set for at least thirty minutes a day to reserve time to complete my outlined task (NCFDD nd).

What I learned from this practice was that thirty minutes per day was rewarding personally as an accountability mechanism. Furthermore, I was assigned to a group of other faculty to discuss my progress and weekly goals with. This was and still serves as a great way for me to discuss my accomplishments as well as my struggles in my career path with others who have the same struggles that I do. This practice helped me see where and how I was utilizing my time. It helped me learn to prioritize what matters most given daily constraints. It also helped me to see how collectively thirty minutes per day could help me reach my larger goals for the month, for the semester, and for the academic year. The program's support for the creation of personal strategic planning also encouraged me to create intentional goals for the semester in various aspects of my career. This was then translated into a routine for creating healthy habits to support my best work personally and in each area of my career development. I was then able to establish realistic weekly plans to help me revise research projects step by step starting with just a block of time per day.

Mentoring Programs

Research conducted by public administration scholars Scutelnicu and Kneeper (2019) recognizes the importance of mentorship programs in academia as a means for increasing women's academic careers. The mentor relationship in academia according to Todoran (2023) has been defined as a collaborative process of engagement and learning between someone experienced in the field (the mentor) and a new or transitioning faculty (the mentee). Todoran's research defines formal mentoring as planned programs, while informal programs are those lacking institutional design. In her research, she surveys faculty from the Network of Schools of Public Policy, Affairs and Administration (NASPAA) member schools. Faculty respondents stated that both formal and informal mentorship in higher education aided them in their pursuits to advance their careers.

The results of her studies also reveal that African Americans faculty and other marginalized groups reported higher benefit rates from formal institutionalized mentorship programs (Todoran 2023).

Interestingly, according to a study in Higher Edu Jobs by Sarah Jacobs from March 2023, only "one in four colleges have formalized and uniform faculty mentorship programs across all departments." This statistic is concerning for higher education institutions for many reasons.

Shane Desselle et al. (2011) note numerous benefits that an organization can gain from investing in a strong mentorship program. They find that formalized mentorship programs across a university can lead to increased academic success for faculty. Research notes there are numerous best practice approaches that can be implemented to support mentorship programs in higher education for faculty. Upon review of these works, the model below summarizes these findings (see Figure 7.1).

Formalized mentorship programs are important, but support is needed from top authorities in the university's organizational structure for it to work. Successful mentorship program models are those structured

Figure 7.1. University System of Hierarchy. *Source*: Created by the author.

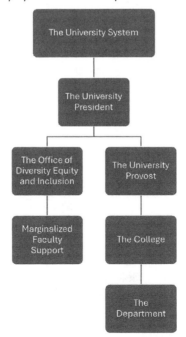

hierarchically, with support flowing from the top down. Additionally, for the programs to work, they need to be formalized for their saliency to be understood. For example, immediately upon hire, faculty members need to know that the president, provost, DEI office, deans, and department chairs are committed to employees' success by offering resources to aid in such programming. That means that faculty need to know that their participation in such programming is supported across the university.

Having the support of a formalized mentorship program integrated into the university could include hosting regular mentorship sessions for faculty members from marginalized groups. At my previous institution, I was very fortunate to have a vice-chancellor of institutional diversity who was committed to the recruitment and retention of faculty from marginalized groups. The institution hosted regular mentorship sessions for women and marginalized faculty where panels of tenured faculty across the campus would share their insight regarding best practices that they had learned to help them gain success in their various fields of study. This helps to demonstrate that the institution recognizes the challenges that these groups are faced with in higher education, particularly regarding advancement and networking. From my experience, these work best when housed in the university's diversity office. This is important since they have knowledge regarding the various resources that faculty may need across various disciplines.

The importance of a formal mentorship program at the college/school level is also vital. This is important for marginalized faculty so that they can establish connections and learn more about the norms and expectations regarding promotional advancement in the college/school where their tenure/promotion will be decided. This is key for the deans of the colleges to help establish connections for marginalized groups to connect with others like them in their college. I was also very fortunate to have experience with having a successful tenured mentor from my college. The interesting aspect of having a college-level mentor was that I was paired with another faculty member in the college, so she understood the expectations for the college regarding promotion and tenure. This interaction aided me tremendously, as I was able to ask questions and seek advice regarding my career but removed from the faculty in my department whom I interacted with daily. The unique perspective and insight provided to me from this tenured faculty member allowed me to have candid conversations with someone outside of my department. What

I think also made this a successful and meaningful connection for me was that the dean of the college was intentional about identifying other women in the college who shared some research and teaching interests. She was able to share with me experiences and lessons learned on her career path.

Lastly, it is equally important to have a formal mentorship program at the department level. This may require training by the university's DEI office, but it is needed and should be understood by department chairs that this can be a great asset for the recruitment and retention of faculty. Higher education institutions must be intentional regarding the creation of strategic plans for hiring diverse faculty. This requires investing in the resources identified for minority faculty members to succeed.

I was also assigned various mentors across campus who helped to guide my career trajectory. I was also a participant of a second mentorship program, which focused on partnering women mentors with mentees across campus. These programs were very influential in helping me learn the norms and expectations of the institution. From my experiences with these individuals, I was able to ask difficult questions that I might not feel comfortable asking of people who would not have a direct impact on my promotion and tenure decisions.

Although I was very fortunate to have been assigned various formal mentors throughout my career, it is vital to note that finding a mentor is a process that requires some work. What can be done if your institution does not have a formal mentorship program in place? What can be done to identify a good one? What steps can be taken to avoid those who might work against you?

Consider identifying a mentorship as a process that is similar to an interview. It may require several trials of meeting with others to see if you are a good fit for each other. Sometimes this might require stepping outside of your comfort zone and taking a risk to ask someone who you admire in the field if they will serve as your mentor. Another suggestion is to outline your goals for the relationship with the mentor. What do you expect to gain from the relationship, what type of information or advice are you seeking? Rockquemore (2016) notes that in order for mentorship programs to be successful, the mentee must recognize that "you are responsible for your success." This means that if you do find a mentor that does not work for you, take charge and create a network of mentors to help you meet your professional goals. In her NCFDD program, Rockquemore calls on mentees to create a "mentor map" (2016). This is a tool that I utilized to help me identify personal goals and then take steps to try to identify the best fit for someone to help me reach these goals. This tool suggests identifying not only one general mentor but mentors for the various areas of my career development. The key here is to take the lead in identifying multiple individuals who can help you best meet your needs and goals.

According to a summary of best practices for faculty mentorship programs, it works best when mentees have multiple mentors. Mentorship program assignments should be promoting the protection of mentees, particularly regarding confidentiality (Jacobs 2023). This is important as it helps mentees feel seen and heard. Maine (1995) as cited in Desselle et al. (2011) found that faculty participants in formal mentoring programs reported "job satisfaction, commitment, turnover reductions, and higher productivity." Their research found that mentorship programs do work.

Implications for Future Research

In conclusion, the theoretical lens of representative bureaucracy can shed some much needed light on how to address the issues of promoting diversity in academia. However, we must not assume that the key to ensuring the success of future generations to come is simply having a workforce whose numbers "match" the student body that they are serving. Institutions of higher education must invest equally in the recruitment and the retention to ensure that inclusion and diversity are promoted as a principle across universities.

This process begins by higher education institutions first recognizing that gender gaps exist in academia. Second, they must begin to create and implement policies that help to address the disparities that exist. Lastly, they must find ways to monitor these trends and their efforts in academia. This requires intentional and deliberate commitment from both the faculty and the higher education institutions to be successful. When students see faculty in the field of study that "look" like them, passive representation, this can lead to better representation of others that "look" like and seek to actively represent them in the field of study in their program. For public administration, this means that we have public administrators who seek to work toward an inclusive workplace environment where the views and interests of everyone are considered in practice.

Note

1. Figure 7.1 may not accurately reflect the organizational structure changes occurring across higher education institutions in some states. This figure may need to be updated to reflect state legislative actions banning Diversity, Equity, and Inclusion (DEI) Offices across higher education institutions. In some states, this legislation may also restrict programs and initiatives targeting marginalized groups of employees.

References

American Society for Public Administration (ASPA). 2020. About ASPA. https://www.aspanet.org/ASPA/About-ASPA/ASPA/About-ASPA/About-ASPA.aspx?hkey=ca893802-9bb7-4541-a68e-6d24c185ad77.

Desselle, Shane P., Gretchen L. Peirce, Brian L. Crabtree, Daniel Acosta Jr., Jonnie L. Early Jr., Donald T. Kishi, Dolores Nobles-Knight, and Andrew A. Webster. 2011. "Pharmacy Faculty Workplace Issues: Findings from the 2009–2010 COD-COF Joint Task Force on Faculty Workforce." *American Journal of Pharmaceutical Education* 75, no. 4: 63. https://doi.org/10.5688/ajpe75463.

Drezner, Daniel W. 2020. "The Hullabaloo about Calling Jill Biden 'Doctor,' Explained: An FAQ about a Bad Wall Street Journal Op-ed." *Washington Post*. December 16. https://www.washingtonpost.com/outlook/2020/12/16/hullabaloo-about-calling-jill-biden-doctor-explained/.

Epstein, Joseph. 2020. "Is There a Doctor in the White House? Not If You Need an M.D.: Jill Biden Should Think about Dropping the Honorific, which Feels Fraudulent, even Comic." *Wall Street Journal*. December 11. https://www.wsj.com/articles/is-there-a-doctor-in-the-white-house-not-if-you-need-an-m-d-11607727380.

Jacobs, Sarah Ruth. 2023. "The Most Effective Approaches for Mentoring New Faculty." May 8. https://www.higheredjobs.com/Articles/articleDisplay.cfm?ID=3448&Title=The%20Most%20Effective%20Approaches%20for%20Mentoring%20New%20Faculty.

Kennedy, B. 2014. "Unraveling Representative Bureaucracy: A Systematic Analysis of the Literature." *Administration & Society* 46, no. 4: 395–421.

Kettl, Donald. 1999. "The Future of Public Administration." *Journal of Public Affairs Education* 5, no. 2: 127–33.

Kindelan, Katie. 2020. "Women Rally around Jill Biden after Controversial Op-ed Calls for Future First Lady to Drop 'Dr.'" December 14. https://abcnews.go.com/GMA/News/women-rally-jill-biden-controversial-op-ed-calls/story?id=74713599.

Maine, L. L. 1995. "Recruitment and Retention of Faculty: A Faculty Member's Point of View." *American Journal of Pharmaceutical Education* 59, no 3: 304–11.

Naff, Katherine. 1995. "Subjective vs. Objective Discrimination in Government: Adding to the Picture of Barriers to the Advancement of Women." *Political Research Quarterly* 48, no. 3: 535–57.

National Center for Faculty Diversity & Development (NCFDD). nd. "Faculty Success Program: Achieve Academic Success and Better Work-Life Balance." https://www.facultydiversity.org/fsp-bootcamp.

———. 2020. "Changing the Face of Power in the Academy." https://www.facultydiversity.org/ncfddmission.

Rauhaus, Beth M., and Isla A. Schuchs Carr. 2020. "The Invisible Challenges: Gender Differences among Public Administration Faculty." *Journal of Public Affairs Education* 26, no. 1: 31–50.

Rockquemore, Kerry Ann. 2016. "Why Mentor Matches Fail. Inside Higher Ed." February 2. https://www.insidehighered.com/advice/2016/02/03/most-mentoring-today-based-outdated-model-essay.

Rubin, Marilyn. 2000. "Women in the American Society for Public Administration: Another Decade of Progress but Still a Way to Go." *Public Administration Review* 601: 61–71.

Russell, Tonya. 2020. "Dr. Jill Biden Deserves Her Title. Saying Otherwise Demeans Teachers and Community Colleges." December 15. https://www.nbcnews.com/think/opinion/dr-jill-biden-deserves-her-title-saying-otherwise-demeans-teachers-ncna1251321.

Scutelnicu, G. and H. Knepper. 2019. "A Tale of Two Journals: Women's Representation in Public Administration Scholarship." *Public Integrity* 21, no 1: 38–53. https://doi.org/10.1080/10999922.2017.1421009

Scutelnicu, Gina, Hilary Knepper, and Rebecca Tekula. 2018. "The State of Women in Public Administration Scholarship: Where We Are, Why We Are Here, and Why It Matters." *PA Times* 4, no. 2: 32–33.

Selden, Sally C. 1997. "Representative Bureaucracy: Examining the Linkage between Passive and Active Representation in the Farmers Home Administration." *American Review of Public Administration* 27, no. 1: 22–42.

Scutelnicu Todoran, G. 2023. "The Contribution of Formal and Informal Mentorship to Faculty Productivity: Views of Faculty in Public Affairs Programs." *Journal of Public Affairs Education* 29, no 4: 404–20. https://doi.org/10.1080/15236803.2023.2220096

8

When the Discipline Disciplines
Stories of a Black Female Political Scientist

JULIA S. JORDAN-ZACHERY

Tippin' on the Tight Rope:
Navigating the Academy without Falling Off

I write this from a place of wholeness.

    I met such resistance as I sat to write this piece. I often thought to myself: Why did I agree to write this? There was a part of me that had reached the point of not wanting to write anymore about the pain I endured as a Black immigrant woman in higher education. As I read the literature on Black women's experiences in higher education, I thought, what is there for me to say? It has been said. In summary, academia is harmful to Black women. I was so tired of writing about my pain and the pain of other Black women. And so, that stubborn part of me resisted writing this piece. Or maybe, just maybe, the part of me that chose to be whole resisted writing this piece. I was tipping on a tightrope, my balance nebulous at times. The resistance I felt was real, so I could not deny it.

    Resistance has been and continues to be a part of my story—the part that centers me as a Black female political scientist. Resistance, in some cases, has served me well, even if it has come at a cost that, at times, I was unsure that I could bear then and into the future. So, it is no surprise to me that I longed to tell a different story. Yet, I did not want to deny the pain. I also did not want to glorify the pain by making it the center of this story. I am apt to say that I do not believe that we have to suffer to be great. To me, it is like justifying race-gender oppression by suggesting something good comes out of it. And I also think of all the women, the Black women, who do not necessarily get to utter the words *I write this from a place of wholeness*.

It has become harder for me to speak of the heartaches I have experienced in academia as a result of the race-gender violence I faced. And it is not because I am in a place of denial. But more so because I am no longer interested in reliving it. When I speak of race-gender violence, I am speaking of actual violence and not the symbolic and theorized violence often discussed by academics and pundits alike. Race-gender violence is structural, physical, and emotional violence intended to cause harm or hurt or kill the physical body and soul of an individual based on the simultaneity of their embodied race and gender. My ambivalence toward writing this chapter not only stemmed from me not knowing what was new to add to the story of Black women in political science but also from not wanting to have that violence revisited in the (re)memory[1] of my body.

All of this left me in a conundrum, and I got to the point of questioning what I had to say. What story needed to be told at this moment? And was I available to tell it? Honestly, I do not know how I survived. My therapist tells me to this day how proud he is of me for doing the work, the deep work, of healing. I smile. And I think, what if I never had to do the work of deep healing—healing from the harm caused by race-gender oppression and violence? What would my experience as a Black immigrant political scientist have been if I did not have to heal from race-gender violence?

Well, I have had to heal. It was not pretty, but I did it. Healing has led me to reimagine and reconstitute myself in the academy and within political science. As I have written about before, healing has led me to exit (Jordan-Zachery 2019). But now, I want to tell you about a different type of exit I had to perform in order to heal. This exit led me to chart a Black Girl Blueprint, which then allowed me to confront the disembodiment I have experienced as a Black female political scientist.

Charting a Black Girl Blueprint

Like many Black women in the academy and political science specifically, I often find myself in that space of being the only one. Years ago, I had a therapist who told me that isolation can make a healthy person unhealthy. She spoke truth. But here is the thing: I wanted to be well. I wanted to be whole. As Toni Cade Bambara (1980, 9) in *The Salt Eaters* writes, to be whole, I "got to give it all up, the pain, the hurt, the anger and make room for lovely things to rush in and fill you full." But there was no blueprint for me to follow within political science that showed me how to "make room for the lovely things." Even more so, there was no path birthed by Western understandings, which tend to privilege individualism, that showed me how to be well. So, like Black women are apt to do, as a means of self-articulation and survival, we invent (see Hill Collins 2000; Walker 1983).

And so, I made my own blueprint.

My Black Girl Blueprint was, in part, my response to determining how to exist within a power structure that did not, consciously or unconsciously, have the capacity to make space for me. Creating space allows me to challenge neoliberal understandings of dominance, suffering, and individuality. Such space creation provides me with an ontological basis of Black feminine freedom. This Black Girl Blueprint is the outgrowth of not just my theoretical understanding of Black feminism but also my personal praxis of such. In other words, I do not simply write about Black feminism; I also try to practice Black feminism. I needed my words and my actions to align. My Black Girl Blueprint is grounded in Black women's epistemologies and is designed as a means of not simply resisting the ideological, discursive, and material of the race-gender oppression I faced but also charting a way of being that is grounded in my corporeality. In some of my other writings, I refer to this as my epistemology of being (Jordan-Zachery 2020). My epistemology of being, my Black Girl Blueprint, is grounded in truth; it is unfolding; it is adaptive; it is grounded in the legacy of my Divine Feminine African Ancestral lineage; it is feminine and pure. The epistemology of being allows me to recognize my pain, name it, analyze it, and take what knowledge I need from it to craft a response. My Black Girl Blueprint gives me a way of existing in white, patriarchal, sexist, classist institutions such as higher education in general and political science specifically.

Part of making a blueprint started with me writing my vision of myself in the academy. I wrote, in part, that I wanted to help create space for others by living my truth. Space-making, specifically Black feminist space-making, became my mission as a political scientist. This has caused me to reimagine and repurpose the spaces that I have access to while recognizing that, as a Black woman, some spaces remain closed to me, given the functioning of race-gender structures and processes. Black feminist space-making allows me to confront the disembodiment so many of us experience as members of the academy. As Johnson (2013, 11) writes, disembodiment "lead[s] many to exist and persist disjointedly as intellectual workers." Disembodiment involves the use of violence, and violence in many forms, and the resulting fear that accompanies this violence. This makes me wonder, is it isolation that makes a healthy person ill, or is it the violence that one experiences in isolation that can make a person who is raced and simultaneously gendered in a particular way ill? Black feminism allowed me to grapple with this question and to resist and exit as needed.

In my pursuit of space-making, I engage in a politics of the practice of turning inward—going into my Black feminine interior. Quashie (2012, 23–24) understands interiority as "emerg[ing] from a place of quiet—at once 'irreverent, messy, complicated, representations that have . . . human texture and specificity.' " It "is inevitable, essential. . . . It is already there, if one is looking to understand it" (23–24). Interiority for Castiglia (2007, 135–37) is self; selfhood; self-knowledge; self-cultivation; a place of "imagination, fantasy, affect, aesthetics, and sensation"; it is that "amorphous space located somewhere 'inside' the human body, generating conviction, satisfaction, and . . . identity." Interiority is autonomous subjectivity. But it was the words of Audre Lorde that helped me to understand better and go deeper into my Black feminine interior. In her poem, "A Woman Speaks," Audre Lorde speaks of worth and power, long-standing themes that cut across her writings. In the first stanza of the poem, Lorde (1997, 234) pens, "but when the sea turns back / it will leave my shape behind." These lines remind me of what the sea, which I interpret as a Black woman (given the end of the poem), holds on the interior and how it knows its/our shape. This knowledge is held in the interior, deep in the vastness of the sea, and serves as a metaphor for how Black women have held on to their truths—their understanding of self (as represented in their shape). I read shape as Black women's knowledge that comes from deeply knowing self—which is to know the physical, the spiritual, and emotional. By going into the interior, Black women can resist disembodiment. That was the first step in creating my Black Girl Blueprint.

By going into my interior, I was better able to align my values and manage the disembodiment that so many Black women experience in the academy. This then allowed me to engage in action—space-making action. To this end, I worked to organize the Black Women and Girls

Collaborative. The Collaborative was a direct response to the hegemonic practice that disqualifies Black feminine knowledge. We imagine the Collaborative as offering physical and discursive spaces, thereby inviting participants to engage Black women's and girls' subjectivities (https://www.bwgsymposium.org). Darlene Clark Hine (1994, 43) captured my intention in creating these types of spaces when she stated, "It was imperative that they [Black women] collectively create alternative self-images and shield from scrutiny these private, empowering definitions of self" as a means of protecting themselves from negative oppressive constructions. This space, given COVID-19, has moved from physical to virtual. Most recently, I organized We Won't Stop! This is a virtual writing workshop for Black-identified women to continue to write as we face not only COVID-19 but also the continued assaults on Blackness and an economic decline. I offered a Black feminist care of ethics to organize the space. The feminist care of ethics allowed us to be in community, first with ourselves, by aligning our minds, bodies, and spirits, which then allowed us to be in community with each other. I did this in response, in part, to the fact that I often did not find space—physical or intellectual space—for me within political science.

Second, my Black Girl Blueprint allowed me to create a space of joy. Part of the disembodiment we often face is that we are not allowed to be our full selves in the academy. I remember once asking the department's administrative assistant if she had ever heard the then-chair of the department laugh. She said no. This made me pay attention to the sounds of the department. There was never the sound of laughter. One of the unwritten scripts I often encounter in academia, and I see this even at our annual meetings, including those hosted by the American Political Science Association, is that there never seems to be a place where joy can happen and happen publicly. I could never understand what it was about the neoliberal institution that seemed to disallow public displays of joy.

The administrative assistant and I (the only two Black women on the floor) would often have these moments of laughter. At times, we would be looked at strangely as we enjoyed a moment of laughter. These looks served as a kind of reminder that academia has no place for joy and celebration, particularly Black women's joy and celebration. I remember when I consciously realized this and resolved to detangle myself from this way of being. I was untenured and decided to attend a political science academic conference wearing a purple dress. Here I was in a sea of whiteness, with bodies (both men and women) cloaked in black, blue, or gray, and then there was me in a purple dress. I can remember how free I felt, how it allowed me to meander through the cacophony of symbols that vibrated the message—you don't belong. My scholarship did not belong—writing on Black feminism, and especially Black women, seems to always leave me on the fringes of political science panels and the discipline as a whole. My body did not belong—here I was, a Black woman with locs (early in my career, that was not commonly seen and remains so until this day). Just like my scholarship did not belong, I received messages (sometimes subtle) that my joyful spirit did not belong. My public presentation of self, my intellectual presentation of self, was told over and over again that I did not belong. How does one resist the ideology that you do not belong?

I tapped into the memory of Black women to carve out my sense of space. As Esther O. Ohito (2020, 3) writes, "Black feminist memory work extends a long lineage of Black women subversively creating alternatives that defy the body-numbing demands of the death and decay-inducing knowledge production normalized in academia." I found myself ferociously reading the words of Black women, those in and outside of the academy, for how they understand and, more importantly, practice joy as a means of engaging in subversion. I need my joy not to be based on capitalism and neoliberalism. Otherwise, my joy would be tethered and not free. Audre Lorde's writing gave me a place to land, a wellspring of sorts to imagine joy in political science. Lorde (2007 [1984]) asserts, "Another important way in which the erotic connection functions is the open and fearless underlining of my capacity for joy, in the way my body stretches to music and opens into response, harkening to its deepest rhythms so every level upon which I sense also opens to the erotically satisfying experience whether it is dancing, building a bookcase, writing a poem, or examining an idea" (56). Furthermore, Lorde, in thinking through work and how our work can be joyful if it rests in the erotic, wrote,

> The principal horror of any system which defines the good in terms of profit rather than in terms of human need, or which defines human need to the exclusion of the psychic and emotional components of that need—the principal horror of such a system is that it robs our work of its erotic value, its erotic power and life appeal and fulfillment. Such a system reduces work to a travesty of necessities, a duty by which we earn bread or oblivion for ourselves and those we love. But

> this is tantamount to blinding a painter and then telling her to improve her work, and to enjoy the act of painting. It is not only next to impossible, it is also profoundly cruel. (55)

I wanted to stretch across my work, all aspects of it, in a way that fed my joyful spirit. To stretch across my work in a joyful way meant that I had to disentangle it from the disciplinary techniques used in political science, the part that saw my production only in a language of profit.

Enter in reflexivity as a tool in my Black Girl Blueprint. Reflexivity gave me the space I needed to find joy in my work. On March 8, 2019, while I was in the throes of managing the trauma that resulted from race-gender violence, I gave a talk on what I called "Dwelling in the Space between Knowing, Not Knowing, and Unknowing." This talk was part of the Cross-Generational Echoes International Conference on Intersectionality. I was to talk about methods. I will not dwell too much on the actual speech but instead highlight a few key questions that I posed that were central and remain central to my practice of existing in that space of knowing, not knowing, and unknowing. These areas helped me find joy in my work; in essence, this is how I resist the disciplining practice of political science and academia in general.

Question one: What is the story that is calling me? One of the things I did in creating my Black Girl Blueprint was renaming what I do. So, instead of research, I refer to what I do as storytelling. Storytelling is aligned with the Black feminine energy into which I was birthed. Posing this question allows me to sit with a project to ask if the ancestors are giving me the story or if it is based on ego. Not that ego in and of itself is a bad place to operate from. But what I have learned is that the neoliberal institution called academia can severely damage the ego. Consequently, we (at least some of us) operate from a place that is not always or fully grounded in truth, thus resulting in harm—our own harm or in the harm of others.[2] Truth is central to what I do. This is how I experience joy. And so, when I am given a story, I ask if it allows me to tell the truth—particularly my truth and the truth of my Black feminine divine. When I stop to ask what is the story that is calling me, I can sit in truth. And this is liberating.

Question two: Are existing words failing me? Much of academia is grounded in reproduction, which involves using words to categorize the "other." These words are so filled with power, white, heteronormative, sexist, and capitalist power, and, consequently, they fail me and the story that I am called to tell. Thus, my use of these words and, in essence, ways of being mean that I am reproducing the same power structures that I claim to be challenging. During that talk, I said, "Do not be afraid to create words to grapple with and dismantle power." One of the words I have struggled with is "intersectionality" and how it is often used to limit or box in the nature of the research I do. I am a Black feminist and write from this position. Furthermore, I write on Black women and their interactions and responses to power and am rather explicit in stating that. Yet, I have been told that my research is lacking because I do not use the term *intersectionality*. Given the politics and practice of intersectionality, I have backed away from using it. Instead, I prefer to explicitly state the population I am engaging with—Black women.

In thinking of the use of words, I also grapple with how I put words on paper for public consumption. Political science often requires that when we put words on paper, we follow a particular format—an introduction, followed by a literature review, methods/methodology/approach, analysis, and conclusion. I understand the impetus for this disciplining technique. However, given how Black women sometimes produce knowledge, this process can be constraining. And so, as part of my Black Girl Blueprint, I have had to confront the words I use and how I put them on paper. I want my work to be grounded in lived experiences, and this is not just a research method/methodology but a lived practice. Writing in the prescribed manner that is often required of political science journals, I realized, was robbing me of the joy that I could experience from doing work—because it was robbing me of my creativity and the ways of knowledge production that were part of my lived reality.

Existing in this place of knowing, not knowing, and unknowing seems to bring me deep joy, although it sometimes pushes me further onto the margins of academia. But I am reminded of the words of bell hooks whenever I contemplate what it is to be on the margins. I want to quote bell hooks at length as her words capture much of what I attempted to articulate during my talk. hooks's (1990) words read in part,

> I am located in the margin. I make a definite distinction between that marginality which is imposed by oppressive structures and that marginality one chooses as site of resistance—as location of radical openness and possibility." Marginality [is] much more than a site of deprivation; in fact . . . it is also the site of

radical possibility, a space of resistance. It was this marginality that I was naming as a central location for the production of a counter-hegemonic discourse that is not just found in words but in habits of being and the way one lives. As such, I was not speaking of a marginality one wishes to lose—to give up or surrender as part of moving into the center—but rather of a site one stays in, clings to even, because it nourishes one's capacity to resist. It offers to one the possibility of radical perspective from which to see and create, to imagine alternatives, new worlds. (153, 149–50)

So yes, my Black Girl Blueprint involves me living and locating myself on the margin as it involves "radical openness and possibility." As a result, I can see me when others cannot. I am able to see the Black women whose stories I try to tell even when others ask, "Is there enough to write a book on Black women?"[3] Or when that well-respected Black male political scientist reads your manuscript and tells you that it is not Black politics and you should send it to women's studies.[4] I have actively created and curated myself as a Black immigrant woman in political science. It has not been easy but necessary since "survival isn't some theory operating in a vacuum. It's a matter of my everyday living and making decisions" (Lorde 2017, 53).

My Black Girl Blueprint allowed me to create the space I needed to survive. Creating space allows me to challenge neoliberal understandings of dominance, suffering, and individuality. It provides me with an ontological basis of Black feminine freedom. This is how I survive the disciplining techniques of political science and the existential threat so many of us face as we walk the hallowed halls of higher education.

Existential Threat

Saying that Black women in the academy and Black women in political science face an existential threat seems a little extravagant. But that is only the case if you have never read or listened to the stories shared by Black women. This existential threat can cause disembodiment. Black women often describe disembodiment as existing in the margins/being marginalized. According to bell hooks (1990, 149), one experiences marginalization when one is "part of the whole but outside the main body."

I turned to "diversity statements" issued by some political science departments and research on Black women's experiences in academia to explore how the marginalization of Black women and other groups is understood and reckoned with. I admit freely that the data sets are not necessarily comparable. There is so little written on Black women's experiences in political science; thus, I was compelled to look at academia as a whole while recognizing that political science is a subset of this larger structure. And I guess that the political science statements are reflective of the larger institutional statements often issued in response to anti-Blackness (see Appendix). I then created two word clouds to capture the diversity statements and Black women's experiences. Below, I explore the themes that emerged from the word clouds.

Power and Inclusion. Academia promises us academic freedom, open dialogue, a community of thinkers, and equity, a space where differences are respected and even valued. And then we, Black women, get to walk in these hallowed halls, and our reality is different. This can cause disembodiment.

The existential threat faced by Black women occurs because of a clash of values. Black women are often perceived as "other" and treated as such in the academy. Thus, while Black women are advocating a power shift, academia, in essence, is advocating for inclusion. Only one statement issued by a department that I was able to unearth via my online search explicitly deployed the term *power*. Inclusion does not change power structures because it fails to account for the past (see Ahmed 2014). Chanequa Walker-Barnes (2019) reminds us that

> We know that intercultural contact will not reduce prejudice or increase racial harmony because we carry the cultural memories of mothers, grandmothers, and other mothers whose service as domestic workers for White men and women provided lots of intercultural proximity during slavery and Jim Crow. We share kitchen table talk with aunts and cousins who labor today as the new domestics: as home care, nursing home, and hospice nursing assistants for elderly White people and as nannies for the young. We know firsthand that such proximity does not protect us from the abuses of racism; it often renders us more susceptible. (14–15)

Black women are speaking of justice within the academy and political science is speaking of inclusion.

Yet, as suggested by Walker-Barnes, Black women hold the memories that allow us to know that inclusion as a policy will not allow us full membership into the academy. This is the underlying fissure that causes disembodiment for Black women faculty members, departments, and institutions writ large. Black women are demanding substantive equality. As Alexander-Floyd (2015) argues, "A substantive equality approach looks to the ways in which members of underrepresented groups experience institutions and the ways in which institutional spaces can be transformed and institutional practices rescripted in order to assure progressive transformation. Substantive equality so conceived constitutes a social justice orientation in direct opposition to bourgeois notions of liberal equality" (465–66). Alexander-Floyd and others capture the value clash faced by Black women.

Black women have long questioned this difference in value positions in the academy. In 1994, Barbara Christian asked whether or not Black feminism could survive in the academy. Christian was interrogating the functioning of power structures and how practices reinforce a mythological ideal of Western culture as superior and, as such, undervalues and often fails to recognize knowledge produced by Black women. What Christian argues is that the perceived and sanctioned academic norms govern what can be validated as scholarly knowledge, which is then used to permit and validate the university's exclusion of Black feminism—and, in essence, Black women's knowledge and their bodies (Hill Collins 2000).

My experiences exposed me to the reality that while academia frames itself as operating in a race-gender neutral and/or benign and, at times, benevolent way, it is other. Academia is a place of deep paternalism, which then renders it blind to how it works to perpetuate oppression. Paternalism works to set up relations of power while simultaneously denying such power relations. The result is that anyone who challenges power hierarchies is often pathologized (see Walkerdine 1990). Given the functioning of paternalism and its intimate relationship with race-gender oppressions, Black women are to be seen but not heard, to speak only when given permission. We are asked to produce knowledge, but only that knowledge that maintains the status quo. To reject this role is to be seen as betraying the norms of the institution without consideration of how the norms of the institution function to betray Black women via its disciplining techniques.

So, how can Black women political scientists walk that tight line between two value systems?

When the discipline disciplines it is a political project to undiscipline yourself to resist the power that tries to twist and shape you into an image of itself while simultaneously resisting you. This is a hard project that requires one to go deep into the interior where truth resides. And that is how we resist being disciplined.

We Be Tippin' on That Tight Rope

How many pieces have you read on how Black women engage with and are treated by academic institutions? As I prepared to write this chapter, I did a cursory review of the literature and noticed the following trends:

1. Over the years, Black women and those concerned about Black women in the "Ivory Tower" have documented the types of harm that Black women experience.

2. Articles and books tend to follow particular formats, signaling to me how Black female bodies are disciplined regarding knowledge production and distribution.

3. Black women report feeling marginalized and isolated. They speak of not being mentored and facing the constant feeling that they are not allowed citizenship in the profession. There is a deep sense that we are visitors and that our time in the academy may be revoked at any time by those who hold the power.

4. Black women speak of their experiences.

We face alienation, isolation, and intellectual marginalization (Diggs et al. 2009; Cooper 2006; Thomas and Hollenshead 2001). This translates into many of us confronting an ethic/power structure/ideology that often requires Black women to habitually prove that they matter. Our studies of Black women's lives and our knowledge production are often treated as suspect, failing to meet the standards of "rigorous" and value-neutral research. As Black women, we are asked to meet criteria that have been determined by a structure that has historically excluded us from determining the "rules" of how to be an academic.

Alienation

Isolation

Marginalization

And we wonder why we are not well.

The narrative of Black women's perilous existence in academia is well documented. We are interviewed, surveyed, or sometimes we write our own stories in autoethnographies/autobiographies—telling the stories of how we are treated in academia and white and Black institutions alike. We are consistently disciplined by the discipline. While Romero (2000) does not necessarily engage in how disciplines discipline bodies, they offer an understanding that I find particularly useful. Romero states, "Within the university disciplines struggled for students, sought prestige through the granting of advanced degrees, and competed for other scarce resources; outside academia, professional organizations enforced boundaries and methodological orthodoxy, journals and peer review systems did the same, and, later, governmental agencies offered grants and financial support to those working within the established pathway" (149). In thinking of how the discipline of political science disciplines, it is important to consider institutional political agendas and power structures that produce knowledge and how they are used to establish boundaries. It is important to think of how institutions do not consider, fully, their history, which is steeped in racism (Wilder 2013)

Early in my career, I sat on a committee on women and political science. Years later, I attended a meeting and was greeted by the same sets of questions that we had offered fifteen years earlier. Some faces in the room were new to me, but so many were familiar—except that we were now grayer and had a few more wrinkles. Something felt oddly familiar, although I had opted to stay away for years. Then, the question was posed: how do we get more women of color into the discipline? The issue of diversity has been and continues to be a long-standing challenge for the discipline of political science. In 2017, Black women were awarded 2065 bachelor of arts degrees and 60 master's degrees in political science. Comparably, white women earned 9837 bachelor's degrees and 411 master's degrees in political science (Political Science & Government 2017). There is a bottleneck in political science that seems to limit the number of Black women who are awarded degrees.

As I sat in that meeting, I was greeted by a range of emotions—sadness, anger, contempt. I was reminded of what my mother often said: "Familiarity breeds contempt." This narrative of diversity was too familiar and coupled with my experience of being "disciplined" by the discipline, I could understand my feelings of contempt. My instinct was to run away and never look back. I did not have the capacity to fix political science's race-gender problem. However, I did not immediately remove myself from the meeting—at least not physically. Instead, I thought to myself, you all need to undiscipline the discipline.

To undiscipline the discipline, there needs to be an honest conversation that centers power and the legacy of racism, specifically anti-Black racism, and how it works to marginalize Black women—mind, body, and spirit. The late Lee Ann Fujii (2017) writes:

> I argue that the abhorrent lack of diversity in our discipline keeps us collectively deaf, dumb, and blind to the larger world around us, the very world we purport to analyze and explain. . . . Setting aside the specious nature of the claim that certain groups are inherently (or structurally) lacking in quality, this would still not explain the lack of diversity in political science. For if the real issue were truly about quality, there should be no problem with diversifying since **the discipline tolerates white mediocrity quite well**. Indeed, many mediocre white scholars enjoy long and successful careers. And if the discipline can celebrate white mediocrity, it should be able to do the same with non-white mediocrity, unless, of course, the real reason is not about "quality" at all but rather, the kinds of bodies that faculty see as capable of embodying quality in the first place. . . . But whiteness is anything but. It operates from a base of unseen and unquestioned power to dictate not only what is worthy of study, but also what the standards for excellence should be across all studies." (emphasis in original)

As I read Lee Ann's words and reminisce on my experiences as a Black woman in political science, I am reminded of my childhood. My mother loved to dance, and so on Sundays, she would pull out her 45s and LPs, and we would dance. She would gently slide her record on, lower the needle, and we would dance for hours. Without fail, a record would skip, or the needle would get caught in the groove. My mum would pause and go over to gingerly lift the needle and place it into the next grove. We knew which records were prone to skip or get stuck. Why? Because we played them every Sunday for our dance sessions. In fact, the malfunctioning was incorporated into our routine.

Political science's dialogues, task force reports, and so on, are like my mother's records, worn from the repetitiveness of this issue of diversifying the discipline. However, unlike my mother, who had a means of addressing the skipping or the stuck record, political science seems to lack the necessary tools to move us forward—to move us forward in a way that would temper and hopefully eliminate the disembodiment we confront.

> Until then,
> Black women in political science,
> at least some of us,
> keep *Tippin' on the Tight Rope.*
> Inventing and creating ourselves
> Because our creativity provides me/us with an ontological basis
>   of Black feminine freedom
> so that we can individually and collectively say:
> *I/we write this from a place of wholeness*[5]

Notes

1. Toni Morrison (1987) in *Beloved*, presents the concept of "rememory." Rememory is thought of as structural remembrance that transcends individual or time-bounded acts of remembrance.

2. An example of such harm occurred when a Black woman political scientist asserted that they were the first Black woman to serve as editor of a political science journal. This assertion erased the labor of four Black women, including mine, who had previously served as editors of a political science journal. One could argue that this was a simple error and easily corrected. What is interesting is that the individual did not correct the error although it was pointed out. This behavior, I argue, comes from the capitalist nature of the neoliberal institution that tells us that our worth is sometimes found in "being the first/only" even if it means that we erase the labor of others. This is, in my imagination, how ego becomes a problem as a result of the disembodiment we face—we celebrate/engage in the same oppression we claim to stand against. And this can happen in our research projects/the work we do.

3. This was conveyed to me by an editor regarding my first book. The editor went so far as to tell me that no one would read the book because there was no market for such a book. *Black Women, Cultural Images, and Social Policy* was published in 2009. I have since worked on several books focusing on Black women and politics.

4. I submitted my manuscript to a Black politics series and was told that it was not Black politics. The manuscript *Black Women, Cultural Images, and Social Policy* focuses on Black women and how they are treated vis-à-vis policy decision-making. At that moment, the discipline told me that Black politics need

only look one way, which was not what I attempted to do in this book. Interestingly, I thought very long about including this experience; after all, one doesn't air "private" dirty laundry in public. This is a different type of disciplining that is beyond the scope of this chapter.

5. As a way of undisciplining myself, I have started using different techniques to write the stories I have been given to tell. So, for example, in this chapter, I use an inversion approach. The introduction comes last, and what is typically thought of as the conclusion becomes the point of entry into this chapter. Finally, the chapter has a repetitive element whereby two lines are used more than once. This is intentional as a way of testifying about the knowledge created by Black women and how it allows me to center this knowledge to mirror how anti-Blackness is repetitive in our lives.

References

Ahmed, Sara. 2014. *On Being Included: Racism and Diversity in Institutional Life*. Durham, NC: Duke University Press.

Alexander-Floyd, Nikol G. 2015. "Women of Color, Space Invasion, and Political Science: Practical Strategies for Transforming Institutional Practices." *PS, Political Science & Politics* 48, no. 3: 464–68.

Bambara, Toni Cade. 1980. *The Salt Eaters*. New York: Random House.

Castiglia, Christopher. 2007. "Interiority." In *Keywords for American Cultural Studies*, edited by Bruce Burgett and Glenn Hendler, 135–37. New York: New York University Press. https://keywords.nyupress.org/american-cultural-studies/essay/interiority.

Christian, Barbara. 1994. "Diminishing Returns: Can Black Feminism(s) Survive the Academy?" In *Multiculturalism: A Critical Reader*, edited by David Theo Goldberg, 168–17. Cambridge, UK: Basil Blackwell.

Cooper, Tuesday L. 2006. *The Sista' Network: African-American Women Faculty Successfully Negotiating the Road to Tenure*. Bolton, MA: Anker.

Diggs, Gregory, Dorothy Garrison-Wade, Diane Estrada, and Rene Galindo. 2009. "Smiling Faces and Colored Spaces: The Experiences of Faculty of Color Pursing Tenure in the Academy." *Urban Review* 41, no. 4: 312–33.

Fujii, Lee Ann. 2017. "The Real Problem with Diversity in Political Science." October 17. https://duckofminerva.com/2017/04/the-real-problem-with-diversity-in-political-science.html.

Hill Collins, Patricia. 2000. *Black Feminist Thought: Knowledge, Consciousness, and the Politics of Empowerment*. 2nd ed. New York: Routledge.

Hine, Darlene Clark. 1994. *Hine Sight: Black Women and the Re-Construction of American History*. Bloomington: Indiana University Press.

hooks, bell. 1990. *Yearning: Race, Gender, and Cultural Politics.* Boston: South End Press.
Johnson, Sekile, ed. 2013. "Introduction: Extending the Boundaries." In *Laboring Positions: Black Women, Mothering, and the Academy*, 1–32. Bradford, Ontario: Demeter Press.
Jordan-Zachery, Julia S. 2009. *Black Women, Cultural Images and Social Policy.* New York: Routledge Studies.
———. 2019 "Licking Salt: A Black Woman's Tale of Betrayal, Adversity, and Survival." *Feminist Formations* 31, no. 1: 67–84.
———. 2020. "Timeless Conversations: How Audre Lorde Helped Me to Move from Race-Gender Violence into the Erotic" (unpublished article, January 15).
Lorde, A. 1997. *The Collected Poems of Audre Lorde.* Norton.
———. 2007 (1984). *Sister Outsider: Essays and Speeches.* Berkley, CA: Crossing Press.
———. 2017. *A Burst of Light: And Other Essays.* Mineola, NY: Ixia.
Monáe, Janell. 2007–2010. "Tightrope." By Janelle Monáe Robinson, Nathaniel Irvin III, Charles Joseph II, and Antwan Patton. Track 7 on *The ArchAndroid.* Wondaland Arts Society and Bad Boy Records.
Morison, Toni. 1987. *Beloved.* New York: Knopf.
Ohito, Esther O. 2020. "Some of Us Die: A Black Feminist Researcher's Survival Method for Creatively Refusing Death and Decay in the Neoliberal Academy." *International Journal of Qualitative Studies in Education* 34, no. 6: 515–33. https://doi.org/10.1080/09518398.2020.1771463.
Political Science & Government. 2017. "Data USA." https://datausa.io/profile/cip/political-science-government#demographics.
Quashie, Kevin. 2012. *Sovereignty of Quiet: Beyond Resistance in Black Culture.* New Brunswick, NJ: Rutgers University Press.
Romero, Mary. 2000. "Disciplining the Feminist Bodies of Knowledge: Are We Creating or Reproducing Academic Structure?" *NWSA Journal* 12, no. 2: 148–62.
Thomas, Gloria D., and Carol Hollenshead. 2001. "Resisting from the Margins: The Coping Strategies of Black Women and Other Women of Color Faculty Members at a Research University." *Journal of Negro Education* 70, no. 3: 166–75.
Walker, Alice. 1983. *In Search of Our Mothers' Gardens: Womanist Prose.* New York: Harcourt.
Walker-Barnes, Chanequa. 2019. *I Bring the Voices of my People: A Womanist Vision for Racial Reconciliation.* Grand Rapids, MI: Eerdmans.
Walkerdine, Valerie. 1990. *Schoolgirl Fictions.* New York: Verso.
Wilder, Craig. 2013. *Ebony & Ivy: Race, Slavery, and the Troubled History of America's Universities.* New York: Bloomsbury Press.

Appendix: Sources for Word Clouds

Black Women in the Academy Literature

Alfred, Mary. 2001. "Expanding Theories of Career Development: Adding the Voices of African American Women in the White Academy." *Adult Education Quarterly* 51, no. 2: 108–27.

Benjamin, Lois, ed. 1997. "Introduction." In *Black Women in the Academy: Promises and Perils*, 1–8. Gainesville: University Press of Florida.

Christian, Mark. 2012. *Integrated but Unequal: Black Faculty in Predominately White Space*. Trenton, NJ: Africa World Press.

Kelly, Bridgette Turner, and Rachelle Winkle-Wagner. 2017. "Finding a Voice in Predominantly White Institutions: A Longitudinal Study of Black Women Faculty Members' Journeys toward Tenure." *Teachers College Record* 119, no. 6: 1–36.

Robinson, Subrina J. 2013. "Spoketokenism: Black Women Talking Back about Graduate School Experiences." *Race Ethnicity and Education* 16, no. 2: 155–81.

Thomas, Gloria D., and Carol Hollenshead. 2001. "Resisting from the Margins: The Coping Strategies of Black Women and Other Women of Color Faculty Members at a Research University." *Journal of Negro Education* 70, no. 3: 166–75.

Walkington, Lori. 2017. "How Far Have We Really Come? Black Women Faculty and Graduate Students' Experiences in Higher Education." *Humboldt Journal of Social Relations* 39, no. 39: 51–65.

Political Science Department's Statements on Diversity

Penn State's Political Science Department
Department of Political Science at University of Wisconsin-Madison
Ohio State University Department of Political Science
Political Science at University of California, Berkeley
The Department of Political Science at Indiana University Bloomington
Massachusetts Institute of Technology Department of Political Science
Cal Poly Political Science Department Statement on Justice, Diversity, and Inclusion
Purdue University Department of Political Science

9

Transforming Political Science

Founding the Transnational Black Womxn Scholars of African Politics Research Network

TIFFANY WILLOUGHBY-HERARD, T. D. HARPER-SHIPMAN,
KIRA TAIT, ROBIN L. TURNER, AND TARA JONES

> The creation of the treasured spaces that have allowed dozens of Africa's feminist thinkers to come together at various African locations and carry out collaborative work on intellectual projects is historic.
>
> —Amina Mama

As established and emerging Black womxn scholars of African politics, we offer a model of Black womxn transforming the discipline of political science.[1] Our model includes (1) the development of a research network that engages the history of Black women political scientists transnationally, (2) claiming space in the public sphere of professional academic political science and sharing opportunities as Black womxn, (3) exploring the ontological and epistemological significance of nurturing our research from these deliberately chosen positionalities, and (4) researching and connecting ourselves to prior Black transnational research networks. Our research network intervenes in and corrects the willful exclusion of Black women political scientists of African politics from syllabi, PhD examination required reading lists, and scholarly citations in the top journals (ASBWP 2016; Alexander-Floyd 2015a, 2015b, 2014, 2008; Alexander-Floyd and Willoughby-Herard 2015). This model is antithetical to the way that political science typically operates. Indeed, the *Chronicle of Higher Education* has documented the extreme underrepresentation of Black women with tenure in US higher education; among the campuses where the founders of this research network teach, tenured Black women range from 1.3% to 2.5% (June and O'Leary 2021). Members of our network are cognizant of our own positionality and work conditions as Black womxn in the field of political science. We have used the seeming deficit and history of discrimination as a salient organizing structure, an analytical frame. Having experienced our own hardships as scholars and recognizing the ways that institutionalized raced and gendered bias operates in the field of political science, we decided to interrupt a scholarly "knowledge production system" that pretends that we do not exist (Robinson 2003). Not only do we intend to demonstrate that Black womxn have contributed in fulsome and critical ways to the study of African politics, but we also mean to create a scholarly network where we could practice solidarity, support, and sharing. In these ways we could change the conditions of exclusion that shaped our own training and that of others in order to create new research possibilities and new research questions. In the following, we describe the work that we have undertaken since March 2020 to build a transnational research network.

The purpose of sharing this history is to reveal what happens analytically when we put several terms under pressure: *Black women* and *political science*. We put pressure on these terms by exploring how Blackness, womanhood, and political science are configured in knowledge production and in academic political science. Our research formation intentionally unsettles Black womanhood from its predictable relationship to gender by using the concept *womxn* to describe ourselves and our future members. With this term, we insist on creating space for all people who identify as womxn regardless of the sex they were assigned at birth. This means that we are enabled to think about Black womanhood (1) through the distinctive experiences of an ascriptive identity, (2) as an analytical category, and (3) as an "ideological imperative" that charges us to "examine and redress the oppressive forces that have constrained the lives of Black women in particular and women of color more generally," including the lethal forces, tropes, and practices invested in using gender itself to disappear and punish us and those we share this complex social and political category with (Alexander-Floyd 2012, 3–4). Second, by prioritizing both Black womxn knowledge producers and African politics, we dislodge racializing notions of the political that may unconsciously or intentionally rely on the premise of the American polity of the last two and a half centuries as the beginning and end of the study of politics. We are demonstrating that politics has geographic and spatial dimensions that can only be best understood by transnational and diasporic thinking. Gendered racisms in knowledge production are cornerstones of hegemonic definitions of "the political." Such gendered racisms effect dominant expectations of who should be studying politics or who can make claims on what constitutes the political. Indeed, Black women and women of color elected officials experience particular forms of misogynoir, obstacles to claiming to represent groups of people and their interests, and are often understudied or deemed usurpers for entering the public sphere and claiming to have interests (Caldwell 2007; Isoke 2013; Brown 2014; Harris 2018). Our research network is a generative and productive strategy for transforming the discipline, its canons, and the histories that are written about who has produced impactful and singular knowledge about Black womxn and African politics. If politics is about far more than the study of achieving one's goals and articulating one's interest within the particular geography and polity that one lives inside of then our insistence that we are suturing our inquiries of the present to those that came before and insisting that we are binding our studies to those conducted in other geographies fundamentally transforms who we think is contributing to the field of political science. We explore how our work is transforming political science by foregrounding narratives by the Black women who have undertaken this work before us. Though the legacy of these Black women scholars has largely been redacted from our formal training in African politics (none of us was required to study or was introduced to any Black women political scientists in any of our formal training; and yet we were duly certified as African politics scholars), through our meeting each other at the National Conference of Black Political Scientists (NCOBPS) in March 2020 and before, we initiated a transformative space that could benefit us and many others. Knowing how transnational research networks and professional organizations have been built inside of NCOBPS and taken flight in other spaces that are NCOBPS adjacent is key to this formal assessment of how we are transforming the discipline.

The Puzzle: Doing Our Work Together as Black Womxn

The Transnational Black Womxn Scholars of African Politics Research Network was initiated at the March 2020 NCOBPS meeting in Atlanta when Kira Tait, Robin L. Turner, and Tiffany Willoughby-Herard presented papers on postapartheid evictions housing policy, rural women's involvement in traditional leadership, and Pan-African scholar activism and praxis as a response to contemporary xenophobia in South Africa at a panel titled Considering, Challenging, and Navigating Wars on Blackness in Southern Africa. Takiyah Harper-Shipman organized a panel on radical political economies that included research from Honduras by K. Melchor Hall, Haiti by Mamryah Dougé-Prosper, and her own work on Ghana, intending to contribute to expanding the geographical scope of NCOBPS scholarship. As program chairs for the African politics subfield, Turner and Harper-Shipman had empirical evidence with which to conclude that we had received a paucity of research papers in African politics or diasporic politics beyond the United States at the otherwise inclusive NCOBPS conference. Coupled with the marginalization of Black womxn's scholarship on Africa at the mostly white fall 2019 American Political Science Association meeting the we also attended, it was clear that we needed a more systematic way to raise the profile of research in African politics by Black womxn scholars.

While scholarship on Africa and the diaspora is embedded in the mission of NCOBPS and has an esteemed history in the organization, there is room for its further articulation and expansion. We continued talking after our panel, attended sessions on the Race and Democracy in the Americas Project, and began to envision creating a sustained and inclusive network for Black womxn scholars of African politics. We see our research network as bridging broader networks of Black and African feminists, womanists, and African gender studies scholars organizing movements, catalyzing political education, and using research to amplify vital contributions to the study of African politics with the vision, longevity, and institutional dedication of the founders and leaders of the NCOBPS. As cofounders of this transnational research network, we have each emerged in different scholarly generations and through a wide range of US-based ideological, political, movement traditions. Despite all these differences as Black womxn scholars, we share the painful, isolating, and wholly preventable experience of being underrepresented, tokenized, and regarded as having no antecedents. Such experiences cause grave injury and reduce our potential numbers as formally trained Black womxn African politics researchers. Much of our work involves opening up space for reflecting on the scholarly and scholarly activist genealogies that were key to our own training—outside of mainstream white American political science—and to other genealogies that we wish to engage. Ultimately, we seek to take up the charge of what one of the cofounders of the African Heritage Studies Association and a former president of NCOBPS, Dr. Shelby Lewis, explained as African politics leadership in the 2014 to 2019 renewal period marking fifty years of the organization (2019). Explaining the charge, Lewis writes that in addition to holding conferences, publishing a book series, erecting a scholarly canon, commissioning murals and curating art exhibits, and catalyzing new research agendas, the tasks of this renewal period included "documenting and explicating the global context in which slavery, colonialism, and imperialism emerged, converged, pillaged the African world and interrupted its development, and examining the impact of historical forces that still resonate and continue to divide, destabilize, exploit and shape relations within and between African peoples and the rest of the world" (Lewis 2019).

Lewis and the genealogy of African politics scholars that she emerges from have produced a vast literature, the founding and funding of institutions of higher education across the African continent, and research partnerships that linked Black movement people across the globe into sustained scholarly networks that have produced us. And yet, their scholarship exists under erasure and is not available on syllabi in political science departments outside of the HBCUs around the world. As an autonomous and Black-led professional research association, the African Heritage Studies Association "challenged conventional views of Africa; interrogated ahistorical ideas of an underdeveloped, dependent, resource poor continent in perpetual need of Western aid and tutelage; collaborated with other disciplinary associations, including holding joint conferences with the NCOBPS and the Black Studies Association and mentored young scholars studying African history and culture. These efforts ignited a proliferation of African-centered research and publications, the expansion of Black Studies, Africana Woman's Studies programs, and the development of curriculum materials on African history and culture for precollegiate school systems" (Lewis 2019). In our variant of the renewal period, we have the opportunity to use our own scholarship, curriculum development, and professional associations to highlight and amplify Black transnational research networks from earlier generations while also nurturing our own contributions to scholarship on Black womxn in political science. Writing about the relationship between those earlier generations and our own is one critical and necessary way to undo practices of erasure and silencing that still occur while situating what we do in a vibrant intellectual scholar-activist tradition. Not only does naming the earlier tradition of Black transnational research networks ground us in our ethical, epistemological, and analytical practices, associating how we are moving and thinking with these prior scholars enables us to upset the forms of despair, loneliness, and self-doubt that tend to accumulate as affective and psychological response to curricular misremembering and intellectual dispossession in African politics. When we say that we emerge from different genealogies and traditions and institutional and citizenship histories, this is a polite way of describing the divide and conquer tactics that operate to construct a multigenerational "matrix of domination" in the academy (Collins 1990). Professional political scientists in major research universities across the world use divide and conquer strategies to dispossess Black women researchers from the field of political science. From tokenizing gestures, to perpetuating inequitable access to rigorous academic publishing opportunities, to excluding from training opportunities and withdrawing such opportunities as punishment for speaking up and protesting, the discipline and its mainstream practitioners in African politics erases our antecedents from syllabi and examination lists and polices those among the faculty who do remind us of the value of self-determined Black political scientists. Our existence and persistence tell a different truth. We have claimed the inheritance of the Black women scholars who came before us, even when we were denied their company and denied being taught their names and their ideas.

If we remained in the restricted nodes that constituted the most limited and demoralizing dimensions of political science training—often focused on the knowledge production of white male and some few white female scholars of African politics, we would not be able to seek out, reconstruct, or repair these historiographical breaches. In such zones there are no Black womxn political scientists that ought to be cited, read, or engaged with. In such zones every Black womxn who enters a graduate program is a *unicorn* and a token, a kind of sixteenth-century conquest era bridge between her people and the world of white knowledge production—an affective burden that results in countless people simply leaving higher education and the discipline of political science. Instead, we are creating new narratives and relationships across the diaspora to promote, water, nourish, and sustain existing and new research collaborations and modes of thought.

Pan-Africanism, African feminism, Black feminism, and African gender studies principles animate the project and how we sought to materialize our commitments and foster collaborative research. Among these principles and commitments are the idea of process-oriented scholarship, collaboration and sharing of institutional resources and time, activist scholarship that is accountable to championing justice, attention to our positionality as people who reside in the United States and who have positions that guarantee that our scholarship will be placed in a knowledge hierarchy above that produced by people who reside on the African continent. Our intention and our practices, to the best of our ability, mean to undermine those dynamics of power and to acknowledge and be in dynamic partnership with scholars based on the African continent.

We are committed to the idea that self-determination and decolonizing knowledge is a key feature of living for people of African descent wherever they are. In pursuit of self-determination and decolonization, we have deep commitments to challenging captivity, historicizing and making sense of the afterlives of slavery and racial colonialism, exploring the logics of gendered racial terror, and dislodging the conditions that enable capitalism to destroy lives and wreak havoc. We do these things through creative engagements, working together, and coming into each other's lives as thinkers and as feminist scholar-activists. As modern-day pan-Africanist thinkers, we claim a deliberate and intentional sense of dynamic and mutual sociality, relationality, and chosen belonging to each other. We are encouraging each other on our own paths of decolonization from the most harmful expressions of racialized gender, imperialist and capitalist violence, and the afterlives of slavery and colonialism. We wrestle with the legacies of being inheritors of dynamic, highly adaptable, and justice-oriented cultural-cosmological and political survivals. Such African survivals are embraced with deliberation and care, as they continue to provide necessary lessons for survival and flourishing. In a 2016 interview, Oyèrónké Oyěwùmí explained decades of research on the violence on gender with the phrases "motherhood is transcendent" and "everything has a mother, even God." For Black womxn scholars to embrace such an ontological claim as a centerpiece for meaning-making requires understanding that this claim and others like it were essential tools for re-creating our value in spiritual terms. Such claims enabled us to defy the violence of being reduced to not quite human property and the tragedy of feverish greedy ambitions of financial prospects tethered to our wombs. Such ontological claims engage epistemologies, concepts, symbols, and ways of interpreting history outside of Western scripts of white knowledge production, wherever they show up. We encourage each other to recognize and experiment with the political, cultural, and social visions that bind us together as Black womxn and to celebrate, value, and admire those parts of our experiences as Black womxn that do not overlap or coincide. In the following, we shift from our principles and analytical frameworks to the institutional and epidemiological history of the research network that we created.

COVID-19 and a Shifting Epidemiological Context for Knowledge Production

During the emergence of the COVID-19 pandemic, Robin Turner, Tiffany Willoughby-Herard, Kira Tait, and Takiyah Harper-Shipman were among the third of scheduled NCOBPS attendees to have arrived in Atlanta prior to campuses and state governors prohibiting faculty travel. In those early days of COVID-19 awareness and spread in the United States as we fumbled through provisional notifications and warnings to shelter in place, information about the transmission of the virus was only beginning to become available. Centers for Disease Control and Prevention notifications, World Health Organization announcements, warnings from those with friends in China and Europe, anecdotes, and confusing hearsay from the White House proliferated. Those of us at the conference followed social-distancing protocols, including greeting with elbow bumps, refraining from touching objects, and wiping down our hotel rooms, podiums, and microphones. At the time, the lethality of the pandemic was largely unknown to us, and daily news reports were just beginning to frame the new normal. All of us had major international travel scheduled for the ensuing months that was subsequently canceled. Not only did this smaller conference facilitate conversations and signal a need to shift to virtual communication, but it also opened up pathways and possibilities that we might have overlooked in other moments.

Perhaps a sense of impending doom and also our own imagined hardiness, as people who travel regularly around the world and had done so for decades, made us realize how important it was at this historical juncture to follow through on a vice-presidential initiative[2] to build out (and in some ways rebuild) the scholarly focus on African politics in the organization through holding workshops and panels and initiating collaborative research projects. NCOBPS has a long-standing history of African politics research and affiliation with political scientists on the continent whose research lives required confronting and navigating spurious racist legacies in the discipline. This kind of transnational research among Black political scientists upends stereotypes about Black political scientists as prototypical "native informants" if continental Africans and "lacking objectivity" if diasporic Africans. The COVID-19 context required web-based communication from scholars across the globe and normalized such communications in a way that compelled people of African descent around the world to affirm each other as independent and autonomous scholars beyond the limited associational frameworks available in existing organizations.

So, when we agreed at the conference to meet regularly to talk about establishing a framework for a lasting writing, thinking, and creative space for Black womxn interested in pan-African and African politics, we were both drawing on a long Black transnational scholarly tradition and creating a new branch in the context of a global pandemic that continues to reveal how racism is a public health disparity—even racism that emerges in scholarly conduct and practices. Key to this agreement was deciding on regular bimonthly meeting times, exchanging articles and publications, sharing reflections on formal training and activist journeys in African politics as a field, trading memories about how and where our research and activism has been received, swapping stories about new books published by scholars that we admire, exchanging syllabi and teaching materials, forwarding relevant opportunities for fellowships and research posts, and joining Sistah Scholar monthly zoom calls convened by Georgetown political scientist Nadia Brown and doctoral student India Lennear.

As researchers with significant experience with constructing, building, and benefiting from existing networks that reflect "transnational network[s] of Black women from across the diaspora who could work together to promote racial and gender equality" (Williams 2014, 9 cited in Hordge-Freeman and Mitchell-Walthour 2016, 8), we would not be daunted by the need to draw on our own network building and organizing skills. Not only did we talk briefly after our panel session about collaborating on something larger in the future, but we immediately set up a phone tree and attended several other conference panels and workshops together.[3] The COVID-19 travel restrictions heightened our awareness and catalyzed our collaborative action as Black womxn who make sense of the world through transnational research and cultural exchange on the African continent.

In this pandemic context, we have had the opportunity to (1) make visible the institutional barriers—across scholarly generations—that have prevented us from being in more sustained contact before; our common struggles to seek out Black womxn scholarly mentors even when they had not ever been on our assigned syllabi; and (2) teach ourselves to speak across the activist scholarly traditions and genealogies. We do not mean to flatten these traditions but create new conditions under which African politics emerges in the learned associations and political formations that matter most to us.

We were faced with the thinned-out participation and the risky possibility of not being able to see each other again, and COVID-19 provided a context of scholarly intimacy to share ideas in a way that we might not have participated in earlier. Despite having all written dissertations (or being at the very end of completing dissertations) and having robust publication records in African politics given our very distinctive activist scholarly genealogies and institutional histories, our paths would not have naturally overlapped. Additionally, the lack of robust citational practices in political science, the lack of inclusive syllabi or doctoral exam preparation, and the very small number of us located in the academy regularly prevented us from being in the same scholarly assemblies. The COVID-19 context shifted the meanings that we associated with these structural and institutional barriers. Thus, we sought to bring these formations into conversation because we did not know how things would be after COVID-19. In this high-pressure context, we developed new sinews of scholarly connection and activist relationality, which meant sharing the analytic tools that we had created in the absence of being introduced to Black womxn African politics researchers that had come before us in the major scholarly journals and on our graduate syllabi. Creating this new research network provided an encouraging lifeline in the uncertainty of the COVID-19 pandemic and the pandemic of grinding anti-Black racial violence that captured the global news cycles for months after the murder of George Floyd.

Founding the Research Network

From the period of May 2020, when we began to meet biweekly and then monthly, we recruited Takiyah Harper-Shipman (author of *Rethinking*

Ownership of Development in Africa published by Routledge) and Adom Getachew (2020 awardee of the NCOBPS W. E. B. Du Bois Book Award for *World Making after Empire: The Rise and Fall of Self-Determination*, published by Princeton University Press); drafted a mission statement; and proposed, applied for, and secured a preconference workshop grant from the Centennial Center of the American Political Science Association in partnership with the NCOBPS and with enthusiastic formal and informal endorsements from the Association for the Study of Black Women in Politics (ASBWP) and the African Heritage Studies Association.

During meetings, we discussed what and who such a research network would make space for, how it would support researchers and new projects, and what draws us to transnational research in Africa. We shared a timeline of diaspora-focused research and African politics–focused research that had grown out of the NCOBPS as the first post-1968 generation professional organization committed to unmasking how what we know as the (bureaucratic administrative and nationalist) regimes of "the political" come to conscript and "limit thought" (Robinson 2016, x). We discussed how its members entered academia and proliferated their contributions to global Black Power protests in higher education through the establishment of alternative learned societies and professional associations, including the African Heritage Studies Association (founded 1968), the Joint Center for Political and Economic Studies (founded 1970), the Congressional Black Caucus (founded 1971), and the National Council of Black Studies (founded 1975).

This meeting and planning space, in effect, became our political education workshop and laboratory for new ideas and initiatives and enabled us to weather the storms that unfolded after the murders of our ever-expanding cohort of much-mourned Black people that continue to catalyze a global racial reckoning. We also shared grant opportunities, fellowships, calls for papers, and job advertisements and talked through thorny research, unionization, and departmental politics. It matters that the scale of our conversation could work through a formal agenda while asking after each other's loved ones, planning a conference, and encouraging each other as people surviving multiple global pandemics. This is not how we were socialized in political science. Indeed the paucity of Black political scientists whose research focuses on Africa in political science departments has meant that we have not had pathways for socialization into the disciplinary organizations. Our experience of underrepresentation is severe, and though we are often recruited for committee work in the largest US political science organization, our voices and perspectives are muted, isolated, and marginalized. Typical committee outreach will overtax one or two Black womxn instead of extending a broad reach and building genuine ties of recognition, curiosity, or concern. By contrast, our transnational research network began from the place of listening to each other and cultivating a process of resocialization into the field and discipline where our lives as Black womxn would be valued and prized.

Throughout our discussions, we regularly infused key practices critical to womxn and politics and Black feminist politics research networks, including shared meditation, groundings, stretching, check-ins, and support of Harper-Shipman and Turner's completion of yoga instructor certification. Such embodied approaches to interpretive work were especially valuable given the extraordinary burdens faced as underrepresented and minoritized Black womxn faculty members, community advocates, union organizers, and scholar-activists at North American universities. We provided an empathetic ear for grassroots organizing and mutual aid and union strikes across our various institutional and regional locations and became a place for collective decision-making and process-oriented African politics scholarship.

From the moment when we began to decide on what our mission would be and what it would entail, we agreed that foremost among our goals would be to support Black womxn scholars writing and working on African politics by creating an intentional space for resource sharing, collaboration, and mentorship.

At present and with full acknowledgment that it is a provisional and beginning living document and that we will seek revision, assessment, and ratification at our first preconference gathering, we proposed the following mission to organize our work:

> We are creating an intentional space for resource sharing, collaboration, and mentorship to support Black womxn scholars writing and working on African politics. By womxn we insist on creating space for all people who identify as womxn regardless of the sex they were assigned at birth. We aim to build a truly transnational network led by Black womxn based in Africa and those based elsewhere. This network will identify and challenge shared and distinct barriers that Black womxn face in researching, writing, and publishing on African politics with a mind toward candid conversation, strategic thinking, and resource sharing that expands resources for all of us. This

network will create and convene spaces to highlight the work of Black womxn; foster collaborative research among members of the network; and generate new research agendas. Solidarity and egalitarianism are always at the center of the network. The network will center the principles of solidarity and egalitarianism and self-determination, self-defense, accountability, in these and other projects. (September 18, 2020)

Our most tangible evidence of the extant need for this framework was a preconference that we designed together and hosted at the 2021 NCOBPS virtual conference. This collaborative project involved several steps, including debating whether we had the capacity to organize it, coming up with and revising our communication strategies, identifying which institution and person would serve as the host for the grant, using our networks in different ways to maximize the infrastructure for the project, dividing up tasks, and cowriting the grant application. The preconference itself borrowed the workshop model from the African Politics Conference Group of the American Political Science Association, as that organization features untenured scholars in their workshops. However, we intended to frame such workshops around the gap that we observed with regard to how Black womxn's scholarship is treated in the discipline of political science. Heading the workshops Celebrated, Centered, and Cited enabled us to reflect on Black womxn Africa politics researchers as worthy contributors that ought to be cited. Black womxn Africa politics researchers and their scholarly outputs are key to the corpus of African politics and have consistently transformed the contours of the field. Careful studies of research by Black women in political science, women of color in political science, and women in political science have found time and again that we are rarely cited, included on syllabi, or featured as key thinkers whose pathbreaking contributions have to be read and engaged with in order to claim that one has conducted significant research work on African politics (ASBWP 2016; Alexander-Floyd 2015a, 2015b, 2014, 2008; Alexander-Floyd and Willoughby-Herard 2015). We marshaled our capacity for resource sharing and intellectual collaboration to bring womxn scholars from various ranks in the profession and diverse geographical backgrounds together to exchange feedback, foment publishing opportunities, and build scholarly community around African politics. We intend to nurture holistic relationships of collaboration that do more than achieve the political objective of developing a sustainable transnational research network. Institutionalizing our goals is as important as careful attention to how we engage with, disagree with, and learn from each other. We mean to have a real and lasting impact on research network members' lives and the work we are doing and to insist that Black women scholars in political science, especially those working in African politics be cited, studied, and engaged. This is another way that we are transforming political science by humanizing how we operate in the field and affirming our presence and scholarship as well as sustaining each other as people outside of our connections to each other in academe. This emerges directly from the ethos of NCOBPS and the way that we have been socialized as Black political scientists to express concern about each other's family members and lives. In order to do this we have built a web of connections that is also concerned about how and whether our political commitments meet our ethical standards for care, nurturance, regard, and integrity.

Partnering with NCOBPS and Developing Long-Lasting Ties

As an organization, NCOBPS is largely known in the discipline of political science as being a long-lasting incubator organization for launching and sustaining pathways for Black and other underrepresented minority graduate students and faculty members. It is acknowledged publicly for supporting the founding of the race and ethnic politics subfield (1995) and its expansion through the launch of its journal, *Journal of Race and Ethnic Politics* (2016). However, as we began our research network, we felt that NCOBPS was a wise institutional partner because NCOBPS's history of building robust and lasting international research networks in Africa and across the Americas was time tested. In fact, Tait, Turner, and Willoughby-Herard attended multiple sessions at NCOBPS 2020 in Atlanta featuring reports on and presentations by US- and Brazil-based scholars affiliated with the Race and Democracy in the Americas Project. According to a cofounder of that research network, David Covin, "Since 1992, NCOBPS has never failed to offer at least one panel on Afro-Brazilian, Caribbean, or Afro Latin politics. Junior NCOBPS scholars continue to be mentored on their work on the politics of the African diaspora" (2016, 39). That is a tremendous, nearly thirty-year history of sustaining "*an international black space*, based in the western hemisphere" (36; emphasis added).

The Race and Democracy in the Americas Project members recruited and convened US and Brazilian Black scholars and activists conducting work on Black social movements both to expand the number of movement building spaces and to link them. They amplified the impact of Afro-Brazilian social movements through research and holding conferences (including NCOBPS Oakland 1993), writing books that published Brazilian and US researchers on equal footing. They operationalized diasporic and internationalist ways of responding to anti-Blackness by creating new ways to be together both inside and outside of formal conference spaces. They treasured the social spaces that they built together through sharing stories and memories and viewed NCOBPS as a movable technology for drawing people together across national boundaries (Covin 2016, 34). Cofounders Covin and K. C. Morrison along with their Brazilian collaborators first met at the 1988 Salvador Bahia Brazil Association of Caribbean Studies Conference and were astounded "by the extraordinary number of black scholars who were attending, most from other parts of the Americas, and particularly because they were coming to conduct serious discussions of African descended peoples" (30). Ironically, attending those international conferences drew them into scholarly networks with US-trained Black American scholars of Brazil whose training in anthropology, history, and even political science might have placed them outside the known sphere of NCOBPS and the National Council of Black Studies and other spaces. There Covin met collaborators that he has continued to write and organize with for the last three decades: Luiza Helena Bairros, Michael Hanchard, Angela Gilliam, and Kim Butler. Like us in the transnational Black womxn scholars of African politics Network, the Race and Democracy in the Americas Project leaders and participants actively cultivated "social space, social narrative, and social memory" far beyond formal conference panels (35–36). Using diasporic narrative, memory, and space-making practices, they wrote to and for each other. They built intellectual kinship and shared space in a community of struggle that witnessed each other contribute to meaningful and significant change in community organizations, public policies, and national elections.

Building a Transnational Space: Leveraging Financial Resources, Prestigious Institutional Networks, and Knowledge Economies

Covin's vivid 2016 study of the Race and Democracy Project offers an extended discussion about the benefits of sharing ideas and writing collaboratively despite resource inequalities that have long histories in colonialism and slavery and their influence on institutionalized and recognized knowledge production. The Race and Democracy Project emerged out of ties that had been cultivated within NCOBPS. In the following quotation we find a useful illustration for thinking about how collaboration can be operationalized and the ethos and culture that NCOBPS nurtures and socializes members through.

> Barrios was insistent that whatever they did should be collaborative, such that Brazilians and NCOBPS members would be coequals. it would have to be interdisciplinary, as she knew of no Afro Brazilians who had completed the PhD in political science. it would have to be funded from the United States because there were no Afro-Brazilian scholars who had direct access to funding sources. Further elements were discussed, including language training; the need to incorporate both junior and senior scholars; the formation of mentor relationships—cross-nationally as well as intra-nationally; the development of cross-national research projects; the development of support mechanisms for junior Afro-Brazilian scholars; and the implementation of mechanisms to ensure that both the conception and inception of the work would be cross-national. the vision and design would derive from cross-national collaboration, deliberately including scholar-activists as full-fledged members of the project. (Covin 2016, 33)

While the transnational network of Black womxn scholars of African politics is not hamstrung by small numbers of political science doctoral graduates or political science faculty across the African continent, there continue to be hierarchies of knowledge based on where scholars are trained. As scholars have taught us, there is a century-long historic legacy of marginalizing refereed social science research produced by Africa-based scholars (Zimbalist 2020, 621; Cakata 2020, 89; Mama 2011, e5; Mafeje 1971, 253, 258, 260). Cakata and Mama write about the necessity of "re-Africanising" or simply "Africanising" knowledge production as one modality for correcting this—identifying concepts that actually answer the social scientific problems and questions most pressing, instead of applying concepts that have no utility, little use, and reinforce colonial power. Not only this but Africa-based scholars and African diaspora–based scholars often have challenged the basic concepts and frames of analysis produced by Eurocentric scholars trained and based in the West both as it exists geographically and ideologically around the globe. Both groups of scholars often have not been able to gain access to decision-making in professional associations associated with the historically white academy due to the implicit and historic racial hierarchies imposed under slavery, colonialism, apartheid, Jim Crow, and their afterlives (Allman 2020, 2019; Pailey 2016). These scholars faced the conundrum of non-Black and non-African social scientists who researched African and African diasporic topics refusing to interpret or perceive variation, change, or difference where it existed, on the one hand, and being ideologically wedded to proving that no intentional *shared* political choices had been made by African and Black peoples when they had, on the other. Africa-based and African diaspora–based Black scholars have faced well-documented commitments to consolidating white knowledge production over Blackness and Black thought as a set of interpretations of the social and the political. They have faced this will to white power over knowledge production across ideology, language, ethnicity, gender, class, and relationship to slavery, colonialism, or imperialism. In the context of Eurocentric knowledge production, Africanness and Blackness existed as states of ontological nonbeing for Enlightenment and as ready objects for study. Being caricatured in such a fashion about our existence has been conveniently packaged within gendered scripts about the bodies of our people at the bottom of dozens of national racial hierarchies across multiple continents. Patterns of physical violence, economic discrimination, and civil and political exclusions included segregated inclusion or exclusion from public life. Often such patterns were entrenched in arenas of social reproduction that are key for transmitting social norms, ideologies, and justifications for prejudice, such as the schoolhouse and the university. These arrangements of power hierarchy also readily utilized the power systems of gender to engulf, extract, steal, brutalize, and suppress the thinking of Black womxn, in particular, but not only. Not only is the construct of gender itself something that has been systematically troubled and dislodged time and again in the work of Black feminists of all genders, this skepticism of the consequences of gender and the project of ungendering has not become hegemonic within Black knowledge production.

She Determined, on That Day:
Black Feminist Transnational Research Networks

One of the most important lessons from the Race and Democracy Project has been that we needed to learn how to connect ourselves to existing research networks like the one we envisioned, networks from which our ideas about Black womxn's approach to political science as fundamentally transnational had emerged. Indeed, a historiographical recovery chapter such as this one is a required output for participating in Shelby Lewis's charge that we prioritize *renewal*. Our first collective writing, the Centennial Center grant sketched out a very preliminary intellectual history of the publications of the Black womxn African politics scholars whose work had inspired our own, teaching us in person in professional associations (away from our graduate programs and campuses) and teaching us through their articles published in long defunct journals and in anthologies and in working papers series (because their rarely cited, seemingly contraband writings were passed to us hand to hand not easily available in research libraries). In the following, we review the reminiscences of several leading Black women scholars who have written about African politics. In an illustrative moment, about the design of our first preconference, our proposed keynote conducted an assessment of our analytical vision before agreeing to present as a keynote. After we began discussions with Professor Amina Mama about being our inaugural preconference keynote, she asked for us to first join the Feminist Africa Network, her long-standing global research network. Then Mama asked us to each send a brief bio about our own work. She was assessing what we were doing, what values we were accountable to while expanding the number of informed and rigorous Black womxn's movement spaces that exist and linking them to their progenitors. Mama was vetting us and our ethics before agreeing to speak to us as a keynote.

Black womxn scholars have contributed to the wealth of knowledge on the origins, dispersal, and maintenance of power in Africa. Despite their invaluable contributions, their work is often absent from the citational practices and course syllabi that form the parameters of the field and the basis for evaluation in the discipline (Okech 2020). Scholars such as Pearl Robinson, Amina Mama, Achola Pala, Shelby Lewis, Oyèrónké Oyěwùmí, Mae King, and Dzodzi Tsikata, some of whom have been key figures in NCOBPS, have expanded our understanding of political economy, institution building, public policy making, and gender relations in African politics.

In the following, we select a sample of these key thinkers in the NCOBPS ecology: Pearl Robinson, Shelby F. Lewis, and Mae King. Pearl Robinson shared a vivid memory during her presentation at the Tribute to Ralph Bunche Panel at the American Political Science Association

2020 virtual conference. Robinson testified in her comments about the barriers to her being able to conduct her pathbreaking research in African politics. Paraphrasing her words as closely as possible here, she said, "Charles Hamilton and Elliott Skinner were [her] professors at Columbia University. [At] that time you couldn't do African American Politics and African politics together because one was American Politics and one was Comparative. If I'd known that Ralph Bunche was doing both in the 1920s I would have not had to petition. His career was very much like mine and though I've been looking at him through the archives I realize that it is now a mind meld of sorts."[4] Not only was Robinson denied access to an astonishingly well-known intellectual forebear and thinker that had already charted a path that she sought to go, but she was told that such a pathway was literally unthinkable. Ralph Bunch was a president of the American Political Science Association in 1953, more than two decades before Robinson earned her doctorate in political science at Columbia. Pearl Robinson's experience of being denied access to Ralph Bunche was reiterated in our own training. Her articles and research were never on any syllabus for any course that any of us ever took in political science.[5] Robinson was made to feel that what she was prepared to do and the questions that she sought to ask were what philosopher Nahum Chandler has called "problems for thought," itself.

Robinson's memory of her graduate education echoes one that Shelby Lewis shared during an interview in December 23, 2019.[6] Upon asking Lewis what took her and her siblings to Uganda and Tanganyika in 1963, she retold a story of a white woman anthropology professor that discouraged her from studying in Africa during her master's program. Her professor told her that African Americans lacked the capacity to objectively study Africa, in particular. Further, she was told that Africans did not like, admire, or welcome African Americans, erasing at least two centuries of well-documented intellectual and cultural exchange and intentional social and political collaboration. Lewis finishes the story by exclaiming that that conversation made it easy for her to leave that graduate program and immediately begin searching out and applying for posts like the one that she eventually took with the British Teachers for East Africa Program, thereby beginning five decades of research, including visiting nearly every country on the continent and raising her children there.

Another key example from within the NCOBPS ecology is Howard University emerita professor Mae King. King conducted and completed sustained and published research on the United Nations crisis in the

Congo, Ghanaian nationalism, international relations of Nigeria, the Southern Christian Leadership Council, the Congressional Black Caucus, the National Council of Negro Women, and the International Association of Black Professionals in International Affairs, and she was the first African American professional staffer to work at the American Political Science Association—an organization whose provenance and financial solvency relied on the acumen of the aforementioned Ralph Bunche in securing a building that the organization still operates out of today in Washington, DC. Clearly King's body of research demonstrates that it is possible to conduct both African politics and African American politics and diaspora politics in the life of one scholar. But beyond these esteemed things, Dr. King is an incredibly humble and accessible mentor for junior scholars. Actively engaged in the ASBWP, and having lent her name to one of their annual awards, she is always a voice for intellectual autonomy for Black people as thinkers. By studying the Black womxn who people the intellectual history of African politics, not only is it possible to develop theory out of the Global South, but it is possible to develop theory out of the intentional choices of diaspora-based Black womxn scholars to amplify the voices and politics of African scholars and to collaborate on an equal footing.

US-based movements like #CiteBlackWomen exposed the need to transform the practice of citation so that Black women's work receives its due credit. Though we are not attempting to provide a comprehensive or encyclopedic genealogy here, we are developing a more formal historiography that addresses the intellectual histories, which we emerge from and have extended in our own scholarship (Malaklou and Willoughby-Herard 2018; Alexander-Floyd 2008; Robinson 2003; Du Bois 1935). Beyond citational practices, Black womxn in political science face numerous barriers that hinder their advancement and exposure in the field (see #BlackInTheIvory). The recent pandemic has only exposed and exacerbated these inequities.

While US-based scholars constitute the planning committee, we aim to build a truly transnational network coled by Africa-based womxn scholars. This is of particular significance since there are long histories of ethnic competition across the United States and Canada in professional associations, academic departments, neighborhoods, and cities. From our perspective this is largely an effect of citizenship restrictions, immigration policies, and other institutional and structural pressures that mirror racial segregationism and Jim Crow with African-descended immigrants as the targets—not a natural social phenomenon (Miller 2020; Carter 2019;

Austin 2018; Greer 2013). We anticipate complex and nuanced dialogues that will enable us to name and learn from the silences across Black ethnicities and not find ourselves trapped within the hyperpatriotism and xenophobia that threads through and shores up so many racial states. This reflects an intentional inclusivity that refuses to allow the fact of linguistic, cultural, and ethnic difference to create rifts, confusion, chaos, and injury. For us, this is one of the most profound insights of transnational feminist political thought: we can wrestle within difference, and we can decide that we have antagonistic interests without destroying shared visions and agendas. This is a key way that our research agenda disrupts the fetish of ethnicity in political science. We transform the discipline by understanding that ethnic conflict is often politicized in ways that legitimize harm between and minimize harm against African people. With our partners on the African continent, we hope to identify and challenge shared and distinct barriers that Black womxn scholars face in writing on African politics (Willoughby-Herard 2019a; ASBWP 2016; Collins 1990).[7] These challenges morph in accordance with geographical location, professional rank, language, institutional affiliation, methodology, limited resources, access to prestigious publishing networks, and even familial contexts. Although these are shared barriers, part of our work requires us to attend to our different locations and positions with a mind toward candid conversation, strategic thinking, and resource sharing that expands resources for all of us.

And the Rockets' Red Glare: Bunker Busting, Poetic Methodologies, and the Stakes of Black Womanhood in Political Science

While historiographical recovery, linking ourselves to prior research projects, and envisioning and building our autonomous space with one hand, in our other hand we hold a necessary war making against the political project of making African studies in a way that minimizes our participation—not as individuals but as members of a variegated yet singular, deliberative, and chosen historic consciousness and set of scholarly and cosmological traditions. We mean to convene spaces that are up to the requirements of research *and* healing. Therefore, we have also introduced cross-genre experimental writing and forms of meditation in this section—identified stylistically with italics and block quotations. To contend with the implications of canonical African studies scholarship in the United States, Europe, and other parts of the West as it is institutionalized across the globe as a form of race making and racist knowledge production requires us to draw on interdisciplinary and creative approaches. In the following, we practice some of these creative approaches.

An African Studies Association former president concurs. Jean Allman's "#HerskovitsMustFall? A Meditation on Whiteness, African Studies, and the Unfinished Business of 1968" (2019) proffers an explanation for the foundational and fundamental whiteness of US African studies scholarship. Steeped in rumination, musing, introspection, and a pose of intellectual vulnerability Allman disavows the first president of the African Studies Association, famed anthropologist Melville Herskovits and his infamous presidential address to the association. Herskovits's 1958 presidential address opened with an argument about what made US-born scholars uniquely suited to the study of Africa. Herskovits, says Allman, argued that Americans had the capacity to be objective about Africa in a way that residents of no other European colonial power could. Allman enters the ring brawling rhetorically, smashing away at the feigned detachment of "lineage, language, or imperial liability" that was deployed in many scholarly directions to illegitimate the actions of diasporic Africans as they might explore, study, or claim linkages of any sort whatsoever to Africa. According to commenters who reflected on the moment, Herskovits gave this racist address to an audience that included Black people.

Not only did Herskovits deny the long geographic continuities between Africa and the Americas, but most importantly he denied that the United States as a geography, as a polity, and as a cultural project making claims on progress, science, and modernity was constructed through the African body, displaced though it was throughout the Americas. One can only imagine how acutely Herskovits's Black audience members must have felt their displacement on that day. Quite literally, there could be no knowledge production in the United States of America that was not nursed, reared, diapered, or taught to walk without Black women's bodies. Indeed, there could be no academy in the United States of America that was not born through the literal womb of Black women.

Willoughby-Herard's published work in African politics has increasingly drawn on experimental cross-genre writing and poetics as a methodology for interpreting the dynamics of racialized and gendered hierarchy in political science. The following offers such a meditation, a kind of breaking of the fourth wall of the scholarly text to render the historical harm using poetry, presented hereafter in italics. This use of poetics as an analytical frame is quite new to the study of political science but has found resonance in scholarly works. Making room for eruptions and signaling the process of disciplinary knowledge norms, poetics have emerged as a necessary multivocal way for Black womxn to indeed sing different songs and code switch analytically and grammatically.

> *Taken wombs, taken bodies, taken land. Stolen. Thiefed. Bartered away, sometimes, yes, as foreigners unwanted within the context of changing polities on the African continent.* Philip Curtin and John Thorton offer so much historical thinking while also playing the blame game of asserting that Africans in the Americas have no significant cultural retentions because they were after all sold by other Africans. Sadiya Hartman's *Lose Your Mother: A Journey along the Atlantic Slave Route* makes the same claim having returned to West Africa as a literature professor, tourist, and a devout American. Finding the selling of Black people by other Black people so odious she concludes that it was the foreignness of language, ethnicity, patriline, and matriline that rendered her ancestors sellable and alienable. As a descendant of those who could be dislodged from Africa she cautions the mythohistoricity that links African Americans to Africa. But, Hartman, uses precisely such "critical fabulations" to construct Black Americans as a tribe that have come into existence bearing the same warrior marks and traumatic scars in the same ways. Indeed, Hartman provides no account for how African Americans could be cleaved away from Africa by their own and then yet have an ethical-cosmological-cultural set of frames for becoming a people again across the very same linguistic, ethnic, and kinship distinctions. That the intention to belong to one another and to regard each other in high esteem without hierarchy could operate across the Mississippi as well as it had across the Senegambia and the Atlantic, too, seems strangely impossible for Hartman. And yet, this belonging to each other as *equals, as companions, as friends*, animates memory and world-making and perhaps more importantly animates the death-defying risk-taking that is so often undertaken by Black people the world over for Black people that they shall never meet or share a table with.

Becoming Black happens in so many different iterative ways both through being born directly to line and then again through being blackened by harm or blackened by falling out of love with white supremacy or being blackened by refusing complicity with white supremacy. The complicity of African people in the slave trade becomes the heart of their argumentation and the fatal flaw that Walter Rodney, in *How Europe Underdeveloped Africa*, and Manning Marable, in *How Capitalism Underdeveloped Black America*, excoriate. At issue is the weight given to African complicity and the premise that it shores up. The premise is that national and ethnic identities and relations minimize the significance of white supremacy in concocting and manufacturing racial polities. What if complicity and violence and trauma can be healed one day? Can we hold out hope that being wayward and without the guidance of a mother tongue can be not just something to be revered to beautify those of us who were cast out and sold? What if there is more to the story about how we came to be discarded and away? What if John Thornton and Phillip Curtin with all their training and access to archives all over the world *lied to us* to make us believe that our kinship was broken by other African people to make us weak and alone? What if instead of being minoritized we are legion—what if the wretched of the Black world is the only world worthy of note? And that Blackness is indeed beautiful?

What if our mother has been searching for us all this time? Kinship and bloodlines do not make us family. It is decisions to share each other's burdens, to bring in the crop together, to mourn together, to receive each other, to see each other's art making and intellect. We become kin every single day in the mundane acts of sharing recorded music and cleaning toilets. Through interdependence we are African. Far more so than by the horrific violence and tragedy of what is daily taken from us.

Or better I might say, we are made African by the choices we make to remain African people in the paradoxical reality that so many wish us subjugated to the will of violence and yet we exceed that diktat again and again.

But mostly stolen and transubstantiated from "neg" meaning *abantu*/people/human into furniture, thing, chattel, property.[8] The wealth of nations relied on the theft of the "lineage, language," and geography embodied in the hearts and minds of African people cannibalized in the belly of thousands of slave ships—the euphemistic cross-generation trauma engendering "hold" (Koné 2019; Popa and Mackereth 2019).

Which African could hear or read Herskovits's piercing words and not feel their blood boil to read exactly how it was stated in a public forum that American objectivity is what made white scholars trained in the United States particularly well equipped to study Africa. What Herskovits meant by objectivity was American anti-Black racism—as protected and consolidated in prestigious elite intellectual circles at the most revered universities; is it ok to write that here and say so just as publicly? Herskovits's claim relied on eclipsing and silencing the history and heritage of African people. This is the same Herskovits, remember, that studied under Franz Boas with fellow student Zora Neale Hurston. The same Herskovits that taught at Howard University according to Pearl Robinson. Hurston learned from Boas how to make anthropological meaning with the proliferation of African survivals and cultural retentions. But Hurston, after writing some of the most memorable ethnography in modern human history had to leave the field behind, taking her extraordinary social scientific talents to filmmaking, short stories, and novels. Until restored again to canonical status in Black intellectual history by beloved 1980s Black womanist writer and essayist Alice Walker, Zora Neale Hurston had been largely lost to social science history. But Hurston was not simply lost. Like many Black womxn political scientists conducting African politics research today, Hurston was buried alive in the middle of the canon formation of anthropology by white anthropologists, who intended to occupy Black knowledge about the African diaspora as certainly as plantation capital meant to/means to occupy Taino and Tongva land. Hurston was catacombed while yet breathing, also by the Black masculinist patriarchal social realism writers of her day. Her Harlem Renaissance playmates did not appreciate her very public accommodationism to white patronage, even when they were being supported by the same patrons.

How dare Hurston speak publicly about Black people in the nadir of American race relations joyfully and earnestly enjoying each other's company? How ridiculous to claim that the proverbs and singing and social and leisure and marriage and land tenure folkways of Southern turpentine workers remembered and reiterated the world-making vision of the African cultures that they had come from. How dare Hurston demonstrate time and again that African descendants in the Americas (Florida, Jamaica, Haiti) had intentionally and deliberately chosen to rebuke the adolescent society in the making that was to be the United States for the remembered company of African people.

Zora Neale Hurston's fellow student of Boas Melville Herskovits fixed his lips to get in front of his white peers and render yet again, a public disavowal of the dynamic, intentional, and massively important cultural processes that Hurston had documented, explored, practiced, and amplified. Herskovits sought to displace Hurston and the other people like her who were most likely to inherit Boas's nuanced and carefully crafted politically informed attention to culture and race. *It is not that Boas was right or that he was somehow above tokenizing. Rather the approach to race and culture that trained Hurston and Herskovits lacked what we might call quality control over the maltreatment of Black women.* Who else but the people both African and Indigenous whose cultures had been stripped by genocide, slavery, and mission education would be the appropriate inheritors of anthropology? Shouldn't the people whose cultures had been so profoundly disrupted over and over again each generation to subordinate them have much to say about how culture is passed on from one generation to the next, how it is experimented with, how it relates to the building of civilizations, how it preserved most adoringly by the people discarded and unwanted and harmed by it? Herskovits could see that Boas had created a veritable monster in the unflappable Zora Neale Hurston. She would not be made to feel ashamed. In order to undertake studies of the ethicocosmological Black worlds that African people made in Eatonville, Florida, and in Haiti and in Jamaica and in the migrant worker seasonal camps that she documented, Hurston had to see her particular and distinctive assets as a Black womxn researcher who centered stories and transnational identities and mobility and cultures. She would not be made to think that there was some falseness or disloyalty in her because she longed to study folklore and anthropology with Boas at Barnard in New York and because she longed to make films about Eatonville, Florida. Hurston's excellent contributions in the study of African peoples were pushed out of the sphere of social scientific research and knowledge production because she was astonishingly courageous as an intellectual. Hurston's written work was placed under exquisite erasure through denying her opportunities to found and lead social science programs—through caricaturing her and her cohort members as emblems of the alleged failure of diaspora Africans intellectually. Herskovits's presidential address had this effect.

Taken wombs, taken bodies, taken land. Stolen. Thiefed. Bartered away.

Herskovits's 1958 speech was about stealing, yet again, this time, an entire intellectual inheritance in the field of anthropology that belonged to other people with other experiences and other ways of moving in the world. And Hurston was not the only woman of color social scientist wrenched out of the intellectual history of transnational research on race and politics; there were also Jovita Gonzalez and Elena Padilla and Ella Deloria (Cotera 2005; Rua 2005; Yu 2001; Harrison and Harrison 1998).

Echoing others, Allman reminds that there is a counternarrative about the history of the African Studies Association and the significance of its contributions to African studies in the United States and globally (Allman 2019, 8). It has neither been the primary organization for knowledge production nor has it been the route by which distinctive research on Africa and African-descended people has been cultivated, prepared, or trained. Instead the African Studies Association has been the bagman for a series of well-orchestrated robberies, crimes, and "forgeries of memory," to use Cedric Robinson's 2007 book title. Federal National Defense Education Act Title IV (1958) and Carnegie and Ford philanthropic funding has been distributed to launch and sustain African studies at universities, including University of California at Berkeley, University of Chicago, University of Pennsylvania, Columbia, Northwestern, Boston. Intermediary government funding agencies like the Social Science Research Council replicated long histories of what Willoughby-Herard (2015, 127–28) describes as the "slavery-foundation nexus." The accumulation of capital during racial colonialism and racial slavery became the basis for corporate capital that sustained its will to govern over African people the world over. In other words, the same organizations that entangled themselves in the political project of melting away how slavery and racial colonialism operated to generate capital—the Laura Spelman Rockefeller Fund, the General Education Fund, the New York Colonization Society, the Commission of Interracial Cooperation, the Phelps Stokes Fund, the Rosenwald Fund—even when doing their utmost to champion an end to white supremacy still sought to insert a notion of a benign liberal white guidance, allyship, and tutelage—especially in the arena of knowledge production. Such intermediary organizations could not ever undo racial hierarchy. They could mop up after bloodshed. They could render service, sympathy, and consolation. Sometimes they could even offer small and large grants.

Confirming these dynamics, Jean Allman concedes it has been Black thinkers—some troublesome for white power and some long-suffering with the vagaries of white power—that have produced the longest and most significant scholarly tradition about Africa and the African diaspora.

> [A] knowledge river that flows through African American intellectual history right back to the nineteenth and early twentieth

centuries through the work of Black scholars such as George Washington Williams, W.E.B. Du Bois, William Leo Hansberry, Carter G. Woodson, Lorenzo Turner, St. Clair Drake, and countless others. These Black scholars, located in Historically Black Colleges and Universities [HBCUs] constitute a far older lineage of African Studies in the United States, a lineage built on and through resilient Pan-African bonds, but marginalized and displaced by the massive inflow of resources to post-war African area studies, located primarily in traditionally white institutions. (Allman 2019)

There are generations of pacesetters worthy of fuller consideration: Nnamdi Azikiwe, Alain Locke, John Henrik Clarke, Nicholas Onyawu, Leonard Jeffries, Shelby Lewis, Melina Kagobe (Lewis 2019). *Legions, really, of Black thinkers growing up at Howard and Clark Atlanta University, and Southern and Fort Hare and Western Cape, among others.* Pearl Robinson unpacks a typology to help us understand how these places were constructed as nurseries of Black thought. A former African Studies Association president (in 2007), Robinson's "Area Studies in Search of Africa" (2003) provides a sweeping historiography of the three worlds of area studies knowledge production about Africa occurring in three spatially differentiated spheres of endeavor:

> 1) the *World* of U.S. Research Universities—particularly the top research tier, which is the domain of the major Title VI African Studies Centers; 2) the *World* of Diasporic PanAfricanist scholars—a highly polyglot realm that includes Historically Black Colleges and Universities (HBCUs), which were the first US institutions of higher learning to introduce African Studies into the curriculum; and 3) the *World* of African Universities and Research Networks. Each of these *Worlds* has its own complex sociology intellectual pace-setters, respected elders, epistemological debates, citation conventions, overlapping memberships, and identity politics. . . . Research agendas differ. Moreover, funding sources have generally treated these spaces as separate and distinct. (Robinson 2003, 1)

The following chart was developed as a teaching tool that Willoughby-Herard has used for the past decade along with Pearl Robinson's insights

Table 9.1. Ideological Domains of Africa

Three Worlds	Space	Trendsetters, Elders' Writing Norms Debates	Tokenism	Funding	Exotica	Vindication
TOP TIER/TITLE VI RSCH CENTERS	Sub-Sahara	European US-Trained Cold Warriors US Empire	Recruit Tokens from World 2, 3, Police and Shame Tokens, Deploy Tokens to do Shameful Dirty Work; "Educated Kaffir" Myth; "None Qualified" Myth	Foundations Govts Fund to Shape US Role in World—Global Whiteness; Kinder Gentler White Supremacy via Liberals	Africa Makes for Good Cocktail Party Chatter	Legitimize Claims of Good Intentions and Well Wishes
DIASPOA/ PAN-AFRICAN SCHOLARS	African Diaspora	George Washington Williams, W. E. B. Du Bois, William Leo Hansberry, Carter G. Woodson, Lorenzo Turner, St. Clair Drake	Recruited then humiliated/ recruited by core, govt, philanthropy.	See Cayton and Drake's *Black Metropolis* for the major sources of funding for Black scholarship	Africa is litmus test for political radicalism; "Not Theory" Myth; "Not Objective" Myth	Challenge marginalize correct caricature, interrupt violence
AFRICAN UNIV.	Continent—regions (Horn, Indian Ocean, North)	Euro/US trained, Cold warriors	Kids of missionary State Dept. cosmopolitan	Goal is Bantu education, useful white intelligentsia	Funding overshadows work actually done in/out univ	Challenge marginalize correct caricature, interrupt violence; work done rigorously can transform economic outcomes nationally/ regionally

in that pathbreaking essay on knowledge production. The chart offers a visual rendering of the variables and ideological domains that determine what Africa is geographically, who is empowered to speak for and about and to Africa, the ways in which scholars enter the field, who pays for training and research opportunities, the stakes of studying Africa for different categories of persons, and how research on Africa might interrupt epistemic violence.

Like Pearl Robinson, Shelby Lewis, and Mae King before her, Jean Allman concluded that outside of the HBCUs the Black scholars, both those based in continental Africa and in the African diaspora were diminished and sidestepped in post-WWII Western colonial social science curricula wherever on the globe they were taught and imposed. The fields of inquiry and methods of study that they created—in the midst of horrific forms of global apartheid and global Jim Crow segregation, legalized brutality, land theft, and torture and rape of countless survivors—were stolen and they were displaced. While they were graduating and training race men and race women committed to fighting racial subordination, these Black institutions of higher learning were subjected to segregated and highly restricted racialized knowledge audiences. Places dubbed by their students and alumni "the Mecca" to signify how critical they were for crafting life worlds—those places like Howard University, Spelman University, Fort Hare, Cheikh Anta Diop University, Makerere, and Southern University—taught and graduated Black thinkers who would largely be prohibited from speaking or ridiculed and defamed when they somehow managed to secure patronizing or tokenizing white audiences. Two antagonistic worlds—one white and "anomalous historically"[9] and several that were Black and African—were created year after year brick by brick.

Let's return to poetics to explore the affective resonances and the rhythm of being placed under erasure as a Black thinker.

Books that were denied publications. Academic and research lecture series that were funded by Black civic, fraternal, and church organizations and not by universities or research foundations—paradoxically produced an African American population far more well educated about international affairs and with deeper ties to international education and international travel.[10] Dissertations that were scuttled. Careers and reputations that were sabotaged. Silenced from speaking about political imaginaries and worlds that their political praxis and research had inaugurated; kicked out of archives and humiliated when they sought out visas to be approved to travel to international meetings that they had organized. Caricatured and misremembered. Uncited and laughed about over brandy and cognac in old boys clubs in every settler colonial capital all over the world. Telegrams and emails sent ahead of them alerting intelligence officials to monitor and observe, to interrupt and disrupt, to threaten and to beat. Becoming a Black thinker writing about Africa or African people in any part of the globe is a testimony of generations of fraudulent, abusive, and unnecessary tests. Games played with human beings lives while white men and women looked on with glee at the horror they had wrought.

Pearl Robinson explains that menacing "racially mediated hierarchies affected access to data determined success in the field" (2003, 8). Robinson goes on to explain that such research institutions and self-named intelligentsias operated as gatekeepers and protectors of white racial empire, even in an era allegedly *after* empire. These forces determined which African Americans would have a chance to gain training and research opportunities, organized the limits and terrain of epistemic communities, and wielded the power differentials and resources gaps to suppress the voices of Black researchers. For Pearl Robinson it was more than common that such dynamics were allowed to literally define the spatial boundaries of where Africa is, who belongs to Africa and in what ways, whose accounts about Africa can and should matter, and whose associations with Africa would be deemed believable and useful for determining US foreign policy and international affairs with African countries. The terms and conditions of securing international recognition and legitimacy as a sovereign power required complex negotiations with long-standing global racial hierarchies and presumptions embedded in organizing the world system. Anti-Black institutionalized racism often enforced in the academy, foundations, and government was taught, upheld, and reinforced by a well-linked cadre of European- and US-trained historians and political scientists. Motivated to correct harmful racial stereotypes and navigating the brittle edges of global and domestic liberation movements and US expansionism and influence seeking during the Cold War, Black scholars have historically found ourselves in the predicament of having to re-excavate this history and these complicated dynamics each generation.

Ultimately, the federal government and a group of corporate foundations led by notorious segregationist philanthropists aided and abetted a group of white universities to train an all-white cadre of scholars who would loot that knowledge that had been produced by Black thinkers.

In 1968 in Los Angeles the scholars of the Black Caucus protested and then walked out of the African Studies Association. They formed the African Heritage Studies Association. In Montreal the following year, the African Heritage Studies Association members disrupted the African Studies Association. According to cofounder Shelby Lewis in her "Historical Milestones" (2019) invited address to the African Studies Association:

> John Henrik Clarke was the Founding President and Chair of the Founding Board that included Nicholas Onyawu, Leonard Jeffries, Shelby Lewis (Smith) and Melina Kagobe. The Board concluded that convening annual conferences was the best way to explore and expand its membership and knowledge base. Thousands of enthusiastic supporters and notable scholars attended well-organized conferences at Howard University (1970), Southern University (1971), and New York City (1972). In 1973/4 AHSA fielded a delegation to the International Meeting on African Studies in Addis Ababa and requested certification. ASA had served as the sole representative of African Studies in America for decades, but since only one US delegation could be certified, a compromise between the two associations was required. John Henrik Clarke, AHSA's President, was elected as leader of a joint US delegation. This was a watershed moment for AHSA, one that was enhanced by a private audience with Emperor Haile Selasse. In 1975 AHSA organized a pilgrimage to Ghana and in the succeeding decades AHSA members challenged conventional views of Africa; interrogated ahistorical ideas of an underdeveloped, dependent, resource poor continent in perpetual need of western aid and tutelage; collaborated with other disciplinary associations, including holding joint conferences with the National Conference of Black Political Scientists and the Black Studies Association; and mentored young scholars studying African history and culture. These efforts ignited a proliferation of African centered research and publications, the expansion of Black Studies, Africana Studies and Africana Woman's Studies programs, and the development of curriculum materials on African history and culture for pre-collegiate school systems.

This rupture constituted yet another history-making pivot away from the whiteness of African studies. It required great personal and collective risk-taking. They decided that what they knew already and the questions that they sought to answer could not be answered by Herskovits and his ilk. Yet, this rupture and the many others like it have been papered over with a farcical account of the production of a nonracial African Studies Association, one that Allman's presidential address and invitation to AHSA cofounder Shelby Lewis acknowledges. This nonracial face remembers its own history pointedly in presidential addresses and journal articles based on this counternarrative. And yet, it cannot effect the change necessary to undo the harms and legacies of its own history. Only building careful and mutual ties with organizations focused on knowledge production in the Black radical tradition can apprehend the massive work that has to be undertaken to conduct an African studies globally that is worthy of that name. Political scientists engaged in African politics research that will not wrestle with this biting history and its legacy are not poised to miss the absence of Black womxn scholars. We have transformed political science by reintroducing this history and the Black women scholars engaged in African and African diaspora research in an interdisciplinary fashion. While these scholars and thinkers are important for the entire political science discipline, we claim them as Black womxn in particular and build from the insights that they make perceivable to us as people positioned to experience the same forms of isolation and erasure in the academy. Understanding the barriers that we face historically and as key ingredients in the manufactured of a white-led and largely exclusively white African studies curriculum has transformed how we enter and relate to the discipline of political science. Turning to counternarratives and other scholarly genealogies focused on recovering the scholars who, like us, have been under threat for being placed under erasure has changed the way we value, defend, and understand the stakes and necessity of our research. When we care for the Black women African politics scholars that came before us and care for each other, we upend the normalized practices of treating Black womxn as unworthy in political science and as what Nikol Alexander-Floyd called "space-invaders."

Notes

1. The authors wish to thank readers Desireé Melonas (Birmingham Southern University), Tiffany Caesar (Margaret Walker Center, Jackson State University), and Onyekachi Ekeogu (Arizona State University) for their careful review of and attention to this chapter.

2. As vice-president of NCOBPS (2019–2020), Willoughby-Herard sought to develop a research network with the Ethiopian Ministry of Science and Higher Education (MOSHE) for aiding in the development and expansion of political science education in that country through regular conferences, three-week intensive miniseminars for advanced master's students and faculty members, and supporting their already established pathways programs for Ethiopian students pursuing a degree in established African doctoral programs outside of Ethiopia. After the devastating loss of 157 people on Ethiopian Airlines Flight 302 on March 10, 2019 in the fiasco surrounding the negligent regulation of the Boeing 737 MAX 8 aircraft and Professor Zegeye's separation from MOSHE, this six-month-old research network had to fold. However, it had learned many lessons for NCOBPS leaders about how to pursue Africa-based research networks in the contemporary period.

3. Turner and Willoughby-Herard attended Safe Spaces training on LGBTQ+ inclusion, affirmation, and diversity convened by the LGBTQ+ Caucus as well as a panel on Black women and Black girls, titled Articulations of Women and Their Labor. Turner, Tait, and Willoughby-Herard also intentionally attended the panels about the Race and Democracy in the Americas Project focused on over three decades of research on Black movements in Brazil with the intention of learning from that long-standing project about how to infuse and reinfuse more attention into African politics in NCOBPS.

4. Willoughby-Herard attended this panel session as an audience member and took detailed notes and circulated them to scholars working on African gender studies globally.

5. Willoughby-Herard notes that her undergraduate Ivy League professors who were teaching African politics in political science only included early post-WWII Frantz Fanon on their syllabi. The only other political science–based course in African politics was taught by a US trained African-born scholar whose syllabus seemed keyed toward repudiating the idea of African independence.

6. Lewis shared this with Willoughby-Herard for a chapter of a forthcoming book focused on activist scholars and their internationalist and pan-Africanist research.

7. In a pointed intervention in the APCG, Willoughby-Herard testifies to the embodied impact of these shared and distinct barriers in the context of what the Tarana Burke–founded #MeToo movement made available for discussion about the nature of the field of political science.

8. H. Vete-Congolo (Presentation at AICRE-Philosophy, University of California, Irvine, November 18, 2020).

9. Ndumiso Dladla (Talk at AICRE-Philosophy Webinar Series, University of California, Irvine, November 18, 2020).

10. Detailed histories of the racist and gendered reception of Black knowledge production in the social sciences focused on race and international affairs can be found in the John Stanfield's *Philanthropy and Jim Crow in American Social*

Science (Westport, CT: Praeger, 1985); Paula Giddings's *In Search of Sisterhood: Delta Sigma Theta and the Challenge of the Black Sorority Movement* (New York: Harper Collins, 1988); and Lee D. Baker's *From Savage to Negro: Anthropology and the Construction of Race, 1896-1954* (Berkeley: University of California Press, 1998); and Ira Harrison and Faye Harrison's *African American Pioneers in Anthropology* (Urbana: University of Illinois Press, 1999); Robert Vitalis's *White World Order, Black Power Politics* (Ithaca, NY: Cornell University Press, 2016); Linda Perkin's fantastic research articles; "Merze Tate and the Quest for Gender Equity at Howard University, 1942-1977," *History of Education Quarterly* 54, no. 4 (2014): 516-51; "'Bound to Them by a Common Sorrow': African American Women, Higher Education, and Collective Advancement," *Journal of African American History* 100, no. 4 (2015): 721-47; and "The Black Female Professoriate at Howard University, 1926-1977," in *Women's Higher Education in the United States: New Historical Perspectives*, ed. Margaret A. Nash (London: Palgrave Macmillan Press, 2017), 117-37.

References

Alexander-Floyd, N. 2008. "Written, Published, . . . Cross-Indexed, and Footnoted": Producing Black Female PhDs and Black Women's and Gender Studies Scholarship in Political Science." *PS: Political Science & Politics* 41, no. 4: 819-29.

———. 2012. "Disappearing Acts: Reclaiming Intersectionality in the Social Sciences in a Post-Black Feminist Era." *Feminist Formations* 24, no. 1: 1-25.

———. 2014. "Why Political Scientists Don't Study Black Women, But Historians and Sociologists Do: On Intersectionality and the Remapping of the Study of Black Political Women." *National Political Science Review* 16: 3-18.

———. 2015a. "Black Women Political Scientists at Work: A Conversation with Nadia Brown and Wendy Smooth." *National Political Science Review* 17, no. 2: 97-106.

———. 2015b. "Women of Color, Space Invaders, and Political Science: Practical Strategies for Transforming Institutional Practices." *PS: Political Science & Politics* 48, no. 3: 464-68.

Alexander-Floyd, N., and T. Willoughby-Herard. 2015. "Introduction: Nobody Can Tell It All: Symposium on How Researching Black Women in Politics Changes Political Science: Methodologies, Epistemologies, and Publishing." *National Political Science Review* 17, no. 1: 59-62.

Allman, J. M. 2019. "#HerskovitsMustFall? A Meditation on Whiteness, African Studies, and the Unfinished Business of 1968." *African Studies Review* 62, no. 3: 6-39. https://doi.org/10.1017/asr.2019.40.

———. 2020. *Academic Reparation and Stepping Aside.* Africa Is A Country. https://africasacountry.com/2020/11/academic-reparation-and-stepping-aside.

Association for the Study of Black Women in Politics (ASBWP). 2016. "Scandal in Real Time National Conference on Black Women, Politics, and Oral History May 11–13, 2016." https://www.youtube.com/playlist?list=PLQw7KTnzkpXeNrqS-jZHDCbkO3lWfbfr2.

Austin, S. D. W. 2018. *The Caribbeanization of Black Politics: Race, Group Consciousness, and Political Participation in America.* New York: SUNY Press.

Brown, N. 2014. *Sisters in the Statehouse: Black Women and Legislative Decision Making.* Oxford, UK: Oxford University Press.

Cakata, Z. 2020. "South Africa Belongs to All Who Speak Colonial Languages." In *Sasinda Futhi Siselapha: Black Feminist Approaches to Cultural Studies in South Africa's Twenty-Five Years Since 1994*, edited by Derilene Marco, Tiffany Willoughby-Herard, and Abebe Zegeye, 87–100. Trenton, NJ: Africa World Press.

Caldwell, K. L. 2007. *Negras in Brazil: Re-Envisioning Black Women, Citizenship, and the Politics of Identity.* New Brunswick, NJ: Rutgers University Press.

Carter, N. M. 2019. *American While Black: African Americans, Immigration, and the Limits of Citizenship.* Oxford, UK: Oxford University Press.

Collins, P. H. 1990. "Black Feminist Thought in the Matrix of Domination." In *Black Feminist Thought: Knowledge, Consciousness, and the Politics of Empowerment*, 138, 221–38. 2nd ed. New York: Routledge.

Cosby, K. 2016. "Scandal in Real Time National Conference on Black Women, Politics, and Oral History May 11–13, 2016." https://www.youtube.com/playlist?list=PLQw7KTnzkpXeNrqS-jZHDCbkO3lWfbfr2.

Cotera, M. 2005. "'Native' Speakers: Ella Deloria, Zora Neale Hurston and Jovita Gonzalez in the Borderlands of Ethnographic Meaning-Making. Decolonizing Methodology: Women, Race, and Ethnographic Meaning-Making Panel." Paper Presented at the American Studies Association Conference, Washington, DC, November 4.

Covin, D. 2016. "The Genesis of the Race and Democracy in the Americas Project: The Project and Beyond." In *Race and the Politics of Knowledge Production: Diaspora and Black Transnational Scholarship in the United States and Brazil*, edited by Gladys L. Mitchell and Elizabeth Hordge-Freeman, 27–39. Houndmills, Hampshire: Palgrave Macmillan.

Du Bois, W. E. B. 1935. *Black Reconstruction in America: An Essay toward a History of the Part, Which Black Folk Played in the Attempt to Reconstruct Democracy in America, 1860–1880.* New York: Harcourt, Brace.

Greer, C. M. 2013. *Black Ethnics: Race, Immigration, and the Pursuit of the American Dream.* Oxford, UK: Oxford University Press.

Harris, D. 2018. *Black Feminist Politics from Kennedy to Trump.* New York: Palgrave Macmillan.

Harrison, F., and I. Harrison, eds. 1998. *African American Pioneers in Anthropology*. Urbana: University of Illinois Press.
Hordge-Freeman, E., and G. L. Mitchell-Walthour. 2016. "Introduction: In Pursuit of Du Bois's 'Second-Sight' through Diasporic Dialogues." In *Race and the Politics of Knowledge Production: Diaspora and Black Transnational Scholarship in the United States and Brazil*, Gladys L. Mitchell and Elizabeth Hordge-Freeman, 1–11. Houndmills, Hampshire: Palgrave Macmillan.
Isoke, Z. 2013. *Urban Black Women and the Politics of Resistance*. New York: Palgrave Macmillan.
June, A. W., and B. O'Leary. 2021. "How Many Black Women Have Tenure on Your Campus? Search Here." *Chronicle of Higher Education*. May 27. https://www.chronicle.com/article/how-many-black-women-have-tenure-on-your-campus-search-here.
Koné, M. 2019. "Black Zombie: Capture, Slavery, and Freedom: Symposium: Politics and Film in *Get Out* 2017." *National Political Science Review* 20, no. 3: 150–64.
Lewis, S. 2019. "Historical Milestones." African Heritage Studies Association Newsletter. July. https://static1.squarespace.com/static/5ab91fc3cef372bf6644569c/t/5d6a85e741111900010b2568/1583431393434/July+2019+Newsletter+.pdf.
Lewis, S., and K. Catherine. 2019. Interview by Tiffany Willoughby-Herard. December 23.
Mafeje, A. 1971. "The Ideology of 'Tribalism.'" *Journal of Modern African Studies* 9, no. 2: 253–61.
Malaklou, M. S., and T. Willoughby-Herard. 2018. "Appendix of 'Notes from the Kitchen, the Crossroads, and Everywhere Else, Too': Ruptures of Thought, Word, and Deed from the 'Arbiters of Blackness Itself.'" *Theory & Event* 21, no. 1: 64–67.
Mama, A. 2007. "Is It Ethical to Study Africa? Preliminary Thoughts on Scholarship and Freedom." *African Studies Review* 50, no. 1:1–26.
———. 2011. "What Does It Mean to Do Feminist Research in African Contexts?" *Feminist Review* 98, supplement 1: e4–e20.
———. 2017. "The Power of Feminist Pan-African Intellect." *Feminist Africa* 22: 1–15.
Miller, C. S. 2020. "'A Hand out over the Water': Racial Terror, Black Maternal Loss, and Cross-Ethnic Passages of Reclamation." *Palimpsest* 9, no. 1: 83–110.
Mitchell, Gladys L., and Elizabeth Hordge-Freeman, eds. 2016. *Race and the Politics of Knowledge Production: Diaspora and Black Transnational Scholarship in the United States and Brazil*. New York: Palgrave Macmillan. https://doi.org/10.1057/9781137553942.
Okech, A. 2020. "African Feminist Epistemic Communities and Decoloniality." *Critical African Studies* 12, no. 3: 313–29. https://doi.org/10.1080/21681392.2020.1810086.

Oyĕwùmí, Oyèrónké. 2016. Interviewed by Zine Magubane. Recorded Interview for the Gender and Motherhood Conference Rhodes University. https://www.youtube.com/watch?v=6NRbvqeY1xw.

Pailey, R. N. 2016. "Where Is the 'African' in African Studies?" *African Arguments.* June 7. Available at: http://africanarguments.org/2016/06/07/where-is-the-african-in-african-studies.

Popa, B., and K. Mackereth, K. 2019. "Vampiric Necropolitics: A Map of Black Studies Critique from Karl Marx' Vampire to Get Out's Politics of the Undead. Symposium: Politics and Film in *Get Out* (2017)." *National Political Science Review* 20, no. 3: 165–78.

Robinson, C. 2007. *Forgeries of Memory and Meaning: Blacks and the Regimes of Race in American Theater and Film Before World War II.* Chapel Hill: University of North Carolina Press.

———. 2016. *Terms of Order: Political Science and the Myth of Leadership.* Chapel Hill: University of North Carolina Press.

Robinson, P. T. 2003. "Area Studies in Search of Africa." *Politics of Knowledge: Area Studies and the Disciplines.* 3: article 6. http://repositories.cdlib.org/uciaspubs/editedvolumes/3/6.

Rua, M. 2005. Decolonizing Methodology: Women, Race, and Ethnographic Meaning-Making Panel. "Intervening in the Field: Elena Padilla, Scholarly Activism and the Study of US Latinos." Paper presented at the American Studies Association Conference, Washington, DC, November 4, 2005.

Turner, R. L. 2015. "Peace-Building without Western Saviors? An Approach to Teaching African Gender and Sexuality Politics to American Students." In *Gender and Peacebuilding: All Hands Required*, edited by Maureen P. Flaherty, Thomas G. Matyók, Sean Byrne, and Tuso Hamdesa, 321–38. Lexington Books.

Williams, E. L. 2014. "Feminist Tensions: Race, Sex Work, and Women's Activism in Bahia." In *Taking Risks: Feminist Activism and Research in the Americas*, edited by Julie Shayne, 215. New York: SUNY Press.

Willoughby-Herard, Tiffany. 2015. *Waste of a White Skin: The Carnegie Corporation and the Racial Logic of White Vulnerability.* Berkeley: University of California Press.

Willoughby-Herard, T. 2019a. "Poetic Labors and Challenging Political Science: An Epistolary Poem." *Journal of Women, Politics & Policy* 40, no. 1: 228–35.

———. 2019b. "Reminiscences of Shelby F. Lewis." Unpublished interview with Tiffany Willoughby-Herard, December 23.

Yu, H. 2001. *Thinking Orientals: Migration, Contact, Exoticism in Modern America.* Oxford, UK: Oxford University Press.

Zimbalist, Z. 2020. "So Many 'Africanists', so Few Africans: Reshaping Our Understanding of 'African Politics' through Greater Nuance and Amplification of African Voices." *Review of African Political Economy* 47, no. 166: 621–37. https://doi.org/10.1080/03056244.2020.1840972.

10

The Duality of Disruption

Black Women in Midwestern White Liberal Arts Institutions

CLARISSA PETERSON

I started to write this account of my life as a Black woman teaching in a private liberal arts college in the Midwest in 2017. I simply stopped writing because it was too painful for me to continue. I felt that I had been beaten down so often and so badly that every single word was just too painful to type. I managed to draft a significant amount, but I was not mentally ready to unpack the years of hurt, neglect, and depression that had become a part of who I was. Yes, I had become the angry Black woman, but that was the result of a transformation after years of working in this environment. My presence disrupted business as usual at my university as well as in my life, and I have been paying for that disruption ever since.

Hiring a Black woman at a selective liberal arts college in the Midwest was a conscious decision by the university. The university president made it clear that he wanted to create a more diverse community, but he had no idea that the pushback from university faculty, students, and staff, as well as the larger community, would be almost unbearable. The faculty and administrators minimized my expertise to issues that only dealt with race, ignoring the fact that I was a trained political scientist, and designating me as the de facto adviser of minority students and minority student organizations. Students challenged the notion that my graduate degree could possibly mean that I knew more than they did about anything. Never could a Black woman be the expert on any subject, especially grades or course requirements. Anything I said could and would often be subjected to a higher authority, more qualified to make the decision as observed by the work of Thomas and Hollenshead (2001). In addition, the people in the community created an isolated environment that seemed impossible for raising Black children or having any semblance of a normal life. Everything from shopping in stores to enjoying an evening walk proved a monumental task. Hiring a Black woman was admirable, but hiring was only the beginning of creating a diverse community (Harvey 1994; Yoshinaga-Itano 2006).

I immediately recognized the disruption I caused to the university, but it took me years to understand the simultaneous disruption the university had on my growth as a Black woman political scientist who is also a mother and a wife. I took the job thinking I had finally arrived. I had a job and could begin to experience the ultimate reward for jumping through the graduate school hoops. Unfortunately when I arrived in the summer of 1997, I had no idea that I would be disrespected over and over again, that I would suffer from a debilitating fatigue from the constant fight for my dignity, or that I would slowly drown as I tried to discover who I would become as a scholar, a teacher, a mentor, a wife, and a mother. Saying this experience was necessary to make me stronger would be as dysfunctional as the experiences I have had. It is true, however, that those experiences taught me how to survive when survival seemed impossible. More importantly, it took twenty years, but my experiences in academe taught me that my presence as a disruption to the norm cannot change that *norm*. The norm reemerges in different ways. As the disruptor, one must be vigilant in protecting oneself. I eventually decided when and how to engage. I learned to fight when I needed to fight and to pass the baton when necessary. What emerged from the years of abuse on the part of colleagues, staff, students, and an unwelcoming community was a mature Black woman who understands the importance of knowing when and how to engage.

My work below is my experience as a Black woman disrupting my campus. The events are extremely difficult to write, and I am sure they are as difficult to read. It is likely that reading this manuscript will remind us of the many ways we, Black women, sacrifice ourselves for the greater good. The raw emotions may be more than anyone can handle, but I tell the story nonetheless hoping that anyone who is trying to make sense of their career can find support in knowing they are not alone. In my eyes the story must be told even if it is far from the work I usually do.

The culture I refer to in this essay is the culture of the marginalization of Black people that universities regularly participate in. The culture in my university is one that regularly elevates white students, faculty, and staff above any other group. Moreover, university actors within this culture do everything in their power to justify their existence in this institution and their maintenance of power (Jordan 1974). In their eyes the lack of Black faculty and staff and failings of Black students are due to the individuals, not the institution.

Entering the University

I was hired in 1997 as a part of my university's efforts to consciously diversify the university. My cohort included two Black vice-presidents and three Black faculty members. The president at the time created the two vice-president positions to lead our public relations and to lead student services, and the faculty members were hired in English, math, and political science. I am the only one of the five still employed at the university. The Black woman hired in math left the following year, one vice-president left around five years into the job, another vice-president left when the presidency changed, and the final faculty member retired after years of feeling marginalized under subsequent administrations. We all had unique experiences at the university that could fill a volume.

Although I was coming to a small town in Indiana, no one or nothing could have prepared me for what I was about to encounter. I was the first and last Black person to be hired in this department through a national tenure-track search. In fact, the *university* would not hire another Black person through a national tenure-track search until 2017, twenty years after my hire. The university certainly hired Black people in tenure-track searches, but all were hired outside of the normal tenure-track search. This was possible because departments continued to request tenure-track positions and were granted those requests. When it came time to making offers, they never hired the Black candidate (if there was one in the top). Not only did my department never complete an on-campus interview of a Black candidate, the committee accused me of sabotaging the search when I raised an objection to the lack of diversity in the pool. I suggested that we follow the university written policy on the way to handle pools that lacked diversity. The policy was to cancel the search and resume the next year with more targeted recruiting. My colleagues balked at this suggestion and ended the meeting by saying I had convinced Black political scientists not to apply for our open positions. They never even considered that their treatment of me may have been a factor, but the problem was misidentified. The problem was the treatment of their only Black colleague, not the communicating of the treatment. Of course, they could not imagine they had done anything wrong in this matter.

The only real process for Black tenure-track faculty to enter the university was the opportunity hire process. In this case, the person had either been hired as a pre-/post-doc or a term appointment, and that appointment was later converted to tenure track. When a university chooses to accomplish their diversity in this way—only hire Black people through special positions, never through the normal procedure—it demonstrates the strength of the dominant culture that makes this place such a difficult experience for Black women. It remains an arduous task to convince departments that have never had a Black colleague that Black people are as skilled as they are. Non-Black faculty use excuses about potential candidates' lack of experience in liberal arts institutions and the caliber of their graduate degree–granting institutions to support the notion that they do not belong in these white spaces. The *culture* is multilayered and will not—cannot—be dismantled in a short period of time, in all likelihood not my lifetime. The toll this *culture* can take on the emotional and physical health of naïve Black women is unconscionable. We are naïve because we falsely think we can miraculously change something so profound as the *dominant culture*, which existed before any of us could even dream of being a college professor.

It is important to note that this environment is not unusual at a university and in fact is more of the *norm*. Moreover, it is important to understand there are dire consequences for bringing Black women into these spaces. Black women are significantly underrepresented throughout all ranks of university professors, and while many are quick to connect the experiences of Black and white women, their experiences are not the same. White women outnumber Black women in academe, and the proportion of white women faculty is much closer to their population than the proportion of Black women faculty is to their population (Holmes 2008). The dismal number of Black professors creates a deep feeling of loneliness with an overwhelming burden that others conveniently overlook.

Black women quickly find that minority students rely on them for guidance and support throughout the university, and this work with minority students threatens their jobs because this work is undervalued by the university. As a result, Black women face high stress, burnout, and low research productivity (Holmes 2008). Like many Black women colleagues across the country, I was overworked and found myself in unappreciated mentoring positions (Edghill 2007).

Unfortunately, my experience with being isolated and overworked would remain consistent with the experiences of other Black women (Parker Terhune 2008; McKay 1983; Abercrumbie 2002; Edghill 2007). Black women easily become modern Mammies, overworked and unappreciated, at the universities where we work (Walkington 2017). I entered this new phase of my life thinking I was ready to conquer this small town by being a resource for the minority students who I felt had no idea what they were facing. The truth is that I had no idea what I was facing. I advised almost every Black organization that popped up at the university, even the ones that were newly founded. I was called upon for every racist incident that happened on our campus, even incidents that happened in the larger community, like when the Black kids were kicked out of the high school. I took on some of this work because of my calling to politics as a political scientist. My English Department colleague always supported me but did not have the same drive to change the culture of the university. We understood that every meeting and event needed a face, and I naturally became that person. Black women in political science likely have an additional weight on their shoulders, put on by ourselves and others. Not only is there an expectation that we are more than the modern Mammy, we expect and are expected to have special skills to be an *effective* modern Mammy.

My husband and I had two children during my first three years in this job, still I continued my advisory role to the students, the administration, and other faculty whenever they were incapable of guiding Black students. I even authored several letters to the president regarding the racial atmosphere at the university. My work resulted in some small feats, but the results were limited because we were up against the *culture* of marginalization that could not easily be changed. Creating an experience that valued Black students was not part of the dominant culture, yet this was at the core of our requests. Black students continued to have different experiences with campus police than white students. Courses, even those that purported to be about Black people, continued to be taught from a

Eurocentric perspective, with faculty making racist comments in class. Faculty questioned whether Black students were prepared to be at this university. The university was successful in creating two different experiences, one for white students and one for Black and Brown students, and each campus climate report came to this same conclusion. Yet we were oblivious to the entrenchment of this *culture* so our work asking for changes continued. At the time I did not understand that the university never intended to create a place that did not center the white experience, and that is exactly what we were asking for.

Power on a University Campus

As political scientists, we are used to understanding these complex problems that lead to power disparities between groups. Perhaps this ability to explain power led me to naïvely believe I could change the power dynamics at my institution. To the contrary, this *culture* and power dynamic could never change with the small incremental changes the university was willing to make. While we know that incremental changes keep institutions from making sweeping changes, we also know that sweeping changes are necessary to change systemic inequalities. Incremental changes have a way of keeping marginalized people in their place, while allowing those with power the time to adjust so that the power dynamics never change (Hochschild 1984). This *culture* takes its toll on Black women. I quickly became the receiver of the discrimination many warn permeates this environment (Combs 2003), and like my sister colleagues, I became unmotivated and experienced several health problems (Jones and Shorter-Gooden 2003). The incremental changes were enough to make whites concerned that it was a zero-sum game, which meant to them that if Black people received more of their interests, other groups would receive less. Their response made me fight harder for what seemed like minuscule changes.

The discrimination I faced my first few years was nothing short of horrible. Over the years I have tried to understand what was happening to me by looking at the experiences and writings of my Black sisters. While misery loves company, it is disturbing to know that these experiences are not isolated. Wilson (2012) finds that Black women have a unique experience whereby together other faculty, administrators, and students create an environment that makes it difficult for Black women to succeed on their campuses. Black women across the academy are faced with challenging environments that threaten their livelihood, their sanity, and their physical health. Most of my non-Black colleagues could never comprehend the constant ways in which we battle to be seen as capable people who are smart and deserving of the positions we hold. Black women experience "subordination of their work, isolation, and exclusion, while their credentials, educational background, expertise, and experiences as Black women are all called into question" (Walkington 2017, 61). We are constantly having to prove that we deserve to be where we are, all while often managing a family and dealing with the unique situations that come with motherhood and as a spouse.

I constantly bumped heads with the students in this privileged school. Football players would tower over my short stature contesting grades before class started and after class was over, while other students whispered racist and sexist things about me to each other during our class sessions. Students flooded websites with negative comments about me and my ability to teach. There is no doubt that Black women tend to have harsher experiences, especially owing to white male students (McKay 1983; Pope and Joseph 1997). I was so overwhelmed with these particular experiences that I went into early labor with my daughter which caused me to have long-term health problems. As I disrupted the university, it disrupted my health and the survival of my family.

I was expected to give deference to my white colleagues and students (Seo and Hinton 2009; Wilson 2012), but I chose to *resist*. I resisted by being a competent professor—requiring students in my courses to read and perform at the level that I decided was appropriate for a passing grade. Colleagues visited my office to discuss their prized students' work in my class, reminding me that they were very bright students, but the students often still earned less than an A in my class. Some faculty and administrators suggested that I avoid focusing on race because the students were uncomfortable or having anxiety, but I continued to teach the way I saw fit. A top administrator that no longer works at the university once said we should not scare away Johnny by making him learn these uncomfortable subjects. As I was learning daily, my *resistance* to the concerns of my colleagues and administrators came at a price. These experiences expose the consequence and duality of our disruption to the discipline. When we disrupt the centering of whiteness, disrupting can cause Black women their lives!

My journey has been one of exploration, where I have been knocked down over and over again until I finally decided to fight back after *twenty* years in academe. No one told me my career would be a constant battle. To the contrary, I left graduate school believing I had arrived, only to be slapped back down to a status of irrelevant. It would take *twenty years* to get to the point where I understood how to hold others accountable so that I could not be ignored, but this was not until I experienced some of the most disturbing acts of my career. These acts disrupted the core of who I thought I was and caused me to reinvent who I would be in the future.

Blurring the Lines

Because as a Black woman I felt that my needs were invisible to the university, I chose not to report incidents that should have been reported. No other person should ever be made to believe that they should not report criminal behavior because of what others may think about them. That is essentially what I did, and it underscores the tendency of Black women faculty to care more about our colleagues than our own well-being.

One of the most disturbing experiences at my university happened the day I was granted tenure. I was so excited that I announced the tenure decision in our department suite. Several faculty members were in the suite and all said congratulations. I then walked into my office and was followed by a male colleague. Once he shut the door, which I thought nothing of, he extended his hand to say congratulations again. Although everyone knows I do not like touching people, I was so happy that day that I put out my hand to shake his. He pulled me up toward him and then kissed me on my forehead. The kiss was followed by the words I'll never forget, "I would have done that out there, but that would have been awkward." Another visiting male colleague used to visit my office quite often. One day we sat and talked for a very long time. During this conversation he informed me that he had received a penis pump and his wife loves it. I could not stop thinking about why he felt so comfortable telling me this and how this conversation never would have happened if I were a white woman. White women are afforded too much respect at my university for anyone to ever cross that line. This situation still bothers me because I had so much respect for this colleague and never told a soul what he had dared to say in my office. I kept telling myself that he did not mean any harm and that it was not so bad after all.

There certainly has been some resolution by telling the story, but I tell the story because I know that I am not the only person who this has happened to. Because Black women in academe are isolated, ignored, marginalized, and deemed irrelevant, it becomes easy for us to believe we have to keep these moments to ourselves and just power through. Those two incidents made me vow to never allow anyone else to shut my office door and also made me realize how much I needed a support system.

Working in my institution has meant a series of blows to who I am as a scholar, a professor, a woman, a mother, an African American, and an individual. I quickly became open season for anyone who wanted to gain clout across the university. The irony is that while I was teaching my daughter not to become a permanent victim at school, I had slipped into becoming the permanent victim at work. Many joined the department as tenure-track or term hires and quickly understood that I did not matter. Some were bold enough to ignore me during the interview process, but others waited until they got the job, saw the law of the land, and then decided that no one cared about me. Junior colleagues *without* tenure even felt empowered to challenge my teaching and to try to mandate that I teach my courses a certain way. I repeatedly saw signs of the reality noted by Aparicio (1999): that people see me as both aggressive and incompetent. Political scientists are especially equipped to understand power and what it means to have power. Unfortunately, that meant I was often sized up as lacking power and treated accordingly.

No Permanent Allies

Believe it or not, all of these issues did not compel me to write this account of my experiences. I am writing this piece because of the unexpected antagonism from my colleagues that continued to exist twenty years into this job. I was no longer that young new professor, so dismissing all of my earlier interactions as "that's what happens when you're new and young" no longer worked. It was time to reconcile my reality with the stories others told of their unwavering support for diversity and inclusion. We must face the reality that no one really wants to admit: They are the problem. Yes, their tendency to ignore and reframe the issues I have had these last twenty years is as much, if not more, of a problem than the students who called me a "bitch" when they thought I could not hear them.

My time in academe has led me to conclude that universities and the people within them lack empathy for Black women. A lack of empathy leads to Black faculty feeling isolated since many other faculty are too afraid to become their allies (Abercrumbie 2002). No one wants to spend that social capital. I have been attacked by Black colleagues for being an outspoken Black woman. Imagine having your email criticizing the president forwarded to him and every Black person on campus along with a note saying that the only reason the students have become politically active is because you are on campus. As horrible as that might sound, and believe me, it was horrible, the president did not even respond saying this was an inappropriate conversation for him to be brought into. No one on that list thought enough to point out the ridiculousness of the accusation that students only protest because I encourage them to. Not one person said the email was malicious to the sender's face. Instead, most of them apologized to me when they saw me in person, making sure they never let that person see them talking to me. This behavior was classic. I was labeled aggressive (Seo and Hinton 2009), and this label got in the way of my deserving the empathy that my university colleagues would show to any other person. Perhaps even worse, like so many of my sisters at other universities, my voice had been muted (McKay 1983).

My breaks were not immune from the constant intrusion into my life when my colleagues believed they needed to chastise me. One Christmas break I was called in to a department meeting in early January. Unbeknownst to me, the meeting was about *my* course. My colleagues conveyed to me that my course on research design was being taught incorrectly and I was stunned. I quickly realized that was the impetus for this at the spur of the moment meeting. My colleagues were convinced by the students that this was a course they should not have to take, and they quickly acted on the students' behalves to save them from my terror. This had been one of many instances where students complained about me and I was told to change what I was doing, rather than being supported by my colleagues. This was even worse because apparently all of my colleagues had discussed this beforehand and I was the last to know. I shut down by the end of the meeting and later that day broke out in a rash that we think was a reaction to the stress. In fact, the medical issues that I have experienced, which can be connected with my work at the university, have had a profound impact on my life.

As ridiculous as it might sound, the university had an initiative to address diversity and inclusion across the university. One part of this included a departmental meeting with the vice-president of academic affairs, the person in charge of Title IX, and the dean of faculty. Our meeting started with the department claiming that "we" address diversity by the courses that "I" teach. We then quickly moved into a discussion about how I teach research design and that my research design should be revised to spend more time discussing qualitative methods. No one could make this up if they tried. A conversation about diversity and inclusion ended with the only Black person in the department being told she must do what no one else in the entire department has ever been told to do: teach her classes the way the department tells her to teach them. This argument lasted for at least three to four years, until I went on sabbatical. We repeatedly fought over this, and it always ended with me telling them this was an unfair precedent we were setting. No one in the department had ever been told to teach a course a certain way, and we prided ourselves on our ability to recognize the unique contributions we brought to the curriculum. When I called them out for being racist, the department changed forever. I had the audacity to tell people who prided themselves on being aware of racial issues and always being on the right side that they also harbored racist feelings and acted in a way that continued systemic oppression. They never saw themselves as part of the problem that they had indeed become. Rather than take inventory of their own actions, they buckled down on the principle that this was about the discipline, not personal. My colleagues were incapable of acknowledging they had done what they knew so much about; they succeeded in marginalizing another person. They undermined the only Black woman in the department in a way that they had never undermined anyone else. In a department that prided itself on allowing faculty to have academic freedom, they decided that I could not be afforded that freedom. Qualitative methods was the excuse they used. Because I refused to spend time on qualitative methods, they maintained that I was "marginalizing" this approach to political science. It was a done deal. I had been labeled incompetent in any area that was outside of studying race, and it was now the job of my colleagues to guide me as their apprentice. My doubly bound status as Black and as a woman (Aparicio 1999) relegated me to being an apprentice.

My experience has shown me that people who share my gender, my race, and/or my interests are more damaging to my emotional well-being than opponents could ever be. I call them the pseudoallies because (1) they say they are in your corner, (2) you can have a conversation with them about issues of racism and sexism and they say all the right things, and

(3) everyone on the campus thinks they are your ally. Unfortunately, it is pseudoallies who called me loud in a meeting, blamed me for unhappy Black students, told students they didn't have to use what they learned from my courses, and demanded that I teach my courses to their liking. These pseudoallies remind me that this political science world can be extremely lonely and perhaps was the most surprising part of the disruption. Do not dare make the mistake of confusing friendship with work, because like most coalitions in politics these relationships are usually short-lived. Identifying people on your campus like this is necessary so that you will always know who is playing on your team. You should never be surprised by what happens in a meeting and, when you are, you have to find your voice to say the meeting is troubling. This means more work, but the consequences of being quiet can create a level of stress that compromises your emotional and physical well-being.

Conclusion: How to Survive and Thrive

The stories above are extremely emotional for me and for the reader, but they also suggest that I persevered. It is important to contextualize my experiences by concluding with how I created an environment that allowed me to thrive in my personal life while my professional life seemed disastrous and then learn to thrive in my professional life as well.

My decision to move away from the campus in 1999 was looked down upon at the time, but it turns out that it was one of the best decisions I made. I moved about an hour away from the campus to create distance from the university and its larger community but also to allow my children to have a more normal life. This move meant that I paid a cost for teaching at the university; I always needed reliable transportation, gas prices skyrocketed, staying late for events might mean I needed a hotel, snow-covered roads could be dangerous, and late events might mean not seeing my family for an entire day. However, there was peace and hope in creating the physical space between the campus and me. Weekends were my time when I did not step foot on the campus. I used the driving time to transition to my home life, and while I would repeat some of the stories to my family, I never transferred the anger to my family. I could remain the bubbly person my children, husband, and friends knew me as, as long as I left the campus. My children's schools and activities had nothing to do with the community where I worked, so I did not have to communicate with my colleagues outside of work. I did not have to recall the many acts of racism I had experienced from my colleagues in my personal life. We created lives that did not intersect with the community where I had been so disrespected and that was great for my family. My personal life improved as soon as I physically moved from the area.

Our experiences as Black women underscore the fact that it is imperative to create relationships with people outside of your department and often outside of your university. The number of Black women professors is extremely small, and the number of Black women political scientists is even smaller. If you are not careful, this isolation will reinforce your feelings of being devalued. You must attend conferences that include people who are collegial and friendly. My academic home became the National Conference of Black Political Scientists (NCOBPS). Each year the NCOBPS conference gave me the space I needed to exhale and return to do the job I was hired to do. I learned that not only was I valued by my NCOBPS colleagues, they understood what I was going through and several others were having the same experiences. Many of them were also feeling undervalued, disrespected, and overworked by their respective institutions. My colleagues at NCOBPS thought my work was important and interesting. Some of us became good friends and completed projects together. I could not have made it through my experiences without this network of friends and scholars. They knew my husband, my children, and my work! NCOBPS managed to connect the personal to the professional. While my institution prevented me from merging these two parts of my life, my professional organization had a way of filling that void by accepting me and my family.

My time at my institution would eventually change after I had been teaching there for twenty years. Make no mistake about it, my colleagues did not think differently about me. Rather than wait on them changing the way they felt about me, I changed the way I interacted with them. I became more vocal on issues that I thought were important. I recognized that tenure meant I did not have to sit in silence when I was mistreated or other people were treated unfairly. I spoke up during faculty meetings. I filed complaints against colleagues who were being racist. I challenged faculty who had been racist toward Black students. In the end I realized that my beliefs about their thoughts prevented me from voicing my concerns. Finally, I understood that it didn't matter what I did: I could never change the way others thought of me. My only recourse was for me to make it clear that treating me and others like me badly came with consequences. There would be no closing the door to hide private acts of racism and sexism. All doors would remain open for everyone to see the ways my university colleagues marginalized Black people. People across the institution are uncomfortable with having someone call their acts racist and seem to be more careful about what they say and how they act as a result. I take this as a win.

I have never been able to marry my personal and professional lives at my institution and probably never will, but I have certainly matured to have a healthier professional life. I returned to my passion of creating political science scholarship and making a difference in the lives of Black students. I came into academe as a bright and vivacious young African American woman and morphed into an angry Black woman. While there is no indication that I am actually more angry than before, I am definitely more vocal than before. Becoming the angry Black woman in their eyes is not so bad if it means that others stop demeaning Black women. If people at my institution think twice about the things they say and do because they think I might respond negatively, that is good for all of us. When I chose a path of silence, I was miserable and people walked all over me. The payoff for finding my voice after twenty years is a peace that I could not have imagined in 1997. Never again will I sacrifice my emotional and physical well-being so that others can feel comfortable. I am no longer struggling to survive: I am thriving!

References

Abercrumbie, Paul E. 2002. "There Is Peace in the Midst of a Storm." In *Our Stories: The Experiences of Black Professionals on Predominantly White Campuses*, edited by M. Taylor-Archer and S. Smith, 46–56. Cincinnati, OH: John D. O' Bryant National Think Tank for Black Professionals in Higher Education on Predominantly White.

Aparicio, Frances R. 1999. "Through My Lens: A Video Project about Women of Color Faculty at the University of Michigan." *Feminist Studies* 25, no. 1: 119–30.

Combs, Gwendolyn M. 2003. "The Duality of Race and Gender for Managerial African American Women: Implications of Informal Social Networks on Career Advancement." *Human Resource Development Review* 2, no. 4: 385–405.

Edghill, Vernese E. 2007. "Historical Patterns of Institutional Diversity: Black Women in Race-Specific Positions on Predominantly White College Campuses." New York: Howard University Press.

Harvey, W. B. 1994. "African American Faculty in Community Colleges: Why They Aren't There." *New Directions for Community Colleges* 22, no. 3: 19–25.

Hochschild, Jennifer. 1984. *The New American Dilemma: Liberal Democracy and School Desegregation.* New Haven, CT: Yale University Press.

Holmes, Sharon L. 2008. "Narrated Voices of African American Women in Academe." *Journal of Thought* 43, no 3: 101–24.

Jones, Charisse, and Kumea Shorter-Gooden. 2003. *Shifting: The Double Lives of Black Women in America.* New York: HarperCollins.

Jordan, Winthrop. 1974. *The White Man's Burden: Historical Origins of Racism in the United States.* New York: Oxford University Press.

McKay, Nellie. 1983. "Black Woman Professor—White University." *International Forum* 6, no. 2: 143–47.

Parker Terhune, Carol. 2008. "Coping in Isolation: The Experiences of Black Women in White Communities." *Journal of Black Studies* 38, no. 4: 547–64.

Pope, Jacqueline, and Janice Joseph. 1997. "Student Harassment of Female Faculty of African Descent in the Academy." In *Black Women in the Academy: Promises and Perils,* edited by Lois Benjamin, 252–60. Gainesville: University Press of Florida.

Seo, Byung-ln, and Dawn Hinton. 2009. "How They See Us, How We See Them: Two Women of Color in Higher Education." *Race, Gender, and Class* 16, nos. 3–4: 203–17.

Thomas, Gloria D., and Carol Hollenshead. 2001. "Resisting from the Margins: The Coping Strategies of Black Women and Other Women of Color Faculty Members at a Research University." *Journal of Negro Education* 70, no. 3: 166–75.

Walkington, Lori. 2017. "How Far Have We Really Come? Black Women Faculty and Graduate Students' Experiences in Higher Education." *Humboldt Journal of Social Relations* 39: 51–65.

Wilson, Sherée. 2012. "They Forgot Mammy Had a Brain." In *Presumed Incompetent: The Intersections of Race and Class for Women in Academia,* edited by Gabriella Gutiérrez y Muhs et al., 65–77. Boulder: University Press of Colorado. *ProQuest Ebook Central,* https://ebookcentral.proquest.com/lib/depauw-ebooks/detail.action?docID=3442895.

Yoshinaga-Itano, Christine. 2006. "Institutional Barriers and Myths to Recruitment and Retention of Faculty of Color: An Administrator's Perspective." In *Faculty of Color: Teaching in Predominantly White Colleges and Universities,* edited by C. Stanley, 344–60. Bolton, MA: Anker.

11

Truth Telling

The Limits of Institutional Liberalism, Neutrality, Objectivity, and Meritocracy

ANGELA K. LEWIS-MADDOX

> So it is better to speak
> remembering
> we were never meant to survive
>
> —Audre Lorde, *A Litany for Survival* (1978)

In May 2021, the national news revealed that the University of North Carolina, Chapel Hill (UNC) had denied tenure to Nikole Hannah-Jones. Hannah-Jones is a Pulitzer Prize-winning *New York Times* journalist who launched the 1619 Project, which examined the role of slavery in American political development. Hannah-Jones's case was not the first and will not be the last case of a Black woman being denied tenure in the ivory tower. Tenure is a commitment to a scholar from an institution, an assurance that their work matters enough to make an offer of a job for life, allowing them the freedom to explore and study whatever they choose, as well as the freedom to present that information in an instructional format. It is outside the norm for tenure cases to make national headlines the way Hannah-Jones's case did. In fact, hundreds of Black academics face the same denial Hannah-Jones faced, often in silence. Hannah-Jones was ultimately granted tenure by UNC, but she declined and accepted an offer from the prestigious, historically Black Howard University.

UNC faced additional scrutiny when Irma McClaurin, PhD, award-winning author, anthropologist, and former president of Shaw University, revealed her own experiences at the university. After detailing the Hannah-Jones story, McClaurin (2021) states that "even when BIPOC candidates have exceptional credentials, we are bumped by whites who 'meet the minimum.'" McClaurin, too, applied for a position for which she was more than qualified, but she did not receive an invitation to interview. UNC gave the position to someone much less qualified, a young white woman with a master's degree.

The Hannah-Jones tenure case at UNC brought national attention to the number of Black female professors with tenure. June and O'Leary (2021) reported that in 2019 at public and nonprofit four-year colleges, only 2.1 percent of tenured associate and full professors were Black women. The article presented a table showing the number of Black female tenured professors and their percentage of the overall total of tenured professors in American universities. The universities with the highest number of Black female tenured professors were historically Black.

My Story

For years I struggled with whether to remain silent about my experiences in higher education. Even as I write this chapter, I wonder how to share what I went through without placing my career on the line. I cannot say that I have an answer to the dilemma. When it all began, I was drawn to revealing the truth about institutions of higher education, how they are lauded nationally as models of diversity, equity, and inclusion, yet on the ground, many institutions, particularly in their middle management, lack serious effort to embrace the same ideals. In fact, one could conclude that not only is there a lack of effort but there is a system in place to ensure a lack of diversity in leadership and a lack of equity in salary increases, tenure, and promotion.

I work at an institution that is the largest employer in my state, having over 26,000 direct employees and supporting over 64,000 jobs that were created because of its existence (Tripp Umbach, nd). The institution has a web page devoted to all the accolades it has received nationally and internationally. In 2018 it was recognized as being one of the most diverse campuses in the country. The Princeton Review also ranked my home institution as number three in the nation for diversity of the student population. In February 2021, *Forbes* named it America's best large employer (Koplon 2021). And in April 2021, Forbes again highlighted it, ranking it as the fourth best employer for diversity (Rohan 2021). The university has eleven colleges and schools and one graduate school. Over half of the colleges and schools have nationally ranked programs (Shepard 2019).

From the outside, the institution is acclaimed as a place that is diverse, inclusive, and equitable. Yet all institutions are created by people and are run by people. Although there are varying understandings of institutions, Shinji (2018) argues that "institutions are defined as a system of rules, beliefs, norms, and organizations that conjointly generate a regularity of behavior" (vi). And Plaut and colleagues (2020) maintain that dominant groups create institutions to keep out nondominant groups. In other words, institutions are only as good as the people who run them.

As a political scientist who studies the intersections of race and gender, I understand that relationships are shaped by institutional structures of power and vulnerability. It is well documented that there are disparities in the number of Black women in higher education. Black women are underrepresented at almost every level, even as we celebrated the 2016 election of the nation's first woman of color, Kamala Harris, as vice-president of the United States, and the first Black woman confirmed to the US Supreme Court, Associate Justice Ketanji Brown Jackson, in 2022. The dearth of Black women in higher education as professors and leaders seriously limits the size, diversity, and equity of the pool of scholars, undermining the goals of equity and inclusion in our pluralistic representative democracy (Jeffries 2021).

These issues and insights are particularly relevant for those of us who seek shared governance and diverse representation and inclusive leadership in the academy. As a Black woman who is a full professor, I have seen and participated in the search processes for university leadership posts ranging from department chairs, deans, and provosts to university presidents. The pool of candidates rarely includes women of color, even when our institution has hired high-profile search firms to conduct nationwide searches for qualified applicants.

Utilizing Black feminism and critical race theory (CRT), I share my personal experiences regarding promotion, retention, and advancement in an institution of higher learning. I have over two decades of research, study, and institutional fieldwork as a participant observer to draw from in my analysis of policies and procedures, mindsets, and models meant to increase the diversity, equity, and inclusion of colleagues and leaders on campus. The aim of this work is to contribute to a vibrant and critical conversation about how Black women navigate the path to becoming a full professor and beyond.

Black feminism and CRT both offer a theoretical framework for analyzing higher education administration. This piece draws from Wolfe and Dilworth's (2015) research on how institutional gatekeepers limit or expand opportunities for Black women candidates. How do women of color, specifically Black women, navigate the hills and valleys of professional development from recruitment, promotion, retention, and advancement in the academy? Do Black women receive the same advancement opportunities as other scholars, or are they confined to nontenure or assistant or associate professor positions? Women faculty, particularly those who are women of color, often identify increased demands for service in the department as they advance in rank, and they note that service assignments interfere with their ability to conduct the research necessary for promotion to a full professorship (Hirshfield and Joseph 2012; Porter 2007; Turner 2002). Since the path to appointment in higher education leadership requires professional achievement commensurate with the rank of full professor, increasing the number of Black women eligible for leadership depends upon increasing their number among full professors. As a result, it is central to determine whether there are gatekeepers acting to limit or expand leadership opportunities for Black women in higher education.

Theoretical Framework

Black Feminism

> And yet there is no healing in silence.
>
> —bell hooks (2015)

In *Sisters of the Yam*, bell hooks (2015) provides a guide for healing from racism, sexism, capitalism, and the other societal issues that Black women confront. For hooks, the first step toward healing is truth telling. She ties truth telling to healing because of a connection made by M. Scott Peck (1985), who states that one part of mental illness is related to the lies we tell ourselves and those told to us by society. To be whole, we must disentangle ourselves from lies and be honest about our experiences. hooks argues that the very foundation of white supremacy is based on a lie, that the enslaved were inferior. hooks goes on to say that the enslaved knew that survival meant deception because cultural domination can only occur with deception. In other words, the enslaved knew that "skillful lying could protect one's safety" (hooks 2015, 12). To tell the oppressors the truth often meant death, so the enslaved hid "behind a false appearance in the interest of survival" (hooks 2015, 13). Even after slavery ended, rejecting dissimulation was not in Black people's best interest. Yet, she insists that this dissimulation, the act of being deceitful, no longer serves Black people in society. In fact, it harms us, causing a great deal of stress, and as Peck (1985) suggests, it is tied to mental health. Being open and honest frees us because there is nothing to hide, no stories to tell, and no webs to weave. As hooks says, "It hurts to live with lies" (hooks 2015, 19).

Paul Laurence Dunbar gives witness to this harm in *We Wear the Mask*:

> We wear the mask that grins and lies,
> It hides our cheeks and shades our eyes—
> This debt we pay to human guile;
> With torn and bleeding hearts we smile,
> And mouth with myriad subtleties.
> Why should the world be over-wise,
> In counting all our tears and sighs?
> Nay, let them only see us, while
> We wear the mask.
> We smile, but, O great Christ, our cries
> To thee from tortured souls arise.
> We sing, but oh the clay is vile
> Beneath our feet, and long the mile;
> But let the world dream otherwise,
> We wear the mask! (Dunbar 1922)

Audre Lorde also discusses the importance of not remaining silent: "Tell them about how you're never really a whole person if you remain silent, because there's always that one little piece inside you that wants to be spoken out, and if you keep ignoring it, it gets madder and madder and hotter and hotter, and if you don't speak it out one day it will just up and punch you in the mouth from the inside" (Lorde 2007, 42). Why are we silent? Why am I silent? Why do we not tell our stories? As I was thinking about truth, my daily devotional took me to Ecclesiastes 3:1–7 (Biblia nd), which reads:

A Time for Everything

1 For everything there is a season,
   a time for every activity under heaven.
2 A time to be born and a time to die.
   A time to plant and a time to harvest.
3 A time to kill and a time to heal.
   A time to tear down and a time to build up.
4 A time to cry and a time to laugh.
   A time to grieve and a time to dance.
5 A time to scatter stones and a time to gather stones.
   A time to embrace and a time to turn away.
6 A time to search and a time to quit searching.
   A time to keep and a time to throw away.
7 A time to tear and a time to mend.
   A time to be quiet and a time to speak.

So, in my efforts to remain silent, I continue to read and see things that tell me there is a time to be quiet, but there is also a time to speak.

A major component of Black women's healing involves speaking the truth. When faced with a possible cancer prognosis, Lorde reflected on her life, and the one thing she regretted most was her silence. She explains that there is a cost to silence, particularly to the person who remains silent. These costs are the emotions and feelings silence conjures up in the person who does not speak their truth. This cost is in addition to whatever comes, whether a person remains silent or speaks the truth. For example, speaking truth may lead to pain, but pain also comes from remaining silent. Likewise, death is imminent whether someone is silent or speaks the truth. Lorde concludes, therefore, that "Your silence will not protect you" (Lorde 2007, 41).

Despite this desire to speak, we remain silent—for a variety of reasons, including fear. The fear that we will not be heard, the fear that danger will come from speaking our truth, or just the fear of people knowing the truth. Or, as Lorde says, the fear of visibility, because although Black women are highly visible or hypervisible, we are also rendered invisible within America. This hypervisibility derives from how Black people are scrutinized in society. For example, in entertainment and sports, Black women's bodies are policed. From tennis star Serena Williams to head basketball coach at Texas A&M University, Sydney Carter, society seems obsessed with Black women's bodies (Odihi Empowers 2021; Bernabe 2022). Settles, Buchanan, and Dotson (2019) found that this hypervisibility in higher education comes in tokenism, where Black faculty are easily noticed because of their numerical minority status. They are often singled out for being "the" representative of their respective group. This tokenism has led faculty of color to work harder because they felt someone would accuse them of not being good enough or the faculty member believing themselves succumbing to impostor syndrome (Fields and Cunningham-Williams 2021). The #SayHerName movement points out the invisibility of Black women in the racial justice movement, noting that numerous Black women also suffer at the hands of the police (Crenshaw and Ritchie 2015). Within political science, invisibility comes from the absence of Black women as political subjects (Alexander-Floyd 2018). The invisibility of Black women extends beyond the academy to the private sector, where Black women make up less than 2 percent of executives and no Black women run *Fortune* 500 companies. Our visibility makes us vulnerable, and yet it is our greatest strength. With visibility comes scrutiny, judgment, and maybe risks, as McClaurin (2021) reveals about her speaking out about UNC. Likewise, there are risks to my visibility in telling my story.

Consequently, I ask, as Lorde does, "What do you [I] need to say? What tyrannies do you [I] swallow day by day and attempt to make your [my] own, until you [I] sicken and die of them, still in silence?" (Lorde 2007, 41).

A trusted friend encouraged caution with this truth telling, particularly if I wish to continue to advance my career. This piece feels like a David and Goliath story. After all, my institution is the largest employer in the state. Although I am more than midway through my career, damage could still be done, promotions withheld, or, as one administrator stated, I might be labeled a troublemaker. I have higher aspirations in the academy.

I have already seen the harm that comes because of silence. I am sure there are risks involved in my speaking out. I also know there are risks if I remain silent. So. I. Speak.

Critical Race Theory

> The way to right wrongs is to turn the light of truth upon them.
>
> —Ida B. Wells (2014)

Truth telling is to Black feminism as counterstorytelling is to CRT. CRT originated and was developed in US law schools by scholars frustrated with the slowness of racial reforms. It is a multidisciplinary race-centered theory that scholars use to analyze the academy (Parker and Villalpando 2007; Smith, Yosso, and Solórzano 2007; Hiraldo 2010; Wolfe and Dilworth 2015). CRT's framework includes a critique of liberalism and meritocracy, the permanence of racism, whiteness as property, interest conversion, and counterstorytelling (Bell 2000; Crenshaw 1997; DeCuir and Dixson 2004; Delgado 1995; Harris 1993; Ladson-Billings 1999; Ladson-Billings and Tate 1995).

Parker and Villalpando (2007) note the importance of CRT in higher education administration as "a valuable lens with which to analyze and interpret administrative policies and procedures in educational institutions" (519). Hiraldo (2010) argues that CRT helps expose social inequities in higher education. It legitimizes firsthand experiences of discrimination—or discrimination narratives—by exposing how color-blind policies that rely on "merit, equality, the market, and objectivity" (Parker and Villalpando 2007, 519) often assist gatekeepers in limiting opportunities. A reliance on color-blind policies remains unquestioned in larger society. For example, color-blind policies are employed to deny opportunities utilizing the tools of meritocracy. King (2023) finds that the term *fit* is often used in denying opportunities. Hiring managers state "that a candidate does not 'fit in' with the department, its personnel, culture, performance measures, or status in the discipline" (118). These fit measures are unrelated to qualifications. Still, they are used as if they are and are unquestioned. Thus, counternarratives, stories of those who have experienced a denial of opportunities, are a key aspect of CRT.

The academy, at its best, is an interdisciplinary and multicultural scholarly community dedicated to education, research, and service that welcomes everyone to the table with their ideas, questions, and concerns. CRT suggests, however, that racism remains a norm in many predominantly white institutions (PWIs). In fact, Wolfe and Dilworth (2015) note that "although U.S. higher education institutions endorse egalitarian principles which champion the ideals of liberty, justice, and equality in their language, historical records show clear patterns of engaged practices that reinforce beliefs and values antithetical to those ideals. Many of those practices are centered on White male dominance" (678). Despite efforts to appear progressive and equitable, higher education is a bastion of white male dominance, reminding us that dominant groups establish institutions to exclude nondominant groups (Plaut et al. 2020). As such, dominant group members serve as gatekeepers to positions of prestige and power in the academy. King (2022) states that "many departments across disciplines—including political science—continue to be composed of mostly (or entirely) middle-aged, white, heterosexual (ostensibly) cis-gendered males" (118). Thus, for someone to obtain a position as a professor or gain tenure or a leadership position, they must make it past the gatekeepers, who are mostly people from the dominant groups. In short, higher education lacks diversity because it was meant to lack diversity.

Black feminist bell hooks also discusses how institutions navigate toward an overabundance of white males, particularly in leadership in the academy. She notes that Black women have long existed as scholars despite the web of economic, political, and ideological systems of oppression. But only recently have Black women held leadership positions in universities, media, publishing houses, or other institutions that validate knowledge. Wooten (2019) echoes this sentiment in her work on how Black women are portrayed in the media by analyzing two television shows, *Scandal* and *Insecure*, with Black female leads, creators, and producers, providing them with the power to move away from stereotypical images of Black women on screen. The historical exclusion of Black women, along with other marginalized groups, leads to the elevation of "elite White male ideas and interests and the corresponding suppression of Black women's ideas and interest in traditional scholarship" (Wooten 2019, 60). The elevation of white men follows institutional biases where individuals rely less on qualifications and more on references, informal contacts, recommendations, referrals, and fit to determine if a candidate for an administrative post receives a position (Wolfe and Dilworth 2015). Thus, if a candidate from a marginalized group does not have the right connections, gatekeepers utilize the fit argument to justify not hiring the candidate. King (2023) suggests that fit is a "catchall" term to justify not hiring the candidate. For example, fit could be used to justify not hiring a woman candidate because she would not "fit" the boys club. Likewise, candidates from marginalized groups would not be hired, because of "fit" if a member of a search committee or department cannot see themselves socializing with the candidate.

Using the tools of Black feminism and CRT, here is my truth telling and counterstory of how gatekeepers employed practices centered on white male dominance to limit my promotion opportunities, while claiming that neutrality, objectivity, and meritocracy were the essential criteria they relied on.

Majoring in Political Science

The Undergraduate Years

I am a first-generation college graduate and the first in my entire family to receive a PhD. The path to graduate school to study political science was bumpy. As an undergraduate, I wanted to attend law school and be a politician. However, my introduction to politics was on the campus of the University of Alabama (UA) and the infamous "Machine," described by the student newspaper as a "not so secret" society made up of white Greek organizations that influence campus elections (Boiling 2020). The university suspended the Student Government Association due to violence when a non-Machine candidate for SGA president was assaulted. After I saw how dirty and violent politics could be, I set my sights on law school and graduate school, majoring in political science. While studying political science at UA, I had one white female professor, no Black female professors, and one untenured Black male professor who taught the African American politics course.

Although I had good grades and I graduated a semester early, I suffered the same as many other students from underrepresented groups when it came to standardized tests like the Graduate Records Examination (GRE) and the Law School Admissions Test (LSAT). Despite the hurdle concerning my test scores, I was admitted to the University of Tennessee at Knoxville (UTK). This was after being denied admission by the political science department of a smaller state university in Chattanooga. And my admission to UTK was made possible through my participation in the Ronald E. McNair Postbaccalaureate Achievement (McNair) Program.

The McNair Program is a US Department of Education TRIO program designed to prepare students from disadvantaged backgrounds with strong academic promise to enroll in graduate programs. The summer before my admission, I took courses and worked with a white male political science professor who was a nontraditional PhD, having attended community college before receiving his graduate degree. Fortunately for me, he was dedicated to creating pathways for all students and worked to ensure my admission. Like my experience at my undergraduate institution, at UTK I had one white woman professor, no Black women professors, and no Black male professors. I did, however, have a community of Black support from the McNair Program and my sorority, the Oak Ridge Alumnae Chapter of Delta Sigma Theta Sorority, Inc.

Graduate School—One Pathway

As a graduate student in political science, I was introduced to two methods of conducting research, qualitative and quantitative. Although I don't aim to enter debates about which is better or the need to choose one over the other, it is essential to note the differences and how political science chooses to focus on one over the other. There are no steadfast definitions of qualitative and quantitative methods within political science. Still, a straightforward way to understand the distinction is to consider quantitative methods as a large N and qualitative methods as a small n, where n is the number of cases studied. One could also view the differences between the two where qualitative methods are used to explore or understand while quantitative methods focus on causation and explanation, with the ability to have precise measurements and data that can be manipulated (MQHRG nd). Scholars suggest that there are distinctions between studying natural sciences and social sciences and that qualitative methods are best "used to understand human meanings" (Morçöl and Ivanova 2010, 257).

In contrast, quantitative methods "aim to make generalizations about objectively existing phenomena" and are best suited for studying everything else (Morçöl and Ivanova 2010, 256). Much of my graduate training was in quantitative methods, accessing and analyzing data. There were few, if any, discussions of qualitative methods. The focus on quantitative techniques in the social sciences is validated by Schwartz-Shea and Yanow (2002) in their study of research methods, where they conclude with a few exceptions that "the best research is quantitative research" (476). Because of this training, and because I loved working with data and was not exposed to other ways of knowing, I decided to do quantitative analysis. Looking back over my training, it would have been nice to have a better understanding of how different scholars produced knowledge.

As a graduate student, I loved statistics, one of my comprehensive exam fields.[1] I did well in the classes. I also desired to learn as much as possible because I wanted to have a concentration in political behavior, which required understanding advanced statistics. Along with my decision to be a quantitative researcher, I found an interest in studying Black public opinion. While my dissertation was in the American government subfield[2] of political behavior, I did not choose it as a concentration because the major professor in that subfield and I had a racially insensitive incident that I believed caused me harm. The instructor referred to Black people as Black in front of his classroom, but in one particular office visit, with the door closed, he referred to Black people as *Negroes*. I shared this information with my mentor, who was a white man who encouraged me to report the faculty member. My mentor even went as far as to visit the diversity office on campus. As a result, I did not take my comprehensive exams in political behavior. I instead took it in state and local government, which was odd because my research was in political behavior. In some ways testing in another field was advantageous because I could be viewed as someone who had a subfield in both state and local government and political behavior. I was part of the norm of political scientists studying political behavior, except I decided to study Black political opinions. There were, however, various scholars studying Black political opinions before I completed my degree, so my topic was not provocative. My goal was to conform to the field, blend in, and do what some Americanists did, study political behavior.

I eventually finished writing my dissertation about Black conservatism (Lewis 2000). I chose this topic because at the time, my voting behavior professor and much of what I read in graduate school lumped Black voters into one ideology and one party. Sure, more often than not, Blacks vote with the Democratic Party, and Blacks are more liberal, but as a Black southerner, I knew there was something more to Black voters than the homogenous ways in which the literature in my field referred to them. Moreover, the topic seemed to be a fruitful one. Studying political behavior and public opinion provided me with a steady flow of secondary data from the American National Election Study. From my perspective, this research path could potentially provide me with years of publications to guarantee, to the extent that anyone could, longevity and tenure. Early in my career, I was ready and willing to learn the most sophisticated statistical techniques to ensure my future in the field as a behaviorist in political science. I bought into the idea that if I mimicked behaviorist work, I would be successful in my career. I had it all planned out, or so I thought.

Teaching, Teaching, and More Teaching or Research

The year I graduated was a tough year to be on the job market. I started my job search in August, applying to schools in geographical areas that I considered diverse, which limited my search. I landed a job at a teaching school in North Carolina that required faculty to teach four courses a semester, a four/four load. It was an interdisciplinary department that combined political science and history. By the time I arrived on campus, the department chair with whom I had spent most of my time during the interview had left, leaving me in a department composed mostly of white men, including the new department chair. I had four new class preparations, and research was not a priority for the institution. Instead, I had to strive to be an effective instructor and collect good student evaluations. As a recent graduate, I had elevated expectations of students, often too high for an institution with an open admissions policy. I left that institution because it was not a good match. I decided I would rather work in a research institution and got a job teaching at UA, my alma mater. I was delighted to return home to teach at my undergraduate institution.

UA had more than double the number of students as the North Carolina institution. I was responsible for teaching a large undergraduate course with over two hundred students. Although I had a graduate assistant, it was still tough being a new assistant professor. UA was a research institution, so I had to shift to focusing on my research and not spend as much time on teaching as I did in North Carolina. My plan was to have my dissertation published as a book. I had publishing houses interested in publishing my dissertation, so I was excited to be able to focus on research and completing my book.

The first year I spent time prepping new courses and ensuring that I was ready for the classroom. Between the large undergraduate course and a new graduate course, I was swamped. When I did have time to work on the book project, I realized that my dissertation left me with more questions than answers. In short, I knew some Blacks identified with the conservative ideological label, but I was unsure of exactly what that label meant to them. I needed to collect more data, which meant I needed research funds. While networking with other Black scholars in the state, I discovered an institution in the same system with a job opening and funding for Black scholars as assistant professors. I applied for the job and received the position along with a generous startup package and a more competitive salary. Although I did ask UA for a counteroffer, their offer could not match the one at my present institution, and I left.

Third Time's a Charm

Within five years of completing graduate school, I was on my way to my third institution. UAB was an urban university located in the heart of Birmingham, Alabama, with a woman as president. When I interviewed, the department had a focus on urban affairs, which was attractive to me as a newly minted professor. Although a PWI in the deep south, they appeared to be more diverse than other universities in the south. It was composed of faculty who taught political science and public administration. The job offer was quick and generous, and I received funding to conduct my research.

The department was housed in the School of Social and Behavioral Sciences (SBS). The university would later merge SBS into a College of Arts and Sciences (CAS). For a political science department in the south, the faculty looked different from other departments. There were numerous women faculty and faculty from diverse cultures and countries. Although we interviewed a few Black candidates, I was the only Black faculty member for over a decade.

By the time I was up for promotion and tenure, the department continued to be gender and culturally diverse but not racially diverse. My promotion to associate professor with tenure was a unanimous vote. Although my book wasn't finished, I had published articles and book chapters. The advice I had received from senior colleagues in my department was "Don't put all your eggs in one basket." They suggested that I should not rely on the book manuscript for tenure. The year before I went up for tenure and promotion, my child was born. I planned to take a few years to catch my breath before moving forward to continue publishing.

I had tried to get the book published with the publisher who expressed interest in the project while I was still in graduate school. But because

I was at a teaching university first and then moved to two additional institutions, time was not on my side. The editor who was originally interested in my book was no longer at the press, and I had to find another publishing company. I found one and sent the completed manuscript, but the reviews were unfavorable, and the press lost interest in my project. In addition, the political landscape in America had changed, and I did not feel comfortable writing about conservatism in the Black community largely because conservatism is viewed as hostile to Black interests and incompatible for the Black freedom struggle (Lewis 2013; Smith 2010). The idea for this project had come in a graduate school class during the Bush administration in the 1990s. Bush and the Republican Party utilized an electoral strategy of "compassionate conservatism" to build relationships with Democratic voters (Wallace and Lewis 2007). In 2008, Barack Obama was elected president, which shifted the ability of Republicans to gain ground in the Black electorate.

About two years after receiving tenure and promotion, I met a senior professor, Clovis Semmes, a sociologist at the University of Missouri, Kansas City, who encouraged me to keep working on the book. A year later, with the assistance of world-renowned political scientist Hanes Walton, I found a press that was interested in my manuscript. It is worth noting that the two professors who mentored me were Black men, not Black women. Although I was part of a small network of Black women political scientists, none were senior scholars who could mentor me through the process to full professor.

Two years later, I had preliminary reviews of my book proposal and was working to collect more data. My recruitment funds were expended, and I had to find additional funds to do more research. With the assistance of my department chair, dean, and the vice-president of diversity, equity, and inclusion, none of whom were Black women, I received funds and collected the data. Approximately three years after the chance meeting with Clovis Semmes, I submitted a full manuscript to the press, and my book, *Conservativism in the Black Community: To the Right and Misunderstood* (2013), was published the following year. During this process, I also completed journal articles and maintained involvement with professional associations.

The Path to Full Professor and Beyond

Years earlier, when I first started working at UAB, I had shared my ambition to be a full professor with the department chair. Over the years, she and

I worked together to build a professional relationship of mutual respect, trust, and achievement. Because she knew and understood my desire for promotion to full, she mentored me before I submitted my dossier.

Promotion to full requires a distinguished record of scholarship, teaching, and service. At some institutions, being a full professor is a necessary requirement for administrative posts such as department chairs, deans, and provosts. Despite my university's receipt of a major grant to advance women in higher education in sciences, technology, engineering, and math, it did not have a university-wide mentoring program for faculty at any level. I did not have the benefit of a formal mentoring program, but my department chair sought to communicate clearly and often to me the importance of focusing on my scholarly agenda. Conference travel, grant opportunities, peer-reviewed publication with highly ranked journals and presses—are all part of the measurement for promotion outlined in departmental, college, and university guidelines. The chair reviewed these guidelines with me, and we talked about everything from service to research to ensure I was ready for promotion. Before submitting my dossier for consideration, I served and chaired the CAS promotion committee, furthering my knowledge of policies, procedures, and expectations across disciplines and departments. My book was published. The time had come for me to submit the dossier for the rank of full professor.

For years, I had prepared for this moment. I read and reread the departmental guidelines for promotion to ensure I met the criteria and I served as cochair of the college's Tenure and Promotion Committee. I wrote my personal statement and put together the dossier. The external reviewers were chosen by both the departmental committee and me and submitted to the department chair. I did not have any senior Black women political scientists on my list as possible external reviewers because there were few if any that had specializations within my area of political science.

The guidelines for promotion outlined the process, which consists of reviews from the departmental committee, the department chair, the college committee, and the dean. After the department receives the external reviews, the departmental committee meets, votes, and submits a letter to the department chair. The department chair then reviews the file, votes, and submits both their letter and the departmental committee's letter to the college Tenure and Promotion Committee. This committee examines the departmental committee's letter, the external letters, and the department chair's letter. The college committee votes and recommends promotion or not to the dean, who also votes. The file then proceeds to the provost's office, who either approves or rejects the promotion.

Institutional norms dictate the academic rank of reviewers for promotion. For example, candidates for the rank of full are reviewed by those who are at the rank of full. There was a shortage of full professors in my department. There were three full professors, including the chair. Because the department chair has a separate vote in the process, the chair could not participate in the departmental committee, leaving two members. Of the two full professors in the department, one predated my arrival and was familiar with my work. The other full professor located within my departmental committee was relatively new, having no knowledge of my performance over the years or my research. They were a spousal hire who joined the department the summer before I submitted my file. Having only two full professors in the department meant a third full professor was necessary for the departmental committee.

The recently appointed dean would appoint a full professor from outside the department to form a committee of three for the departmental committee. The dean would not just appoint a full professor from another department but appoint a department chair (who had not served a full year) as a member of my departmental committee. This practice of choosing a department chair, and not simply a full professor, as the third person on a departmental committee was not documented in any of the college's tenure and promotion processes or procedures. Thus, two of the three, a majority of the departmental committee members, were outside my department, having little to no knowledge of me, my work, or departmental norms. Moreover, all three members of my departmental committee were white men, and none of them were traditional political scientists. In fact, one was in international relations and one was an anthropologist.

The departmental committee voted two to one against my promotion. The department chair was shocked. Recalling the years of mentoring, she did not understand how or why the vote was no. Despite the negative vote, I still had the support of the department chair, whose approval was a separate step in the process. After the department and chair's vote, my promotion was in the hands of the college committee and the dean.

Shortly after discovering the departmental vote, I received a one-page letter from the dean stating that the college would not recommend me for promotion. As I look at the letter now, I remain perplexed over the events that took place. Although the dean's letter ended my candidacy, it encouraged me to submit my dossier later. The letter did not indicate a reason; it only stated that I did not receive a recommendation for promotion. There were, however, some interesting sections in the letter. It declared, for example, that the university guidelines for promotion and tenure said that candidates must "have excellent, meritorious, and substantial performance." The letter added that "further peer-reviewed works would strengthen your application. I encourage you to publish additional works and resubmit your application."

At this point, I was exhausted. The academic year I submitted my dossier was fraught with personal upheaval. First, I was going through a difficult divorce. A month or two before the deadline to submit my dossier, I experienced what I believe was the intent to portray my eight-year-old son as violent by the private elementary school he attended. I received a call from the head of the school stating that my child was choking and punching another student. I gathered my support system and made a visit to the school to find out that he was only being an eight-year-old, simply touching another child, not choking or punching him. My response was to withdraw him from the school. Then I had to decide what public school he would attend. Because I was dissatisfied with the schools where we lived and knew that because of the divorce I would eventually relocate, I made the decision to move that same week. Between the divorce, the move, the withdrawal from one school, and registration in another school, I had nothing left to give once my candidacy for promotion ended.

However, after consultation with the department chair, colleagues outside the college, and the chief diversity officer at the institution, I made the decision to appeal. It was a tough decision, but as a woman who is deeply spiritual, I was at peace with moving forward with the appeal. I would be remiss if I did not mention a chance meeting with a Black woman at a coffee shop. After I met with the department chair to go over my appeal letter, I was walking to my car and saw a sister with locs sitting outside. We both said hello. Then she told me that God said to move forward with what I was doing. To me, that was confirmation to keep moving forward.

I wrote a short letter to the provost that succinctly provided the basis for my appeal. My argument was that there was no indication that I did not meet the departmental criteria and that the suggestion to publish additional works was arbitrary because it provided no substantive information. Instead, the negative recommendation for promotion used the words "excellent, meritorious, and substantial," claiming they derived from university guidelines. To this day, I have no idea what guidelines they were referring to or what documents contained this language. In fact, other parts of the letter provided references in policies, but there were no references to this language that implied that my candidacy was not excellent, meritorious, or substantial without any evidence supporting such claims.

It was another month before I knew the fate of my case. During that time, I experienced a personal health challenge and ended up having emergency surgery. I got news about my appeal during my recovery. I remember vividly the early morning call from the department's administrator one day in June 2014, asking if I had read my email. Although I wanted to sit up in my bed, I could not. I asked her to hold, and I searched my emails. I found the letter from the provost overturning the decision and promoting me to full professor. As I cried, I could only thank God for guiding me through this tough season.

In hindsight, I wonder about the makeup of the faculty and administrators who reviewed my candidacy. All reviewers were white men except for the department chair, one external reviewer, and the provost who overturned the decision. In other words, both the department and college committees consisted of white men. The dean was also a white man.

The pathway to leadership in higher education often begins as individuals reach the rank of full professor. Wolfe and Dilworth (2015) argue that diversity in leadership challenges homogeneity in leadership. My contention is that because a majority of those reviewing my candidacy were white men in a setting that is still disproportionately heavy on white male leadership, there was social closure: "Social closure exists when a group of individuals actively engage in efforts to retain their positions of power and control because outsiders are considered inferior and ineligible" (Wolfe and Dilworth 2015, 685).

Denying my candidacy to full professor was part of these efforts to maintain power. Moreover, during this dean's administration, more than half of the department chairs were replaced, and the college's leadership looked like the old boy network instead of being reflective of the student body, which hovers around 20 percent Black. Wolfe and Dilworth (2015) note that Black administrators in higher education often face marginalization, a lack of formal ranking and promotions processes, and a tradition of biases that excludes nonwhites in leadership positions. In short, positions, particularly those in leadership, in higher education sometimes rely on informal networks and recommendations that depend less on qualifications and more on whether a candidate fits into the governing/leading group.

In many institutions, faculty must attain the rank of full professor to be in leadership. Efforts to stop my promotion to full professor would have in essence stopped my efforts to be in leadership. Thus, the only way to hinder my ability to move into leadership was to create some additional requirements that would be deemed meritorious. Although I was selected to serve as the interim department chair and received a decent evaluation, I was told that I was not chosen to be a finalist for the permanent position. After the first search for a permanent department chair failed, I specifically asked the dean what I needed to do to strengthen my application for the permanent position. I was told that I would need national stature to be competitive, which was not listed as a qualification to be chair. Thus, my "perceived" lack of credentials was used to exclude me from leadership via the path of promotion. The people making decisions appear liberal, neutral, and objective, while maintaining that meritocracy is what precipitates tenure, promotion, and pay raises. But the reality is that these same concepts, particularly meritocracy, are used to limit career advancement without concrete evidence to support the lack of merit. Scholars' use of critical race theory along with discussions with others in higher education helped me understand the intricacies of what has taken place in my career over the last decade. I thus conclude in my case that gatekeepers worked to limit my opportunity. Despite all that happened, I share this story to help others in dismantling stories of institutional liberalism, neutrality, objectivity, and meritocracy so they will know that they too have a counter story and that

> it is better to speak
> remembering
> we were never meant to survive
>
> —Audre Lorde, A Litany for Survival (1978)

Notes

1. My graduate program required students to pass comprehensive exams in three fields within political science. The fields offered included American government, public administration, methodology, comparative politics, international politics, and political theory. I chose public administration, methodology, and American government.

2. One of the fields I chose, American government, required an additional, comprehensive exam in at least one subfield, which included political parties and interest groups, political behavior, state and local government, or institutions. I chose state and local government.

References

Alexander-Floyd, N. G. 2018. "Why Political Scientists Don't Study Black Women, but Historians and Sociologists Do: On Intersectionality and the Remapping of the Study of Black Political Women." In *Black Women in Politics: Demanding Citizenship, Challenging Power*, edited by J. S. Jordan-Zachery and N. G. Alexander-Floyd, 5–26. New York: State University of New York.

Bell, D. A. 2000. "*Brown v. Board of Education*: Forty-five Years after the Fact." *Ohio Northern Law Review* 26: 1–171.

Bernabe, A. J. 2022. "Texas A&M Basketball Coach Pushes Back after Criticism for Wearing Pink Pants on the Court." February 18. https://abc7chicago.com/sydney-carter-coach-pink-pants-texas-am-basketball/11577310/.

Biblia. nd. *Ecclesiastes* 3:1–7. New Living Translation. https://biblia.com/bible/nlt/ecclesiastes/3/1-7.

Boiling, Jessica Reid. 2020. "Tracking the Machine: A Timeline of UA's 'Underground' Greek Organization." *Crimson White*. https://cw.ua.edu/65356/news/tracking-the-machine-a-timeline-of-uas-underground-greek-organization/.

Crenshaw, K. 1997. "Color Blindness, History, and the Law." In *The House That Race Built: Black Americans, U.S. Terrain*, edited by W. Lubiano, 280–88. New York: Pantheon.

Crenshaw, K. W., and A. J. Ritchie. 2015. "Say Her Name: Resisting Police Brutality against Black Women." Say Her Name. https://www.aapf.org/_files/ugd/62e126_405fa83edf564e58b122d14560fac4b9.pdf.

DeCuir, J. T. and A. D. Dixson. 2004. "So When It Comes Out, They Aren't That Surprised That It Is There: Using Critical Race Theory as a Tool of Analysis of Race and Racism in Education." *Educational Researcher* 33, no. 5: 26–31. https://doi.org/10.3102/0013189X033005026

Delgado, R. 1995. *Critical Race Theory: The Cutting Edge*. Philadelphia, PA: Temple University Press.

Dunbar, Paul Laurence. 1922. "We Wear the Mask." *The Complete Poems of Paul Laurence Dunbar*. New York: Dodd, Mead.

Fields, L. N., and R. M. Cunningham-Williams. 2021. "Experiences with Imposter Syndrome and Authenticity at Research-Intensive Schools of Social Work: A Case Study on Black Female Faculty." *Advances in Social Work* 21, nos. 2/3: 354–73. https://doi.org/10.18060/24124.

Harris, C. 1993. Whiteness as Property. *Harvard Law Review* 106: 1707–91.

Hiraldo, P. 2010. "The Role of Critical Race Theory in Higher Education." *Vermont Connection* 31, no. 1: 53–59. https://scholarworks.uvm.edu/tvc/vol31/iss1/7.

Hirshfield, L. E., and T. D. Joseph. 2012. "'We Need a Woman, We Need a Black Woman': Gender, Race, and Identity Taxation in the Academy." *Gender & Education* 24, no. 2: 213–27. doi:10.1080/09540253.2011.606208

hooks, bell. 2015. *Sisters of the Yam: Black Women and Self-Recovery.* New York: Routledge.

Jeffries, M. 2021. "POV: Where Are the Tenured Black Female Professors? What We Need to Do to Support Black Women in Academia." September 14. https://www.bu.edu/articles/2021/pov-where-are-the-tenured-black-female-professors/?fbclid=IwAR2FJqd3d-1A4UPXjzU1yaPyZgdUaUsvIqSHsw-ZljWc3-hwCj04gmbSahk.

June, A. W., and B. O'Leary. 2021. "How Many Black Women Have Tenure on Your Campus? Search Here." *Chronicle of Higher Education.* May 27. chronicle.com.

King, Athena M. 2023. "Let's Retire the Term 'Fit': Strategies to Improve Faculty Heterogeneity." *PS: Political Science & Politics* 56, no. 1: 118–22. https://doi.org/10.1017/S1049096522000853.

Koplon, S. 2021. "UAB Named America's No. 1 Best Large Employer 2021 by Forbes." February 11. https://www.uab.edu/news/campus/item/11852-uab-named-america-s-no-1-best-large-employer-2021-by-forbes.

Ladson-Billings, G. 1999. "Just What Is Critical Race Theory, and What's It Doing in a Nice Field Like Education?" In *Race Is . . . Race Isn't: Critical Race Theory and Qualitative Studies in Education*, edited by L. Parker, D. Deyhle, and S. Villenas, 7–30. Boulder, CO: Westview Press.

Ladson-Billings, G., and W. Tate. 1995. "Toward a Critical Race Theory of Education." *Teachers College Record* 97: 47–68.

Lewis, Angela K. 2000. "African-American Conservatism: A Longitudinal and Comparative Study." PhD dissertation, University of Tennessee. https://trace.tennessee.edu/utk_graddiss/1998.

———. 2013. *Conservatism in the Black Community: To the Right and Misunderstood.* New York: Routledge.

López, G. R. 2003. "The (Racially Neutral) Politics of Education: A Critical Race Theory Perspective." *Educational Administration Quarterly* 39, no. 1: 68–94. https://doi-org.uab.idm.oclc.org/10.1177/0013161X02239761.

Lorde, Audre. 2020. "A Litany for Survival." In *The Selected Works of Audre Lorde*, 283–84. New York: Norton.

———. 2007. *Sister Outsider: Essays and Speeches.* Berkeley, CA: Crossing Press.

McClaurin, I. 2021. "Airing UNC Chapel Hill's Dirty Diversity Laundry—My Experience & You Be the Judge." *Medium.* https://irmamcclaurin.medium.com/airing-unc-chapel-hills-dirty-diversity-laundry-my-experience-you-be-the-judge-5afb7d25a9ea.

McGill Qualitative Health Research Group (MQHRG). nd. "Qualitative or Quantitative Research?" https://www.mcgill.ca/mqhrg/resources/what-difference-between-qualitative-and-quantitative-research.

Morçöl, G., and N. P. Ivanova. 2010. "Methods Taught in Public Policy Programs: Are Quantitative Methods Still Prevalent?" *Journal of Public Affairs Education* 16, no. 2: 255–77. http://www.jstor.org/stable/25676125.

Newton, V. A. 2022. "Hypervisibility and Invisibility: Black Women's Experiences with Gendered Racial Microaggressions on a White Campus." *Sociology of Race and Ethnicity* 9, no. 2: 164–78. https://doi.org/10.1177/23326492221138222.

Odihi Foundation. 2021. "It's Time We Stop Policing Black Women's Bodies." Odihi Foundation. April 29. https://www.odihi.com/post/it-s-time-we-stop-policing-black-women-s-bodies?gclid=CjwKCAiAioifBhAXEiwApzCztuLGY2Ejpr EI9C1CttfC3lbOhakAxoU5R_gWFRK2j-9eKiKhGnDDAxoCKVwQAvD_ BwE.

Parker, L., and O. Villalpando. 2007. "A Racialized Perspective on Education Leadership: Critical Race Theory in Educational Administration." *Educational Administration Quarterly* 43, no. 5: 519–24. https://doi-org.uab.idm.oclc.org/10.1177/0013161X07307795.

Peck, M. S. 1985. *The Road Less Traveled: A New Psychology of love, Traditional Values, and Spiritual Growth*. Large print ed. New York: Walker.

Plaut, V. C., C. A. Romano, K. Hurd, and E. Goldstein. 2020. "Diversity Resistance Redux." In *Diversity Resistance in Organizations*, edited by K. M. Thomas, 103–22. 2nd ed. New York: Routledge. https://doi.org/10.4324/9781003026907.

Porter, S. R. 2007. "A Closer Look at Faculty Service: What Affects Participation on Committees?" *Journal of Higher Education* 78: 523–40.

Rohan, A. 2021. "Forbes Names UAB One of America's Best Employers for Diversity." April. https://www.uab.edu/news/campus/item/11983-forbes-names-uab-one-of-america-s-best-employers-for-diversity.

Schwartz-Shea, P., and D. Yanow. 2002. "'Reading' 'Methods' 'Texts': How Research Methods Texts Construct Political Science." *Political Research Quarterly* 55, no. 2: 457–86. https://doi-org.uab.idm.oclc.org/10.1177/106591290205500209.

Settles, Iris H., NiCole T. Buchanan, and Kristie Dotson. 2019. "Scrutinized but Not Recognized: (In)Visibility and Hypervisibility Experiences of Faculty of Color." *Journal of Vocational Behavior* 113: 62–74. https://doi.org/10.1016/j.jvb.2018.06.003.

Shepard, B. 2019. "UAB Graduate and Professional Programs Again Ranked among the Nation's Best." March 12. https://www.uab.edu/news/campus/item/10270-uab-graduate-and-professional-programs-again-ranked-among-the-nation-s-best.

Shinji, T. 2018. "What Are Institutions?" In *The Cognitive Basis of Institutions: A Synthesis of Behavioral and Institutional Economics*, 1–32. Amsterdam: Netherlands: Elsevier Science.

Smith, R. C. 2010. *Conservatism and Racism, and Why in America They Are the Same*. New York: State University of New York Press.

Smith, W. A., T. J. Yosso, and D. G. Solórzano. 2007. "Racial Primes and Black Misandry on Historically White Campuses: Toward Critical Race Accountability in Educational Administration." *Educational Administration Quarterly* 43: 559–85. doi:10.1177/0013161X07307793.

Tripp Umbach. nd. "The Economic and Community impacts of the University of Alabama at Birmingham. Report." https://www.uab.edu/impact/.

Turner, C. S. V. 2002. "Women of Color in Academe: Living with Multiple Marginality." *The Journal of Higher Education* 73: 74–94.

Wallace, S. L., and A. K. Lewis. 2007. "Compassionate Conservatism and African Americans: Politics Puts Faith to Work and Gains New Allies?" *Journal of African American Studies* 10: 75–93. https://doi-org.ezproxy3.lhl.uab.edu/10.1007/s12111-007-9009-2.

Well, I. B. 2014. *The Light of Truth: Writings of an Anti-Lynching Crusader*. New York: Penguin.

Wolfe, B. L., and P. P. Dilworth. 2015. "Transitioning Normalcy: Organizational Culture, African American Administrators, and Diversity Leadership in Higher Education." *Review of Educational Research* 85, no. 4: 667–97. https://doi.org/10.3102/0034654314565667.

Wooten, T. 2019. *Portrayals of Black Women on Television & the Shift in Their Representation: An Analysis of* Scandal *and* Insecure. Carbondale: Southern Illinois University Carbondale.

12

On Becoming a Black Woman Political Scientist

Rising to the Rank of Full Professor at a Major R1 Institution

EVELYN M. SIMIEN

My father always said, "your mouth is going to get you in trouble." To that my mother replied, "You and Evelyn can shake hands. She's just like you."

This chapter is informed by my formative years, from childhood and adolescence to early adulthood, emphasizing parental influences, especially the role of my father. I write as someone who believes she entered the academy with an attitude that was and has been unapologetic and irreverent at times. I urge others to read my story with caution and not as a prescription for how to behave in academe, given the risks. My actions could have easily backfired and been perceived as offensive, resulting in denial of tenure and promotion opposite a different set of actors. Looking back, I am not sure if my behavior is explained by youth and immaturity or a sense of entitlement and brazen self-confidence due to class privilege. I became increasingly aware of my identity in terms of race, class, and gender at various stages of my educational career. More specifically, I developed a sophisticated understanding of interlocking systems of oppression through lived experience and formal training as a Black woman political scientist. I write as an African American woman who holds a unique space in the discipline, with openness about my path thus far.

Recalibrating the way I viewed myself—while navigating barriers on account of my race and gender, including other axes of identity like class, age, and motherhood status—was as impactful in determining my quality of life as my success in the political science profession. I am presently a tenured, full professor in the Department of Political Science at the University of Connecticut. I am the only African American woman at this rank in the College of Liberal Arts and Sciences at the university. While I specialize in American politics, I am recognized as an interdisciplinary scholar. I am widely read and cited in such fields as sociology, history, philosophy, and psychology. I am also the mother of three young children, including two toddlers, and a young teenager. Such an active familial role at this stage in my life course is not the norm, given I am of advanced maternal age—that is, fifty years old as of this writing. Given there is so little about Black fathers who are present and functioning in the family home, I feel it is important to highlight the ways that a father-daughter relationship can influence a Black woman's career trajectory in a predominately male profession. Scholars have traditionally sought to understand gender socialization of Black girls through the mother-daughter relationship. Herein lies my contribution, given the ways paternal presence in a two-parent household influenced my own gender performance and professional socialization.

This chapter is an exploration of how I interpret and make meaning of the father-daughter relationship described here, with the hope that I do not reify notions of respectability or heteronormative patriarchal ideas of being. I consider how interactions with my father and his advice enabled me to successfully navigate obstacles in the profession with willful resistance and strike a healthy work-life balance. This chapter will provide a few examples that attest to the value of such a familial relationship insofar as it might explain the ways that gender, race, and class simultaneously shaped the experiences, behavior, and influence of this Black woman political scientist but *not* from a deficit perspective. If we wish to contest the power-sustaining hierarchies that work in tandem with a bootstrap mentality, I think we might glean a few life lessons from successful Black women in the profession who occupy top leadership positions.

Recognizing the ways that multiple axes of identity simultaneously contribute to differences in our personal and professional lives as well as our representational responsibilities is very necessary to build new pathways forward. Being actively present and publicly visible in academic institutions at every rank, but especially at the most senior and administrative levels, absent any serious physical or mental health constraints is a notable accomplishment. Black women like me are vulnerable to chronic stress, a result of early health deterioration and the cumulative impact of our persistent, high-effort coping with racism and sexism, as we strive to put others at ease and counteract negative stereotypes of ourselves (Alexander-Floyd 2015; Geronimus et al. 2006; Michelson and Lavariega Monforti 2021). As I have argued elsewhere, the belief that Black women are tireless, deeply caring, and invulnerable has helped maintain exploitative hierarchal arrangements at home and in the workplace (Beauboeuf-Lafontant 2009; Simien 2020), while contributing to negative health outcomes and such preexisting conditions as diabetes, hypertension, and heart disease. For Black women in the profession, such "weathering" and aging patterns exact a physical and mental toll. While our health is influenced by a variety of factors, this chapter will spotlight the impact of having paternal involvement as it relates to strategies I've adopted to remain mentally and physically well, knowing disproportionate service and exclusion are not mitigated by my rank as a full professor.

My Backstory: How I Came to Be

It was my father's desire to have a third child, and preferably a son, which resulted in my conception despite advanced maternal age. Whereas my mother was in her late thirties, my father was in his early forties. As I often say, I was no accident. To the contrary, I was negotiated, and the terms of this agreement resulted in my father having to give up smoking cigars and competing in professional automobile races with his 1967 Ford Mustang called the "Texas Rattler." Little did I know, or come to understand, the significance of this sacrifice during my childhood. I was mesmerized by several first-place trophies with cars mounted on top of them, which were safely locked away in a cabinet. As I sifted through family photos, I learned of my father's former smoking habit and past auto racing. As my mother explained, "I was not going to drag no baby to a racetrack," and "you can't be smoking around no baby." In return, my father was granted the privilege of naming me: Evelyn Marie. My mother had named my older siblings: Patricia Ann and Pamela Ann.

Birth Order

The youngest of three girls, I was affectionately called the "baby" of the family. Given I was fifteen years younger than my oldest sibling, I was a toddler when she graduated from high school. In fact, we have a family photo of me smiling alongside her, holding on to her leg as she stands next to me in her cap and gown. I have little memory of having shared space and time with her as siblings normally interact in their family home. I am aware, however, of the racial trauma she faced integrating into the same schools I attended more than a decade later. She had horror stories of being taunted and called the N-word by her white classmates in the 1960s. I was ten years younger than the middle sister, and I have some memories of her being in high school, attending the local university (McNeese State University), and working full-time at the shopping mall. I held her in high esteem, as she graduated with academic honors in the top percentile of her graduating class. Both sisters were out of the house, entering marital relationships and early adulthood, when I was still a young adolescent. Given the age difference between me and these two older siblings, I experienced my formative years as an only child and developed a close relationship with my parents.

About Me and My People: Where I Came From

I was born and raised in Lake Charles, Louisiana. Based on the 2020 US Census, the city is the fifth largest in the state, with a population of 84,872 residents. Located thirty miles from the Gulf of Mexico, it sits on the banks of the Calcasieu River in southwest Louisiana. The city is known for petrochemical refineries and gambling casinos, with the Calcasieu Parish School Board being the largest employer, and L'Auberge Casino resort being the second. I grew up in a low-income, overwhelmingly Black neighborhood located on the north end called Goosport, with 68 percent of children living in poverty. The residents were mostly sales and service employees working minimum wage jobs.

African American entrepreneurs like my father owned beauty salons, funeral homes, grocery stores, and barbershops in this neighborhood. My father, who was a self-employed masonry contractor, owned several rental properties. We lived on the same street as other affluent Black business owners amid the poorest Black residents in the city. Since white-owned businesses did not operate in our neighborhoods, Black business owners did not face economic competition. Our five-bedroom, five-bath home, which included two kitchens, an indoor swimming pool, and an attached five-car garage, stood on the corner of a popular intersection. Our residential property took up a few city blocks.

The Salience of My Dad's Provider Role

My father's paternal role as an economic provider was clear; however, it was not viewed as his singular purpose. His ability to provide a secure economic system facilitated the relationship between his occupational ambition and successful fathering. As my dad would often say before his dementia set in, he was the "top dog" between Black and white. Still, he was no workhorse. My father actively engaged in other male-oriented recreational activities outside the home, like fishing and hunting wild game on the weekends. His personality was bombastic, no-nonsense, and honest. He had quite a sense of humor, which made him affable to others. He was admired and respected for his work ethic. My father possessed only a third-grade education but proudly touted his accomplishments, as they were tied to wealth accumulation and property ownership, absent any debt.

Examples of Nonnormative Parenting for a Black Girl

Most of my father's clients were wealthy doctors and lawyers who spared no expense when building their large, extravagant custom-made brick homes. My father also built large commercial buildings like offices, grocery stores, and banks. He had a special skill set, such that he could customize the brickwork to resemble any image or patterned design if he was provided a picture—for example, a pastor of a church requested that the brickwork resemble a cross above the main entrance. At an early age, I came to understand the costs per square feet to lay brick for an entryway, a floor or sidewalk, even a mailbox, and so on. I was asked to sit down, look at architectural plans for homes, and help him "figure" the cost of building—specifically, the labor and materials. The nature of his work created a powerful dynamic, having a carry-home effect that left a lasting impression on me as a child. These two separate and relatively distinct spheres—work and family—formed a compatible symbiotic relationship such that the occupational sphere facilitated his father-daughter interactions with me.

I was enrolled in the same private schools as the children of his white employers. My father's own limited education fostered his desire for me to acquire the education that he never received, and I was instructed to "focus on my lesson" in accordance with this purpose. He was a father-husband-provider within the family system. His role as such was not that of the traditional patriarch, but he was egalitarian, expressive, and more involved than most fathers of his day; after all, he was born in 1933. That is not to suggest that he attended PTA and other school activities, but he was present and available for other father-daughter activities indicative of his own parental style and paternal involvement. So, for example, I was subject to a "pop quiz" on Saturday mornings. It entailed me showing my father that I could open the hood of my car, identify the engine and other parts, and demonstrate that I could change a flat tire and check the motor's oil level. To his chagrin, I quipped, "Daddy, I'm a girl" to avoid such a test. I had come to understand normative standards of hegemonic femininity and thus expressed little interest in learning that which seemingly conflicted with my identity as a cis female and corresponding gender role expectations of the dominant society. He replied, "Pay attention, little girl. Your daddy ain't always gonna be around, and you got to know how to do these things."

By disrupting normative parenting practices, my Black father set up contradictory expectations of me as a Black girl, who must negotiate femininity within a racialized gender structure. In his view, I was fully capable of learning some basic mechanics of a car and overcoming adverse circumstances related to its maintenance. To change a flat tire or check the motor's oil required that I be self-reliant and independent, not fragile or dependent. I was admonished for my verbal retort associated with such ascribed female traits as submissiveness and domesticity. I was expected to reject gendered societal expectations, replacing them with a more positive understanding of self as being strong and resilient, not vulnerable.

Other agentic stereotypes of men were reinforced by my dad—for example, one of the most influential things he did, which left an indelible mark, was to have me shadow him as a child. He instructed me always to pay attention when he conducted business and negotiated major purchases, for which he always paid in full, and with cash. I recall accompanying him to automobile dealerships to purchase new vehicles and my feet dangling from the chair upon which I sat and being told, "Little girl, watch and learn." My father briefed me before and after these meetings. I can recall my father's mantra: "I pay the cost to be the boss," and those words continue to resonate with me today. He insisted that in negotiations, you tell people what you want unequivocally, as if you demand nothing less. He had a tremendous influence on my life, as did my mother, who also possessed a forthright and assertive personality.

My mother dropped out of school in the eighth grade at the age of sixteen. Her parents had enrolled her in school late (by years), and so she was academically behind. She secured employment as a maid in white households to sustain herself as a single person who lived at home with her father. Her parents had divorced while she was growing up, and it was her father who raised her and her four brothers as a single parent. Upon marrying my father, she left paid domestic work and stayed home full-time. Once my father decided to go into business and work for himself, she began investing in real estate, which translated into a second income and their retirement nest egg. Together, my parents renovated homes for the purpose of renting them. While still in high school, I was asked to collect the rent from their tenants. I remember feeling uncomfortable about this task as a teenager. Being assertive was a male-typical trait, and I felt pressure to perform as my mother did opposite her tenants. She was a tough act to follow. My mother came across as forceful. She was direct and no-nonsense, even courageous. She charged late fees, issued warnings for late payment, called the police, filed eviction notices, and so on. Correspondingly, my mother had her own mantra, "I'm not going to let these people kill me," and those words continue to resonate with me today.

I can't say that I was consciously aware of how my race and gender identities intersected in these sociocultural contexts. I could not foresee how the father-daughter interactions described above, or my mother's own role modeling, would influence my gender role performance and behavior in the adult phase of my life course. At issue for me would be identity salience—specifically, which identities would be enacted in future circumstances and be activated most often. Class had always been at the fore, as was race and gender. Such identities were equivalent, overlapping, and complementary in situations that were tied to hierarchical arrangements and signaled real meaning.

My personal testimony, as it intersects with certain biographic details and identity categories, will not tell the reader everything they wish to know, but I believe it will be instructive, nonetheless. So, for example, to hear my parents' voices at times—specifically, their respective mantras in my head—has always made it easier for me to say no to less prestigious, time-consuming service that would have slowed my research productivity and, at the same time, say yes to more high-prestige service that, while challenging, afforded me the opportunity for career advancement in administrative roles. In the sections that follow, I intend to explore further the extent to which such personal experiences and the identity categories described above have shaped my journey in life and academe.

St. Margaret Catholic School, 1979–1987

Starting in either kindergarten or first grade, I was selected for the gifted and talented program. I remember I was the only girl among a group of white boys chosen to participate in this program. I also recall sitting in the front of the classroom purposely and constantly raising my hand to ask questions because I knew when I went home no parent could help me with my homework. Neither parent could read or write well. At a young age, I felt solely responsible for my learning. And so, I was intentional about asking questions during classroom instruction. I would read and reread the material as much as necessary. No one had to tell me to do my homework when I came home. For me, it was out of necessity that I actively participated in class. As a result, I was often identified as the "student of the month" and rewarded with lots of praise from teachers. My parents, especially my father, always struck me as neutral about my academic performance. I heard the same refrain of praise, "Good job. Keep up the good work. You're doing what you're supposed to be doing." I came to believe what I did was nothing extraordinary but commonplace, despite awards and recognition, even long after graduate school and well into my academic career as a political scientist.

St. Louis Catholic High School, 1988–1992

While all the Black girls sat together in the school cafeteria, I believe the elementary and high schools I attended made a deliberate effort at times to break down cultural barriers between people of different races. I attended predominately white private schools from K through 12. My friends and I were not loud, underperforming Black girls. There was no achievement gap that I was aware of, and we were thriving academically. I don't recall struggling with impostor syndrome. As I progressed from elementary to high school, I began to think more about what it meant to be Black (without fully understanding the ways in which class and gender intersected with that identity). I have few salient memories of elementary and high school; however, I do recall times when as a child on the playground I was singled out because my mother drove a Cadillac and we possessed an indoor swimming pool. Considering how young Black children in reactive defensiveness to white microaggressions in elementary school came to reference a luxury automobile and inground swimming pool as evidence to counter a commonly held stereotype of Black people as poor is vexing to say the least. While I had grown up amid poverty in a predominately Black neighborhood, engulfed by housing projects on a street that was home to wealthy Black entrepreneurs including my father, I would respond with the same reactive defensiveness. I too could not resist the proprietary impulse to confront white peers when they appropriated Black culture or disparaged racial or ethnic identities. One such episode occurred when a group of white students dressed in blackface for a presentation before their English class at my high school. I was in AP (advanced placement) English at the time, and I had only heard of the incident. Nevertheless, we (the clique of Black girls in AP English) demanded a face-to-face meeting with members of this group that had decided to dress in blackface. The teachers accommodated our request. Upon looking back, I realize that our teachers probably regretted that decision. As I recall, the confrontation resulted in one member of that group shedding "white girl tears," and the clique (me included) had no mercy during this difficult dialogue. To put it bluntly, they got their ass handed to them.

The high school I attended was intentional about building community, helping students connect across lines of difference, and cultivating leadership with Christian values at the fore. With an enrollment that averages between 500 and 600 students in total, including grades 9–12, my memory recalls roughly about ten African American students out of sixty or so total students in my graduating class in 1992. I feel I was an average student, even though I maintained honor roll for all four years at St. Louis Catholic High School. It was and remains an academically rigorous high school and ranks favorably—for example, of the Best Catholic High Schools, it ranks 14 of 49 and of the Best College Prep High Schools, it ranks 20 of 109 in Louisiana (as of this writing). I was no straight A student; however, I was on the academic track and college bound, having completed honors and AP courses with As and Bs. I was a solid student. Still, I never thought of myself as an exceptional student. I presumed my academic performance was typical of most students enrolled in the school, including members of my friendship circle. I think this was the case because my friends almost always had higher GPAs than I, with their cumulative grade point averages being closer to a 4.0 or higher. This seemed to be the case while I attended Xavier University of Louisiana (XULA) as well. While not consciously aware, I seemingly gravitated toward overachievers, many of whom I felt outperformed me even though I was no slacker.

Xavier University of Louisiana, 1992–1996

By August of 1992, I had moved into an on-campus dorm and begun my freshman year at XULA, where I majored in political science and minored in mass communications, with a concentration in broadcasting. My choice to attend XULA was deliberate. While I considered applying to Louisiana State University, I was intent on attending a historically Black college or university (HBCU) because I had attended majority white, private schools from K through 12. I had always been one of only a few African American students enrolled in these schools and one of the few among them not receiving a needs-based scholarship. My father took pride in his ability to pay the tuition in full, and he did the same at Xavier. It was not until I walked past the long enrollment and registration lines for students with loans and federal grants that I came to realize my class privilege. I would enter the gymnasium and go to a separate table for those who had paid their tuition and student fees early. While I would be in and out within a matter of minutes, others with such loans were in line for hours. When I was in the campus bookstore, I purchased all new versus used books at the start of each semester. I witnessed other students struggle to make tough decisions over which books they'd purchase. I, on the other hand, went through the aisles shopping for books that were not required for my classes but looked interesting. I purchased clothing and other miscellaneous items at whim.

On one occasion, I told a student to put all her books on the conveyor belt at the register. I had witnessed her struggle with making the tough decision of which books to purchase and which books to leave on the shelf. She could not afford them all. I paid for them. My mother later asked why my bill for books was significantly higher that semester and when I told her this story, she simply replied: okay. I never returned my books to the bookstore for cash, as I recall observing this practice with intrigue. I had no interest in standing in a long line for such a minimum return. I kept some books and donated others to local libraries.

My allowance or budget for the first semester I enrolled at XULA amounted to one lump sum of $5K deposited into a bank account with my name. Still, I called home for more money by midterm. My mother made a deposit in the amount of $500 upon request, as she would again and again. Then, my aunts intervened and reprimanded my mother. I was not happy with my aunts, given I now had a stricter allowance. I was limited to $500 a month. Though I had always had the meal plan, I had not stepped foot in the school cafeteria until I had this stricter allowance. By comparison, I had friends who cooked meals in their dorm rooms on a hot plate. We had no kitchenettes. I had one friend who, like me, called home with similar requests for money. Her parents, who were both schoolteachers, made deposits of $20 into her bank account at a time. Upon learning this, I pulled out my wallet and handed her $20. These experiences left quite an impression on me. My friends were middle class, wealthy, and poor. The experience of attending an HBCU was humbling and inspiring at the same time. Upon entering a friend's dorm room, I asked why there was a single dollar bill in a frame above her bed. My friend replied that it was the only thing her father had ever given her, and it was her motivation for becoming a medical doctor. My friend was from the Mississippi Delta, and she had graduated valedictorian from her all-Black high school. She had also been the school's homecoming queen. Her mother worked in a meat-packaging plant and had raised five kids alone. I was in awe of her. By graduation, she had been accepted into the medical school of her choice.

Purdue University, 1996–2001

In the fall of 1996, I began graduate school at Purdue University. Prior to my arrival, my father expressed concern. He asked, "Don't you care about your family? I mean, if something should happen to you, we can't get to you. Georgia, Mississippi, even Florida would be closer, but Indiana. Oh, you just gonna worry me, worry me, worry me. . . . You already got your first degree; why do you need a second degree?" To that I replied, "Daddy, you just don't understand. I'm trying to get paid. If I get a master's degree, I can double my income." He had wanted me to stay home and apply for a job as a probation officer in the office where my oldest sister worked as an administrative assistant. Despite my father's expressed concerns, he and my mother moved me to West Lafayette, Indiana, that fall of 1996. I recall a huge incoming class of roughly thirty students, with notably three African American women (me included) and maybe six other women. Unfortunately, the other two African American women never completed the program and left early. I recall being one of the youngest members of this incoming class, having only recently graduated back in May of that same year. I observed several of my classmates leave the program in only their first or second year. I would go so far as to describe the program (at the time anyway) as one aimed at weeding out students, with a first-semester course dubbed "boot camp" for new admits. If I recall correctly, the syllabus featured a cartoon image, with a male whose arms were overhead and tied up. The mouth was gagged with a handkerchief.

I personally was stressed for financial reasons, as my funding was determined on a semester to semester basis. The teaching assistantship amounted to tuition remission and a small monthly stipend for nine months only, which meant I had to hustle for employment over the summer to pay rent and other living expenses. By this time, my parents had stopped supporting me financially as they once had during all four years of undergrad. While they continued to pay for my car insurance along with any costly repairs deemed necessary for its maintenance, I was living independently on my own at the age of twenty-two.

While I was not familiar with the financial aid process, because I had never applied for student loans, my white classmates at Purdue assumed that I was familiar with the process. It was just as vexing as when I was singled out as the Black child whose mother drove a luxury vehicle and who had a swimming pool in her backyard, as I had been put on the spot many times to counter stereotypes of Black people as poor. This type of emotional labor in response to microaggressions has since been dubbed the "burden of representation," the "Black tax," and "racial battle fatigue" in academia (Smith et al. 2007). When asked about the financial aid process by white classmates in graduate school, I'd respond with the same reactive defensiveness reminiscent of my early childhood. I would reply, "I know how to write a check, but I don't know anything about a student loan." Given their facial expressions, I think they were in disbelief. To that point, my mother had me write the check and mail in the payment for my college tuition, room, and board at XULA. She would simply glance at the check and add her name to the signature line. For this reason, I could not imagine acquiring a student loan for my degree from Purdue. I intended on graduating debt free. At the time, I had no credit card debt either. So, I went to the director of Multicultural Programs for the graduate school at Purdue and asked to be considered for their Opportunity Doctoral Fellowship. Knowing it was a fellowship used to recruit and not retain students of color, I asked for special consideration. I submitted a revised personal statement, and the committee reviewed my application.

During my tenure at Purdue, I was actively involved in the graduate program. I served as the graduate student representative in the Political Science Department's faculty meetings. I was also highly visible on campus as president of the Black Graduate Student Association. In the classroom, I was outspoken. I could always be relied upon for comment on the reading. Among my peers, I think I am perhaps best known for my direct, and sometimes over-the-top, remarks. So, for example, a fellow grad student who shall remain nameless said the following about my major adviser once he stepped out of the classroom, "Man, he's really busting our balls with all this homework." I replied, "Well, he's not busting my balls because I haven't got any." Besides attending classes, I came into the office daily and worked from the computer lab located on the same floor as the department.

To fully engage and thrust myself onto the scene by holding high-profile leadership positions within the Political Science Graduate Student Association *and* the Black Graduate Student Association at Purdue was a huge benefit to me, given that my service to these respective organizations fostered professional growth and maturation. Still, I had been on the cusp of deciding whether to remain in the graduate program at Purdue or leave with a master's degree because of the stress associated with my funding, as it would be determined from semester to semester. Shortly after deciding I would leave the university; I received the news that I had been awarded the Opportunity Doctoral Fellowship. It is because of this fellowship that I decided to remain in the program, and I completed the PhD in political science within five years. I graduated in 2001 with no student loan debt. By then, I was age twenty-seven.

Purdue was an isolating place. It was ultraconservative. West Lafayette, Indiana, was in the middle of nowhere. When I entered the graduate program in political science, other African American students were far more advanced and closer to finishing their degree with ABD (all but dissertation) status. I was alone in most of the classes I had to take as an Americanist—more specifically, I was usually the only African American student enrolled in the graduate seminars required for those who chose American politics as their major field. I was excluded from study groups that gathered in preparation for the PhD comprehensive exams in American politics. White female members of the study group in question had reported that one white male member of the group had believed I was "an affirmative action student" and made it a condition that I be excluded in exchange for his participation. In this instance, the student in question viewed me as a "token" diversity addition to the graduate program, presumably ill prepared and from low-performing schools.

My exclusion became a matter of controversy in the department, especially when considering I had spent my entire summer under the tutelage of my mentor (Rosalee Clawson) writing answers to past exam questions and meeting with individual faculty for feedback. I think it is fair to say I had become known for possessing an exceptional work ethic as a graduate student in the department. The student who insisted on my exclusion was later referred to as a "son of a bitch" behind closed doors when I was summoned to the department head's office to discuss how the matter could be resolved to my satisfaction.

Such exclusion rendered me an illegitimate member of the graduate program and negated my hard work and accomplishments. Exclusion can take many forms and can occur at the interpersonal and institutional level through such a commonplace practice or norm as organizing a study group in preparation for a comprehensive PhD exam. It is one of the ways graduate students are made to feel excluded, and when we lack said social interactions with our peers it could have deleterious effects and thwart our advancement in the program. Had I been a weaker student and not received mentorship from select members of the faculty in the department, I might have failed miserably. This kind of exclusion can be compounded by research specialization in an emergent field, given that opportunity networks are not universally accessible.

Take, for example, the benefits of conference participation. I traveled to mainstream political science conferences alone—namely, annual meetings for the American Political Science Association and the Southern Political Science Association. I also attended annual meetings of the National Conference of Black Political Scientists (NCOBPS) alone. At the time, there were very few Black women in the discipline, and the membership of NCOBPS was overwhelmingly male, with few (if any) senior Black women who self-identified as Black feminists among its membership. While I had the financial resources to pay in advance of reimbursement, and I was not afraid to travel alone to these conferences, I did so without giving much thought to my status as a "unicorn" in the profession. I was presenting at conferences as my mentor (Rosalee Clawson) had advised me to do. I did so without the benefit of sharing the costs and travel burden with classmates. In the context of NCOBPS, however, it was my gender identity and not my race or class identities that was activated in this professional setting, as was also my ideological commitment to Black feminism. Still, as my father would put it, I was doing what I was supposed to do and that was presenting at academic conferences for professional development and networking opportunities in my "niche" field.

Research agendas have a profound effect on career outcomes, determining the likelihood of possessing a tenure-track job and publishing in peer-reviewed journals (Key and Sumner 2019). As I prepared for the academic job market, I was told I would not find a job by classmates and professors alike on account of my dissertation topic: Black feminist consciousness, using the 1993 National Black Politics Study. Further, I was asked during on-campus visits and especially at job talks: Why is it important that we study Black women? In fact, I told the chair of one search committee at a major research institution who asked me this question repeatedly—at the job talk, one-on-one, and in the presence of the search committee—"I am through explaining to you why it is important that we study Black women. For me it's clear. Matter of fact, it's crystal clear." I returned to Purdue, telling my major adviser that I was confident I would not receive that job offer.

I can also recall being advised to wear a skirt for on-campus interviews versus the pantsuit I wore at the practice job talk by one of the female faculty members who served on my dissertation committee. My reply was this: "What don't you understand? The title of my job talk is Black feminist consciousness." Such unsolicited advice would seemingly suggest that while our assessments of job candidates are formally based on merit and intellectual prowess, adjusting our outward physical appearance can potentially enhance our career opportunities. I was also advised to accept the UConn offer upon receipt and to refrain from negotiation by the same female adviser who suggested that I wear a skirt to on-campus interviews. Instead, I asked the chair of my dissertation for advice. He had been the dean of the College of Liberal Arts and Sciences at Purdue. By the time I had gone on the market, he had stepped down as dean and was serving as the department head for political science. He suggested that I come up with a list of items to negotiate, he'd review it, and we would meet to role play. He and I practiced, or you might say, we rehearsed the negotiation process. I found it to be an invaluable experience.

It has been twenty-plus years since I graduated from the Department of Political Science at Purdue University. Recently, I was selected as a

2024 Distinguished Purdue Alumni Scholar alongside fellow alumni who studied math and engineering—thus, it is a notable accomplishment as a social scientist to be recognized as such. The award is intended to recognize the doctoral alumni of Purdue who have made significant scholarly contributions within their chosen field and in doing so have contributed extensively to the advancement of women in academia. I do not take this award for granted, but continuously strive to be a hands-on mentor. Apprenticing many of whom are first-generation college students, women academics, and faculty of color has been a deliberate goal of mine and one that I have found most rewarding. To that point, I have established an academic "pipeline" program for undergraduate students, launched a summer institute for faculty at any stage of their career who study women and girls of color, and organized a series of wellness retreats for faculty and students alike using discretionary funds, resulting from retention contracts and administrative appointments. My role whether it be as a faculty member or administrator is *not* limited to the classroom, given my identity as a first-generation college student located at the intersection of race and gender identities. Also important is the way in which I "show up" and serve as a role model, helping faculty and students visualize their own professional goals.

My Academic Brand and Work-Life Balance

This subheader and its reference to "my academic brand" says a lot about the commodification of knowledge production and our labor as academics within higher education institutions. It is important to note the ways in which I have experienced the academic culture of exhaustion differently than most, whether that be despite of or because of my own positionality (e.g., race, gender, class, age, marital status, family commitments, seniority in the profession) under stressful and, at times, exploitative work conditions. I am told time and time again by doctors and other health professionals that I am physically fit and healthy—more specifically, my "numbers are perfect." While my medical records show no signs of heart disease, high blood pressure, or diabetes, I do suffer from back pain. I see a chiropractor on a routine basis for adjustments to my upper spine and neck. I am not sure if the pain is solely the result of poor posture, straining to look at the computer or hunching over my desk, or from breastfeeding as well, when there is evidence of scar tissue where backpacks—specifically, the straps—hung from each shoulder in my personal X-rays. The fact that medical professionals have reached agreement that psychological and emotional factors result in back pain worries me and gives me reason for pause. The sheer number of sensational headlines and news reports of biological weathering and its deadly effect on Black women regardless of socioeconomic status run through my mind perpetually. I wonder if there is a silent epidemic in the profession and one we might attribute to interpersonal and systemic abuse in academe, resulting in long-term suffering and premature deaths.

Knowing racial disparities exist, especially for Black mothers, I participate in annual wellness retreats for women of color faculty that are facilitated by two African American women academics who have been promoted to the rank of full professor at research institutions and who are also licensed clinical psychologists. During the retreat, we engage in meditation exercises, circle time, professional development activities, and writing at our own pace. Another practice of mine is scheduling a routine massage and especially doing so when staying at conference hotels with a spa on site. I lost much sleep during the final stages of all three pregnancies, even though I attended the women of color faculty retreat while pregnant and scheduled prenatal massages. I was of advanced maternal age. I feared maternal mortality despite a six-figure salary, first-rate health insurance, paid maternity leave, semester-long sabbaticals, and reduced teaching loads. Notably, I have given birth at the ages of thirty-five, forty-five, and forty-seven without in vitro fertilization. I also exclusively breastfed each child for well over twelve months.

I leveraged my tenured status and scholarly reputation to reclaim my time and focus on my own needs. Retention contracts afforded me course releases and graduate research assistance. I did not teach in the early mornings or late evenings. I did not attend meetings, including faculty meetings, which were scheduled during the lunch hour, because I kept a daily "lunch date" with my infant daughter at the nearby daycare. Prioritizing writing and thinking remained important. I continued to publish peer-reviewed journal articles and scholarly books, albeit moving at a slower pace, ensuring that my own cup was full. My salary afforded me the means to hire someone on the weekends to give me a respite. I also had a partner who leveraged his own senior rank in the US military as a command sergeant major and his career field in human resources, such that he was able to drive or fly on a consistent, routine basis to lend support as well. My own ethic of care required that I establish healthy boundaries and be fully rested at home, which was imperative for me to protect against overexhaustion while nursing a baby and responding to her needs nightly. Taking long baths in my jacuzzi tub and sleeping when the baby slept helped sustain me, as did shopping online for groceries and other necessities that were delivered to my home.

While the academy can disincentivize radical self-care and family growth, it is incumbent upon us to recalibrate ourselves and redefine how we view both our personal and professional lives. The competitive nature of our work and the intense pressure to publish or perish can exact a physical and mental toll. I am acutely aware of this fact. For this reason, I was intentional about my academic brand and the pace at which I met professional deadlines, frequented conferences, and published research. My first monograph, *Black Feminist Voices in Politics* (SUNY Press, 2006), is credited with laying the groundwork for the intellectual advancement of Black women's studies through the examination of Black feminist theory in political science. Using the master's tools—quantitative methods of American behavioral studies—I attempted to mainstream an otherwise marginalized topic—Black feminist consciousness—in a notoriously conservative discipline that privileges large-N survey research. While my line of inquiry, with its emphasis on group consciousness, and research design were compatible with publication guidelines for the most prestigious journals, *Black Feminist Voices in Politics* challenged the narrowness of dominant paradigms that reified race to the neglect of gender while also excluding the perspectives of Black women. Few, if any, political scientists had grasped the importance of mutually constitutive identities in shaping our understanding of American public opinion and political behavior at the time. That single-authored monograph was part of a movement that was paradigm-informing and inspired an astonishing new wave of scholarship (see, e.g., Cohen 1999; Hawkesworth 2003; Berger 2004; Hancock 2004, 2007, 2011, 2016; Simien 2006; Smooth 2006; Jordan-Zachery 2007; Philpot and Walton 2007; Strolovitch 2009; Dhamoon 2011; Harris-Perry 2011; Wadsworth 2011; Alexander-Floyd 2012; Wilson 2013; Brown 2014; Simien 2015; Brown and Gershon 2016). It, along with several peer-reviewed journal articles and book chapters, paved the way for Black women's studies in political science by taking a highly theorized concept (Black feminism) and empirically testing it. The data set on which the first monograph is based, and I am the sole principal investigator—the 2004 National Black Feminist Study—has since been used and referenced by sociologists and psychologists who study feminist attitudes (see, e.g., Harnois 2013; White 2008).

I did this often ignored and undervalued work in concert with others—Nikol Alexander-Floyd, Michele Tracy Berger, Ange-Marie Hancock, Melissa Harris-Perry, Julia Jordan-Zachery, and Wendy Smooth. We were members of roughly the same age cohort, having entered graduate school and begun our professional academic careers as junior faculty with tenure-track jobs at the same time. Early in our respective academic careers, we were labeled "intersectionality scholars" by the discipline and put on a platform at the 2006 annual meeting the American Political Science Association. We were asked to define intersectionality—empirically and theoretically—for the discipline. We conducted research that prioritized the simultaneity of oppression and put African American women at the center of our analysis, much to the chagrin of an even smaller cohort of senior Black women in political science. They, who had essentially built their careers on single-axis approaches that prioritized race over gender, were unsupportive of our research agendas and careers. In my case, there was a deliberate behind-the-scenes effort to sabotage my tenure and promotion to the rank of associate professor by at least one member of this more senior cohort.

Since then, the cohort of Black women previously mentioned and I have all received tenure and promotion from the rank of associate professor to the rank of full professor at major research-intensive universities, and the label—intersectionality scholar—has stuck, emerging as our academic brand. To put it bluntly, however, the study of Black women in politics and women of color studies more generally is not shorthand for intersectionality research despite its intellectual roots and the proprietary impulses of Black feminists to claim it as such (Alexander-Floyd 2012; Nash 2019). Similarly, the study of women and politics does not necessarily qualify as feminist research (Carroll and Zerilli 1993; Lovenduski 1998). While origins and histories are important, as they should be accounted for meaningfully, the theoretical capacity of intersectionality can be misrecognized and distorted by scholars within and beyond the discipline when used only as a demographic or descriptive tool (May 2015). African American women have long been treated as the quintessential intersectional subject in my own work and that of others, but I see no reason intersectionality cannot engage experiences outside of that subjectivity—that being the "holy trinity" of intersectional analysis (race, class, and gender)—by accounting for generational differences, sexual orientation, and marital status, among other axes of identity. To be clear, this recommendation is not to be confused with or misinterpreted as an endorsement of any effort to co-opt intersectionality for broader consumption in the discipline or an "omission project" in the work on intersectionality in political science (Alexander-Floyd 2012; Jordan-Zachery 2014).

University of Connecticut, 2001–Present

This story would not be complete if I failed to mention my introduction to the academy as a junior faculty member starting with my initial hire and the negotiation phase of that process. For starters, I was asked whether I was pregnant. Here's the backstory. I had been offered a one-year postdoctoral fellowship from the Frederick Douglass Institute for African and African American Studies at the University of Rochester at the same time I was offered the tenure-track job in the Department of Political Science as a joint hire with African American Studies at the University of Connecticut. I wanted to accept the postdoc and start the joint appointment at UConn afterward. I requested that the tenure clock be stopped and begin after I had completed the one year at Rochester. It was then that the director of African American Studies at UConn said, "There's only one reason for which you can stop a tenure clock." He then asked, "Are you pregnant?" To that I replied, "Oh my god! That's an illegal question." And so, this was my introduction to the university for which I have now been employed for twenty-plus years. Today, I no longer hold a joint appointment with African American Studies (since renamed Africana Studies), but I am the current director of Africana Studies.

I would describe my tenure and promotion to the rank of associate professor as anticlimactic despite the failed attempt to gatekeep on the part of a senior Black woman in the profession. My department's Promotion, Tenure, and Reappointment (PTR) committee was instrumental in protecting me from this assault and supported my tenure and promotion case without reservation. I would say, however, the opposite about my promotion to the rank of full professor. By contrast, it was extremely negative and involved an appeals process. On September 29, 2016, the Political Science Department's PTR Advisory Committee voted four to one against recommending me for promotion to full professor. I was livid. Since promotion to the rank of associate professor with tenure in 2007, I had produced a second monograph with a major university press (Oxford);

edited an original collection of essays with a highly regarded academic press (Palgrave); edited one symposium for *Polity* and coedited another for *Political Research Quarterly*; and authored or coauthored five peer-reviewed articles, two peer-reviewed book chapters in important collections, and six book reviews; and I had several works in progress. My knee-jerk response was not only to appeal but to go on the job market and apply for faculty positions elsewhere. On October 26, 2016, the PTR Committee met with me to discuss its initial negative findings. By then, I had secured three job interviews from significantly higher ranked PhD-granting programs at aspirant institutions with notable prestige, including an Ivy League. I felt affirmed going into the appeals process.

Despite a total of eight letters out of nine endorsing my promotion to full professor, the department's PTR Committee voted against my case. This alone was extraordinary, considering the minimum number of external letters required by the university was four and I had overwhelming support from twice that number. The committee had reportedly done their own independent assessment of my work, which served as the basis of their decision to override the external reviews. Not a single member of this PTR Committee possessed expertise that aligned with my own—for example, my work on gender and lynching was interdisciplinary and deeply rooted in comparative historical analysis. And so, I asked the question: Which of you is the expert on lynching? Frankly, I wanted to know how members of the department's PTR Committee could justify privileging their own uninformed opinions on this topic over trained experts—specifically, an expert on Black women's history who was recognized by the Obama White House for her contributions to the humanities.

Prior to the meeting, the committee asked me to produce evidence that my articles and books in print had been subject to peer review. I accommodated these requests, knowing I had not published with obscure academic presses or lesser-known journals—for example, Oxford University Press is one of the most highly ranked academic presses in the discipline. *DuBois Review*; *Politics, Groups, and Identities*; and *Politics and Gender* are all highly regarded journals, and each is known for carrying out the standard blind, peer review process. I had received as many as four external reviews for most of my publications, including four external reader reports for the Oxford University Press book. The reviews of the book manuscript were extremely positive and spoke favorably of my scholarly reputation. Given the criticisms select members of the PTR Committee leveled against my forthcoming article, which was scheduled to appear in volume 14, issue 1 of *DuBois Review*, it became evident to me that they had not read my curriculum vitae closely—so, for example, the forthcoming article they criticized harshly had received a best paper award and it had not been the best paper on race or gender and politics but the best paper presented at the conference from which I had received the award. Members of the committee seemed embarrassed when I brought this fact to their attention in addition to my having received a total of three best paper awards over the course of my academic career. Still, they relied heavily on the one negative external letter to build their argument against promotion. I recall asking members of the committee to explain how they could build a case to deny based on one letter when the inverse could not be true—that is, you could not build a case to promote based on one letter in favor and eight opposed, and so I asked directly: Why don't you *want* to promote me?

My impact on the discipline was also reduced to citation counts and impact factor scores. Although I had given several book talks at peer and aspirant institutions and my solo-authored monograph published with Oxford was being taught at Purdue, Stanford, and Princeton, among other schools like Western Michigan State, such examples of impact did not satisfy or qualify as the kind of metric that the majority of members serving on the PTR Committee valued—that is, the PTR Committee said that they had wanted reviews in print of the Oxford book (which had only been released within a few months). Still, there had been several reviews in print for the edited volume, *Gender and Lynching*, and they had been favorable. These same reviews, however, were not referenced in their report. The interdisciplinary nature of my work on gender and lynching had seemingly cost me footing in the discipline—at least, in the minds of select committee members who looked to citation counts as evidence of impact or lack thereof to deny promotion. In response to this line of reasoning, I pulled out a large backpack that I had kept concealed under the table. It was filled to maximum capacity with several texts. I dropped one book after the next for dramatic effect on the table. I had dog-eared, used sticky notes, and highlighted where I had been referenced and quoted in every single one of them. This physical evidence of impact that was undeniable seemingly impressed select committee members. On November 2, 2016, the PTR Committee met for its final deliberations and voted three to two in favor of recommending me for promotion to full professor. From that point forward, I had unanimous support from my department head, CLAS dean, and the Dean's Council. I have since coauthored the guidelines for promotion from associate to full professor and cochaired the PTR Committee for the Political Science Department. I have also served on the faculty review board that assesses specific university-wide cases for PTR at the provost level. Since my promotion to the rank of full professor in 2017, I remain the only African American woman at this rank in the College of Liberal Arts and Sciences at the University of Connecticut.

Conclusion

If you ask me, any woman who has gotten promoted to the most senior rank at a major R1 institution in political science is a bad ass—period. I give credit to my parents for encouraging me to act boldly and to take risks, such that I have been able to ask difficult questions, publish work outside of the mainstream, and leverage my own institutional power for personal health and wellness. No story regarding my ability to balance competing demands absent physical and mental strain that results in debilitating illness for most Black women in the profession would be complete without my reflections on the father-daughter relationship and, to a lesser extent, the mother-daughter relationship described here.

My father passed away on March 21, 2022. I began writing this chapter before his death. The writing process has since felt serendipitous, as I bring closure to my final thoughts on this academic journey, with the influences of my father weighing heavily on me in the aftermath of his funeral. To know me is to know my dad, honestly. He lived to be eighty-nine years old. I reconcile his absence in my life, knowing I was the daughter that grew up to be most like him, living by his example. May he rest in peace.

References

Alexander-Floyd, Nikol G. 2012. "Disappearing Acts: Reclaiming Intersectionality in the Social Sciences in a Post-Black Feminist Era." *Feminist Formations* 24, no. 1: 1–25.
———. 2015. "Women of Color, Space Invaders, and Political Science: Practical Strategies for Transforming Institutional Practices." *PS: Political Science and Politics* 48, no. 3: 464–68.
Beauboeuf-Lafontant, Tamara. 2009. *Behind the Mask of the Strong Black Woman*. Philadelphia, PA: Temple University Press.

Berger, Michele Tracy. 2004. *Workable Sisterhood: The Politicized Journey of Stigmatized Women with HIV/AIDS.* Princeton, NJ: Princeton University Press.

Brown, Nadia E. 2014. *Sisters in the Statehouse.* New York: Oxford University Press.

Brown, Nadia E., and Sarah Allen Gershon. 2016. *Distinct Identities: Minority Women in U.S. Politics.* New York: Routledge.

Carroll, Susan J., and Linda M. G. Zerilli. 1993. "Feminist Challenges to Political Science." In *Political Science: The State of the Discipline II*, edited by Ada W. Finifter, 55–77. Washington, DC: American Political Science Association.

Cohen, Cathy. 1999. *Boundaries of Blackness: AIDS and the Breakdown of Blackness.* Chicago: University of Chicago Press.

Dhamoon, Rita. 2011. "Considerations on Mainstreaming Intersectionality." *Political Research Quarterly* 64, no. 1: 230–43.

Fasching-Varner, Katrice A., Roland W. Albert, and Chaundra Allen Mitchell. 2015. *Racial Battle Fatigue in Higher Education: Exposing the Myth of Post-Racial America.* Lanham, MD: Rowman & Littlefield.

Geronimus, Arline T., Margaret Hicken, Danya Keene, and John Bound. 2006. "Weathering and Age Patterns of Allostatic Load Scores among Blacks and Whites in the United States." *American Journal of Public Health* 96, no. 5: 826–33.

Hancock, Ange-Marie. 2004. *The Politics of Disgust: The Public Identity of the Welfare Queen.* New York: New York University Press.

———. 2007. "When Multiplication Doesn't Equal Quick Addition: Examining Intersectionality as a Research Paradigm." *Perspectives on Politics* 5, no. 1: 63–79.

———. 2011. *Solidarity Politics for Millennials: A Guide to Ending the Oppression Olympics.* New York: Palgrave/Macmillan.

———. 2016. *Intersectionality: An Intellectual History.* New York: Oxford University Press.

Harnois, Catherine. 2013. *Feminist Measures in Survey Research.* Thousand Oaks, CA: Sage.

Harris-Perry, Melissa V. 2011. *Sister Citizen: Shame, Stereotypes, and Black Women in America.* New Haven, CT: Yale University Press.

Hawkesworth, Mary. 2003. "Congressional Enactments of Race-Gender: Toward a Theory of Raced-Gendered Institutions." *American Political Science Review* 97, no. 4: 529–50.

Jordan-Zachery, Julia. 2007. "Am I a Black Woman or a Woman Who Is Black? A Few Thoughts on the Meaning of Intersectionality." *Politics & Gender* 3, no. 2: 254–63.

———. 2014. "I Ain't Your Darn Help: Black Women as the Help in Intersectionality Research." *National Political Science Review* 16: 19–30.

Key, Ellen M., and Jane Lawrence Sumner. 2019. "You Research Like a Girl: Gendered Research Agendas and Their Implications." *PS: Political Science and Politics* 52, no. 4: 663–68.

Lovenduski, Joni. 1998. "Gendering Research in Political Science." *Annual Review of Political Science* 1, no. 1: 333–56.

May, Vivian M. 2015. *Pursuing Intersectionality, Unsettling Dominant Imaginaries.* New York: Routledge.

Michelson, Melissa R., and Jessica Monforti Lavariega. 2021. "Elusive Inclusion: Persistent Challenges Facing Women of Color in Political Science." *PS: Political Science & Politics* 54, no. 1: 152–57.

Nash, Jennifer C. 2019. *Black Feminism Reimagined: After Intersectionality.* Durham, NC: Duke University Press.

Philpot, Tasha S., and Hanes Walton Jr. 2007. "One of Our Own: Black Female Candidates and the Voters." *American Journal of Political Science* 51, no. 1: 48–62.

Simien, Evelyn M. 2006. *Black Feminist Voices in Politics.* Albany: State University of New York Press.

———. 2015. *Historic Firsts: How Symbolic Empowerment Changes U.S. Politics.* New York: Oxford University Press.

———. 2020. "COVID-19 and the Strong Black Woman." *Gender Policy Report*, June 9. https://genderpolicyreport.umn.edu/covid-19-and-the-strong-black-woman/.

Smith, William A., Man Hung, and Jeremy D. Franklin. 2011. "Racial Battle Fatigue and the MisEducation of Black Men: Racial Microaggressions, Societal Problems, and Environmental Stress." *Journal of Negro Education* 80, no. 1: 63–82.

Smooth, Wendy G. 2006. "Intersectionality in Electoral Politics: A Mess Worth Making." *Politics and Gender* 2, no. 3: 400–14.

Strolovitch, Dara. 2009. *Affirmative Advocacy: Race, Class, and Gender in Interest Group Politics.* Chicago: University of Chicago Press.

Wadsworth, Nancy D. 2011. "Intersectionality in California's Same-Sex Marriage Battles: A Complex Proposition." *Political Research Quarterly* 64, no. 1: 200–16.

White, Aaronette. 2008. *Ain't I a Feminist? African American Men Speak Out on Fatherhood, Friendship, Forgiveness, and Freedom.* Albany: State University of New York Press.

Wilson, Angelia R. 2013. *Situating Intersectionality: Politics, Policy, and Power.* New York: Routledge.

13

Racial Discrimination and the Harassment of African American Women in Academia

Sharon D. Wright Austin

> The way to fight wrongs is to turn the light of truth upon them.
>
> —Ida B. Wells-Barnett

I included this quote from Ida B. Wells-Barnett because it stresses the importance of this book. Universities often discuss the need to diversify the faculty and student body, but I question whether they are serious about these efforts. There is a big difference between the rhetoric that we hear on college campuses and the reality. African American women must fight the wrongs that we encounter at our universities by speaking truthfully about them. These wrongs often take the form of microaggressions. Racial microaggressions are "subtle insults (verbal, nonverbal, and/or visual) directed toward people of color, often automatically or unconsciously" (Solorzano et al. 2000, 60). If "subtle," their effects are serious. The authors of one study of the impact of microaggressions on Black women observe, "Microaggressions are insidious, chronic, and traumatizing. An accumulation of microaggression stressors has debilitating psychological impact, including reduced self-efficacy, heightened feelings of vulnerability, feelings of powerlessness, anger, hypervigilance, distancing, and isolation." The authors go on to explicitly note the commonality of microaggressions in higher education, writing, "Although universities aspire to increase racial diversity on campus, research highlights the disturbing occurrence of microaggressions against both students and faculty of color across race and gender" (Robinson-Wood et al. 2015, 222).

When I enrolled in a doctoral program in 1990 and later taught my first university course in 1992, I had no idea that I would have experiences that were insulting at best and abusive at worst. For many years, I was not aware that many Black women encounter the same level of disrespect that I had. I also had no idea how far many had gone even with all they faced. I wish I had had the opportunity to read about Black women's experiences in the academy early in my career. As a first-generation college student from a working-class background, I knew of no African American female professors. After earning my doctorate, I eventually met women like Drs. Byrdie Larkin, Mae King, Jewel Prestage, Dianne Pinderhughes, and Paula McClain at professional conferences. I had no idea that Black female and male political scientists were doing groundbreaking academic research.

In the course of my career, I have taught at four universities—one urban comprehensive institution and three research universities. In July 2018, I achieved a goal that few African American women achieve in academia when I became a full professor of political science at the University of Florida—a major research university. My focus here will be on two phases of my career—my time in graduate school and my time as a young assistant professor. Both included experiences of what I would characterize as blatant racism and subtle microaggressions. I have tried to recount some of those experiences here as precisely as possible, both to capture what microaggressions look like in practice and to let Black women starting out in the profession know they are not alone. The subtitles for each section are statements I heard from a classmate and a colleague, respectively, during these two phases.

Phase One: "All the Black PhD Students Are Being Passed Through"

As a native of a predominantly Black city, Memphis, I attended my state's flagship public university, from 1990 until I graduated in August 1993. Whereas West Tennessee, where Memphis is located, is mostly Black and urban, East Tennessee, where the university is, is mostly white and rural. I suspect that most of the white students, and some of the faculty members,

I met there had never associated with an African American student before because many failed to respect our intellect. I am a loner by nature and spent most of my time there alone. I went there to do my work, earn my degree, and leave. As a result, I had few friends and associated with few people. I noticed that whites in the community often exhibited hostile behavior toward Black people. I would pay for things and cashiers would refuse to put money in my hand. Instead, they dropped it on the counter.

My white classmates and some of the professors made negative comments about affirmative action and expressed resentment about the supposed benefits Black students received, even though I was the only Black student in most of my classes. I had no funding for the first year that I was there and had a particularly hard time in a constitutional law class. Two white male undergraduates audited the class. They had very conservative views on issues involving race and gender. On one occasion, they offended a white female student by addressing her in a condescending way. The other white students, both men and women, supported her.

I didn't receive the same support when they offended me. A friend of theirs, also a white male undergraduate, had written a number of articles about affirmative action in our campus newspaper insinuating that Black students were lazy and undeserving of admission. I wrote a response to one of the articles that was eventually published. In it, I talked about my experience as a Black graduate student at the school. On the day my article was published, one of the two white male undergraduates asked our professor if the National Association for the Advancement of Colored People (NAACP) had ever had any white members. The professor said yes. My classmate then asked if the Ku Klux Klan had any Black members. The professor looked confused and said, "I certainly hope not." The student then replied, "Well, they have an affirmative action policy if anyone wants to join," looked at me, and laughed. I was stunned and the entire class looked uncomfortable. I raised my hand and asked the student, "What kind of affirmative action program do they have since you seem to be a member?" The student said that he was just making a joke. I then tried to ask him what he meant by his joke, but before I could finish, the professor again tried to change the subject. After class ended, the professor came to me and told me I did the right thing.

There were other occurences, too. During a previous class discussion, the same student said that "all the Black PhDs are being passed through," implying that Black graduate students weren't earning their degrees. To my knowledge, I was the only African American doctoral student in the program at the time. I assumed he was talking about me. Again, the professor and my classmates tried to change the subject. I felt silenced. One student started speaking loudly about the next case we were discussing. I started speaking loudly, too, and told them all that I had a right to speak and they were not going to silence me.

But, that was not the end of it. A few days after the Klan comment, I received a call from the office secretary requesting that I schedule an appointment with our department chair. When I went to the office, the chair did not mention the incident in class. Instead, he started talking about the department's attempts to recruit Black faculty members in the past. He mentioned one time when they hired a Black male professor who only stayed for one year and another Black full professor who only stayed a couple of years. The department, he said, had tried to hire Black faculty but had not been able to. I realized he was responding to another comment I'd made in class. Students were talking about the supposed benefits and privileges Black people get in the workforce. At the time, I said that for every benefit Black people get, they also get misery, harassment, and horrific treatment. I asked my classmates, "If Black people get so many benefits, why are there no Black faculty or staff members in the political science department?" Now it seemed like the meeting with the chair had been scheduled to give me an answer. "They"—meaning Black scholars—"aren't doing any innovative research," he told me, "but they always get the best jobs."

I was hurt and offended. I felt like I was being confronted by the chair simply because I had refused to allow white men to disrespect me during a class discussion. I had always had trouble speaking in class because I was either the only Black student or one of only a few. Some white students would ask me to express my opinion because they wondered what I thought, especially about issues involving race. I usually said nothing, but I felt I had to stop the two students in my constitutional law class from engaging in what I interpreted as disrespectful behavior. It seemed that people wanted to know what I thought until I told them things that did not make them feel comfortable.

Besides the microaggressions on campus, life in Knoxville was very difficult. Racism was common. Local salespersons often followed Black shoppers. I remember one incident that occurred shortly before I left. I had lost a lot of weight because of the stress I had endured and needed to buy a dress at a department store for a job interview. Because I had little money, I had to apply for a credit card and was approved. They gave me a card that indicated that I could use it immediately. A white saleswoman had been following me as I shopped in a store that was practically empty that afternoon. I noticed that she followed me when I was in the misses section, then the shoe section, then the men's section. I purposely walked to different areas of the store just so that she could follow me. Eventually, I started walking in circles from the misses to the women's, men's, and shoe sections of the store. After I had done it three times, she noticed what I was doing and left. When I attempted to purchase the dress with my approved card, she refused to accept it even though she had just accepted the same card from a white woman in front of me. She called upstairs to see if the card was real, and they told her that it was. During the entire transaction, she only made eye contact once. After she rang up the purchase and placed the dress in a bag, I told her that I didn't want it because of her racist and rude behavior. Her face turned red and I left.

I was a Black woman living alone in a predominantly white college town with no support system. I just wanted to go to class, do my work, and go home, but I did not receive the opportunity to do these things in peace while in graduate school. I never have been able to understand why some white people are so uncomfortable with our mere presence in graduate programs. Even if they have negative views about us, why can't they just leave us alone, I used to think?

Phase Two: "We Don't Understand Why We Can't Retain Minority Faculty"

After graduate school, when I became an assistant professor at a midwestern research university, I learned firsthand why universities have trouble recruiting and retaining Black faculty. It's not about how "innovative" our research is. In my experience, Black faculty leave universities because of the inexcusable manner in which we are treated. I endured awful treatment as an assistant professor, especially during the tenure and promotion process. It was so bad that, after being awarded tenure and promoted to associate professor of political science and Black studies, I went on a two-year unpaid leave. During the 2000–2001 academic year, I served as a visiting scholar in Michigan. From 2001–2002, I was a visiting associate professor at Florida. At the end of my unpaid leave, I had to either go back to my institution or resign. I chose to resign and continue to work as a visiting professor at Florida rather than return to a tenured position.

I didn't have to think about it twice. On June 20, 2002, I wrote a letter resigning from my position as associate professor of political science and Black studies and I've been at Florida ever since. After visiting for three years, I received a position as associate professor of political science and was promoted to full professor in 2018.

As with my graduate institution, my first faculty position was at a school in a predominantly white college town. I lived in a working-class, mostly white neighborhood near campus for most of the time I was there. However, during my first year, I lived about an hour away, in the suburbs of a larger city, and commuted to work about two to three times a week. A few other faculty members did, too, but colleagues in my department seemed offended at my choice not to live in "our town," as they called it. Even after I moved closer to the school and asked colleagues not to discuss my personal life, gossip—about how I thought I was too good to live in their town and shouldn't have taken a job if I didn't want to live there—continued to circulate. One graduate student told me a professor, one of my colleagues, mentioned it during a class lecture.

That I was supposed to live in town felt like one of many unspoken rules. For instance, I found out the hard way that faculty were required to attend what I thought were optional social activities but were, in fact, mandatory. As an assistant professor, I worked constantly in the quest for tenure and promotion. Occasionally, my friends and I would go to dinner or socialize at each other's homes. One of my best friends and her partner were huge NBA fans, and so was I. A group of us decided to go to a preseason game and to dinner. We had purchased the tickets months earlier. It happened to be alumni weekend, however, and one of the professors was having a reception at his home on the same night as the game. The following Monday, a few people asked me why I didn't attend the reception, and I told them the truth—I went to an NBA game with friends. Later, one of my colleagues, who was a full professor and a friend, asked me to come to his office. He closed the door and told me I should not tell others when I missed faculty events for personal reasons because some of them were offended that I went to a basketball game rather than a "university function." I knew the professor was having a reception but had no idea it was a required "university function." Again, it became clear that I was continually being talked about and judged.

Teaching posed issues, too. I think it's safe to say, Black professors at predominantly white universities know they are inevitably going to deal with racist behaviors and views from their students. It comes with the job and I personally believe that younger Black professors face more backlash from students than older ones. I no longer have the problems with students I did then, but during that time, I faced frequent challenges in a course I taught a number of times on women and the law. During one semester, a white male student seemed to challenge practically everything I said. One day, after I explained one of the cases we were analyzing, he said to the class that "I think we're reading too much into this." I asked him what his view of the ruling was. He said he had not read it but was questioning whether I knew what I was talking about. He would often ask me questions he appeared not to believe I could answer. It was bad enough that even some of his white classmates confronted him about his inappropriate behavior in class.

On another occasion, a white male student asked about a plaintiff's race after I described the facts of a case. The facts did not mention race but said the plaintiff was a woman who was a high school dropout, living in poverty with her family in a New Hampshire trailer park. She lost custody of her child to the child's father because he "had a better command of the English language." The plaintiff was a US-born native English speaker but the father was more educated and of a higher class. I tried to point out the class bias in the case and asked the student why the court described the plaintiff as it did. He replied, "Was she Black?" In his mind apparently, a woman with this type of background—a poor high-school dropout—had to be African American.

My worst experience teaching the course came in spring 1999. I honestly thought that I was going to have a nervous breakdown. Early during the semester, I gave a white female student a D on an assignment. After class, she yelled at me and told me that I should have told the class the answer I expected them to write. I tried to tell her that professors don't give the answers. We teach the information and students have to figure out the answers on their own. She then said, "I can see that I'm not getting through to you" and left. The university had a policy that allowed professors to expel students from classes for inappropriate behavior. I expelled her from my class.

Then, one day we were having a class discussion about a case with plaintiffs who were a lesbian couple. One student said that she didn't approve of lesbianism and wouldn't want her children around them. A couple of other students responded. Without condoning the student's views, which I took to be an expression of her religion, I defended her right to speak freely. I thought nothing of it until days later. Two graduate students told me they'd heard that my name had been mentioned during the question and answer session of a guest lecture by a celebrity who was openly gay. Apparently, two students from my class told the guest speaker (and an audience of 2,000 people, including the dean and provost) that their professor had made a homophobic statement in class. They said they were afraid to say anything because the professor had kicked another girl out of the class for challenging her. The speaker asked for the professor's name and they named me.

When I went to campus the next week, student reporters started calling me and showing up randomly at my office. I could barely get any work done, but still had to teach the class and pretend as if nothing was wrong. The campus paper wrote articles about me—most of which were supportive, thankfully. I heard that someone even contacted the St. Louis and Kansas City newspapers and ABC News but they didn't write about the incident presumably because there was no incident. After about a month, things died down. Before the controversy ended, however, I felt very unsafe and uncomfortable on campus. With the exception of some students and my closest friends, I received very little support. I was especially disappointed that my colleagues in women's studies only came to my defense later, after my students and I clarified what had happened, despite my working with them for years.

By the following fall semester, it was as if nothing had happened. No one mentioned it. I taught my classes without incident and our campus moved on. I also had more important things to think about—getting tenure and promotion.

During the 1999–2000 academic year, I had a ferocious tenure battle. When I started the process, I had published one book and nine articles and book chapters. Most professors had either one book and a couple of articles or five or six articles and no book. I also had excellent teaching evaluations (despite the experiences I've recounted here), an extremely strong record of service, and unamimous support from the Black studies departmental faculty in my joint-appointed position. The primary opposition came from the political science department and our new department chair.

The tenure process worked as follows. The department chair requested letters from external reviewers during the summer before the person filed their tenure application (usually during early summer). In September, the tenured faculty voted for or against recommending tenure. The department chair then wrote a letter that summarized their votes but also included their independent opinion about the candidate's qualifications for tenure.

In May 1999, I left town to spend the summer with my family in Tennessee and to work on my second book. Before doing so, I left my tenure file, including my publications and information about my teaching and service, with the office staff to be mailed to external reviewers so they could write recommendation letters. (Now everything is online, but back then it had to be mailed.) My department chair called me at my mother's home to tell me he couldn't send anything to the reviewers by the deadline because he couldn't find the materials. I called a staff member, who confirmed she had the materials. I called the chair who eventually told me the materials made it into the mail but that I should have remained in town until after they had been sent. To my knowledge, there had never been any such requirement in place—until now. I didn't get a chance to see the letters but heard that all of the reviewers recommended me for tenure and that the letters were extremely good.

In September, the meeting of tenured faculty members, most of whom were white men, took place. The department voted nine against and six in favor of my tenure. I was allowed to explain why I deserved their support in an appeals meeting and bring a tenured faculty member from another department to voice their support. An African American full professor of history accompanied me to the meeting to speak on my behalf. After the meeting, the faculty voted again. This time the vote was ten against and five in favor. One person changed their vote from a yes to a no vote after the appeal.

The case then proceeded to the college and the dean, the university-wide committee and the provost, and finally to the chancellor. The department chair usually receives notification about decisions and then must inform the faculty member. One day I was in the mailroom, about to go to class. A group of students were standing in line in the hallway waiting to talk to an adviser. As I stepped out of the mailroom, my department chair yelled down the hall, "The college just unanimously turned you down for tenure; do you want to appeal?" I was stunned and hurt, but I said yes and went to teach my class. I appealed before the college committee and the vote changed from six to zero against to a split three-to-three vote. The dean, however, mailed me a letter informing me that he was against my case. It then proceeded to the university-wide committee who also voted against my tenure, although I don't remember the exact vote. I appealed again, now accompanied by the one African American full professor from political science, and this time I received a positive vote. The provost, however, opposed my tenure case. From there, it proceeded to the chancellor's level.

By this time, the spring 2000 semester had ended and I was out of town. Then, on August 2, 2000, I started receiving notes from friends in the department congratulating me. I didn't know what they were talking about but there it was: They were congratulating me for receiving tenure. I thought this had to be wrong. The provost had turned me down and I doubted the chancellor would disagree with him—but he did. I had an exceptional record and, despite all the opposition, I had earned tenure and promotion.

Later that day, after I had celebrated my victory with friends, I checked my email again. The chair had emailed the department to announce that "Sharon Wright has been promoted to associate professor with tenure. I have no idea why the chancellor didn't follow the recommendation of the faculty." No congratulations. No nothing. One of my colleagues replied, "Sweet Nightmares." Some faculty members confronted him about it, but he said nothing to me. Later, I asked the chair if he was going to say anything about the disrespectful message. He said that the department's governance committee would meet in October to discuss the issue but he didn't plan to say anything about it.

I went on an unpaid leave that academic year and moved to Ann Arbor to serve as a visiting scholar at the University of Michigan. In October, my department chair sent me a letter saying the governance committee had unanimously voted that my colleague's message was inappropriate. He ended the note with "We as a department are moving on."

In 2001, I moved from a visiting position at Michigan to a visiting position at Florida. In 2002, I resigned from my tenured position to remain in a visiting untenured position at Florida. It was an easy decision to make. I knew when I went on leave that I was never going back there because I had not been welcome there in the first place. My situation would only have gotten worse if I had returned, and I no longer felt comfortable on campus. At Florida, I have been a visiting associate professor, untenured associate professor, tenured associate professor, and professor of political science. I have had a very pleasant experience at UF overall.

Conclusion

In this chapter, I have discussed the lowest points of my career. Although I have focused on the constant slights and needless hurdles, I have continually practiced creative resistance by mentoring my students. I celebrate every achievement with them while they are enrolled in school and after they graduate. My family has also assisted me with my self-care efforts. Although I work a lot as a professor, I find the time to relax with my husband, my son, and my daughter. As a single woman, I worried about negative work experiences way more than I should have. It's hard not to, especially when your job is on the line. Now, I prioritize my relationship with my family.

Prayer and faith have also helped me cope with the numerous negative situations I have encountered. The Bible tells us to combine our faith with good works. Over the years, I have tried to do just that. However, universities really do need to enhance their efforts to address the racism on their campuses. Louis et al. (2016, 470) state, "Black faculty experiences with microaggression at white research universities should be a major concern to department chairs, dean, and provosts since these experiences can negatively affect the recruitment and retention of faculty of color." I could not agree more.

References

American Political Science Association. 2011. "Political Science in the 21st Century." October. https://www.apsanet.org/portals/54/Files/Task%20Force%20Reports/TF_21st%20Century_AllPgs_webres90.pdf.

Louis, Dave A., Glinda J. Rawls, Dimitra Jackson-Smith, Glenn A. Chambers, LaTricia L. Phillips, and Sarah L. Louis. 2016. "Listening to Our Voices: Experiences of Black Faculty at Predominantly White Research Universities with Microaggression." *Journal of Black Studies* 47, no. 5: 454–74.

Robinson-Wood, Tracy, Oyenike Balogun-Mwangi, Caroline Fernandes, Ami Popat-Jain, Noreen Boadi, Atsushi Matsumoto, and Xiaolu Zhang. 2015. "Worse Than Blatant Racism: A Phenomenological Examination of Microaggressions among Black Women." *Journal of Ethnographic & Qualitative Research* 9: 221–36.

Solorzano, Daniel, Miguel Ceja, and Tara Yosso. 2000. "Critical Race Theory, Racial Microaggressions, and Campus Racial Climate: The Experiences of African American College Students." *Journal of Negro Education* 69, nos. 1/2: 60–73.

14

A Black Unicorn in the Academe

A Testimonial of a Black Feminist Scholar in the Field of Political Science

CAROLINE SHENAZ HOSSEIN

When Professor Dianne Pinderhughes commissioned the *Report on the Task Force on Political Science in the 21st Century* (APSA 2011), it was an indictment of the failure of the political science discipline to hire diverse scholars.[1] For me I saw it as a failing to hire Black women—and a failure that would limit the study of power and politics. As a mature PhD student in the Department of Political Science (2006–2012) at the University of Toronto with more than a decade of work experience, I was hit with a hard reality: that I likely would not get hired into a political science department.

Less than 5 percent of those working as professors in political science were Black women (APSA 2011). This data signaled to me that in Canada the number of Black and Caribbean women academics would be far lower than that.[2] I write this chapter noting that I never had a Black woman political scientist teach or mentor me at any of the places I studied. Professor Dickson Eyoh at the University of Toronto was the only Black political scientist to teach me politics, in 2006.

It was clear to me back then that there were so few Black scholars in political science in Canada. I was being trained in a field in which I would be alone. In the book *The Equity Myth* (2017), Frances Henry, Enakshi Dua, Carl E. James, Audrey Kobayashi, Peter Li, Howard Ramos, and Malida S. Smith made clear through data how few Black women existed in academe and especially in the social sciences. Full professors Lisa Aubrey, Jessica Gordon Nembhard, and Kamala Kempadoo shadow-mentored me for many years on issues about citation blindness, plagiarism, and the microaggressions we encounter as Black women in academe. They all knew about these struggles Black women academics face, especially in the fields of social and political science, and they too left positions due to these traumas.

On Being a Black Unicorn

Lorde, in her poem "Black Unicorn" (1978), makes clear that Black women will never be free, because many Black women routinely deal with hate, misogyny, racism, animosity, and fear in the world. They are despised and surveilled as what she calls the "Black unicorn." Even if I were to study positivist political science, I would be that Black unicorn, no matter how much I tinkered with political science's mainstream methods and theories to be part of the standard method and tools. I refused back then to comply with the standard toolkit, and I chose methods and theories that were reflective of the Africana experience and that have been buried in the knowledge-making process.

Coming into the academy after a decade as a professional in the field of international development, I could not accept that Eurocentric theories would reflect the Black women I wanted to study. Scholar April Few (2007) uses critical race theory and Black feminist theory in family studies research to understand what is going on. Her paper's description of how she was able to do this helped me to bring Black feminist theory into my work. I found the work of Wane and Deliovsky (2002) a very good primer on how to bring African Canadian feminist theory into my own work. I also questioned conforming to the standard methods toolkit that obscured the truth.

To study mainstream political science that prioritizes formal institutions would not allow me to understand power, exclusion, and the structural violence against women in the African diaspora when they want to access financial goods. Lorde's (2007 [1984]) point that the use of tools from the Master's House is not the way to bring change is a strong one. To be able to create anew, we need to be the Black unicorn and use different methods and theories. My role, whether inside or outside of political science, was to disrupt the field so that I could positively affect where the change needed to take place.

Professor Pinderhughes's leadership as president of the American Political Science Association (APSA; 2007–2008) was the main reason I went to one of the few APSA meetings I ever attended. Her 2009 presidential address at APSA calling on members to disrupt the discipline stayed with me from that day forward. Her role pushed the discipline to do more in terms of how it considered political issues and the impact of politics on marginalized people. Hearing a tenured professor who was also a Black woman speak on matters of concern was a turning point for me. As a graduate student, I knew I had to cast a net as wide as I could so that I could find a way to do work on the Black political economy in academe. The field of political science was too narrow, and it had a long way to go in terms of expanding its scope.

In this chapter, I share a testimonial of what it meant for me to be a Black Canadian woman in political science. In part I draw from what I saw is reminiscent of an important chapter "Black/Out" written by Delia D. Douglas (2012), who described her excruciating pain in the Canadian academe as a sessional and how not only faculty but also students would disrespect her and question her expertise. Her chapter as the lone Canadian in the edited volume was relevant to me at the time of its publication because I first read it as a contractual at York University. The issues she cited against Black women academics have been ongoing for decades, and I am not sure there is any end in sight. Now I am here writing this chapter in another book similar to the one Douglas contributed to and I am speaking my truth and attesting to the harms that I endured as a scholar and researcher.

Douglas's work most definitely helped me think about the fields of study to avoid as I looked for secure employment. I also do believe that my own reluctance to be a part of a political science department early on, because of the job prospects, gave me the needed distance from the discipline. This allowed me to go ahead to be able to teach it in a way that I was comfortable with. Today after a decade in academe, I am a tenured professor of global development *and political science* holding a Canada research chair in the University of Toronto at one of the world's best political science departments. The journey getting here was complicated. I am now at a place where I can contribute with a new generation of scholars on what it means to be a political scientist.

In this chapter I will cover the path that I took to get where I am today. The chapter has three parts. First, I will share some of my story, pinpointing my Caribbean roots in the United States and Canada, and suggest why navigating graduate school in political science as the first in the family to go to a college can be difficult, why we must take on nontraditional pathways, and why it is those nontraditional pathways that help up to develop our own line of thinking about politics. Second, I offer a personalized inventory of the kind of terror levied against Black women scholars for speaking up about anti-Blackness in Canada. I end the chapter with ideas on how I found a way to define the field of political science, ensuring we remember that inclusive politics means diversifying our theories and methods.

A Testimonial: The Making of a "Disruptive" Political Scientist

I was born in New York City to very young Caribbean parents, a Black St. Vincentian-born mother of Grenadian stock who was raised in Trinidad and a Muslim Indo-Guyanese father. They fled their homelands for economic opportunities. They had a hard time settling in New York City and also the South Bronx, where many of my family still live, and my parents and I eventually moved to Toronto. We lived precariously, moving around a dozen times to many of the low-income pockets—from Downsview in the west to Malvern in the east—and finally finding a footing in a Vaughan suburb, north of the city, at the end of my high school education.

I was a thirty-five-year-old "mature" student pursuing graduate studies after more than a decade of full-time professional work in the field I was studying. Due to my working-class roots, there was family pressure to work and make money, and this is the pathway that many of us take as part of our cultural and class upbringing. The students I met in grad school who had a similar background also shared this experience. Our class strata and cultural background was at odds with the idea of going on to higher education because that is not what people from humble beginnings usually do. What they do is get a good-paying job, like we did, and stay there for at least a decade to pay bills and support others. The university setting at the time I was there first in the 1990s and then again in early 2000s was the same: hostile and exclusionary. And I was only able to make it through with the right friends and mentors. The system was not made for folks like Black women from lower socioeconomic class backgrounds who were educated in this system of white supremacy.

People like me are often streamed toward budget-end community colleges and the like, not toward prestigious universities. This white supremacy embedded into the system ignores and erases any of our accomplishments as students. Scholar-activist Clelia Rodriquez (2018) makes the point in *Decolonizing Academia: Poverty, Oppression and Pain* that we are made to feel like the "disruptor," but she states that it is the roots of the academic system that are fundamentally racist and corrupt and that alienate other knowledges from taking hold. I use quotations around the term *disruptor* because I am only made to be a challenger because of the systemic bias that is baked into the academic structure.

In an era of "equity, diversity, and inclusion," white colleagues hiding behind the pretense of "collegiality" use it for their own personal gain and a marker to constrain any real change. In my opinion the term *collegiality* is code for making racialized and Black scholars abide by rules that benefit white elite scholars. During my time at my former university, there were certain Black scholars who I felt accepted the norms and abided by the rules and did not question problematic behavior.

Encounters like this made me realize early on that there are some academics fixated on careerist moves and not social change. What I find is that internal grants are often gifted to those who complied with administrators, and I would personally refer to those internal awards as goodies. I remember situations in higher education in Canada with racialized students and scholars, as highlighted in an episode of CBC's *Fifth Estate* about systemic racism on Canadian campuses, entitled "Black on Campus" (aired February 2021). I tried to engage tenured colleagues in supporting the scholars, and, in my opinion, they were concerned with their own goodies. Personally, I felt that, because I was not quiet about my own issues, I was prevented from accessing large internal awards, and that is why I chose to leave the school.

This is my story and what happened to me. I was made to feel that speaking up against the racism, sexism, and nepotism would be an issue. This is why I hired an outside lawyer to listen to my issues. In 2018, I remember being the only Black woman on an unusually large hiring committee with mostly men and white people, and at times the sessions were heated as we discussed candidates. A Black male colleague, who emigrated to Canada for an academic position, scolded me about "the way I spoke to white people." I learned that even within academe Black women are contending with misogyny when they oppose anti-Black racism.

After much conflict in this hiring committee with white colleagues, I was eventually assigned as the chair, and the hire resulted in all three women candidates being hired, including the newly minted PhD and Black woman candidate, whom the largely white committee ranked unfairly low in my personal opinion. These hirings completely diversified the program both gender- and race-wise, but it made me question my tenure in the program due to the politics involved in this hiring. One is the Black unicorn when one confronts uncollegial processes.

Knowing one's place is what I was told growing up in Toronto, Canada, and I seldom followed that advice. I watched how my parents tried to "assimilate" and to "integrate" as struggling immigrants without a university education. My working-class roots are not something many of my colleagues at the university understand—even for many people of color. Many of them have educated parents, or they went to the United Kingdom, the United States, or Canada to pursue higher education or were hired for an academic job. So, they do not have the experience of being schooled in this system, and the class positioning of a Black woman who grew up here explains why there are tensions among faculty of color within academe.

Growing up in Toronto means that I do not have the accent that my white colleagues really want to hear when they justify a Black hire. I also don't blend into the cohort in ways they find visually appealing in terms of class. It is no surprise that some professors, usually men, are likely to listen to the rules because they immigrate as "expats" for a lucrative position, and they have limited experience of the deeply ingrained systemic exclusion of those of us born and bred here.

Antiguan-Canadian education scholar Professor Carl E. James (2012), who specializes in education policy for Black youth, has made the point numerous times that being educated in Canada from elementary school onward provides quite a different understanding of race and racism than when one emigrates for university. I would add that also being Black and Caribbean results in being further stigmatized. Joseph Mensah (2010) in his book *Black Canadians* explained that Haitians and Somalis as well are often labeled in derogatory ways compared to highly trained Kenyan, Nigerian, and Ghanaian immigrants. In other words, not all Black Canadians are treated the same. Those of us who are Black diasporic women of Caribbean heritage who were schooled and grew up in these lands understand the subtleties of racism due to the lived experience of being part of the underclass.

Our encounter with inequities and whiteness was not one that started in higher education; the experience of racial domination expands over a lifetime. So being a part of second-generation immigrants, I defied the odds to be able to attend and succeed in an excellent post-secondary system in Canada, the United States, and the United Kingdom—all places not wanting to have their own "minorities" join the academy. Having passed through that experience has led many of us who are "diaspora lifers"—raised our whole lives outside of the place that our parents came from—to join the academy not just to have a job but to really transform knowledge-making and to influence policy such that we can hear what local people, mainly women, are saying.

Far too often, male toxicity and the white savior complex intrudes on empirical work, and this work I do on cooperativism is driven from the ground up. Even though the trauma exists, Black women are responding through their own collectives and agency to help themselves and others on their own terms. For example, economist Nina Banks (2020) has been writing about the erasure of Black diaspora women for years, and she argues that within disciplines such as economics, Black women's labor is not counted even though it contributes to society's well-being.

My Journey in and out of Political Science

Being a woman of Caribbean descent with parents who struggled to cope—and the first in my family to go to any university—I certainly did not follow the usual trajectory of becoming a professor in Canada. My parents were politically active in local politics and so was I because it meant that if we actively engaged in politics, things could be better for us. I understood at a very young age that "politicking" is important to securing our rights in a society. I also grew up watching the precariousness in which we lived and knew that politics was the way to figure out economic provisioning that would be just for all people.

My first degree was in political science and philosophy at Saint Mary's University (SMU) in Halifax, Nova Scotia. I went to SMU (1990–1993) mainly because it was a small school and I could have one-on-one attention from my professors. We also knew Caribbean people who sent their children there because the differential fees were lower, and I wanted to be there for that kind of cultural connection. All of my professors were white and male. Many of the courses I was interested in were on political economy, and they were mostly taught by men. At some point, I had a woman professor, Jane Arscott, who taught at Dalhousie at the time, and I was given special permission to take her class. She was someone I confided in about not only my writing but also when I was attacked at a college bar, and she mentored me well. My sister, who later also studied at SMU, was fortunate to have political scientist Edna Keeble, a woman of color (from the Philippines), hired into the department; she had a tremendous impact on her life.

My time at SMU helped me to meet many Caribbean students through the student clubs, piquing my interest in politics for those of us in the diaspora. While at SMU, I learned about cooperative economics, and the business courses talked about human good at a time when most places did not do this. In one of my courses, on Irish politics with Professor Chauvin, I learned about colonialism and was introduced to how people collectively organized to topple it through cooperatives. It was at SMU that I learned about the underclass fisherfolk in the Antigonish movement and how they drew on activist pedagogy to discuss the politics of the day and to turn away from commercial forms of business. After that first degree, I knew that political economy would be an important course of study for me as a Black woman.

My parents insisted that I attend law school, and so I did and I earned a second bachelor's degree—in law at the University of Kent at Canterbury (1993–1995). Like many Caribbean parents, especially those not well educated, having a professional occupation like law or medicine was viewed as a success for the family. Though my two years in law school were not enjoyable for me, I met students from every corner of the world, and I learned so much from them about life where they came from. I had friends from Kenya, Iran, Sri Lanka, Zimbabwe, Jordan, India, Ghana, Trinidad, Saudi Arabia, Bermuda, and Sudan. While in England, I also knew a number of feminist law professors, such as Joanne Conaghan Paddy Ireland and Kate Diesfeld, but there were no Black law professors at the time.[3] These feminist legal scholars encouraged me to carry on to graduate school to examine the politics of exclusion among African peoples. So I went off and I completed my Master of Public Administration degree at Cornell University (1995–1997) and studied under Professor Salah Hassan (my first Black teacher and professor) at the Africana Centre and law professor Muna Ndulo, and the only political scientist on my committee, Arch Dotson, was a son of sharecroppers from the south.

I learned a lot and met many engaged scholars: Professors Aussie-Lumumba, Mazrui, Christopherson, Beneria, Bekerie, Edmondson, and Turner. I found connections with a medley of friends, who were Black and racialized, Monica Mason, Khadija Bah, Ibe Ibeike Jonah, Chris Norwood, Shayan Sen, Patricia Campos, Elizabeth Rauseo, and Stephen Belessis, who were mature and sensitive to the politics of being at an Ivy League university. To this day I am still in touch with these friends because they helped me get through the program.

With such a diverse group of friends and mentors, I found the support to thrive; and, thanks to Professor Salah Hassan, I landed an internship at the Arab Lawyers Union in Cairo. For my master's degree, I studied the economic and political exclusion of Sudanese exiles and worked mostly with southern Sudanese refugees in a northern suburb of Cairo. An activist and Sudanese feminist, Dr. Magda Ali, mentored me well. After returning to Cornell, it was Professor Ndulo who urged me to join the US Peace Corps and to get some solid community-based work experience globally before returning to do a PhD degree. I followed this advice and spent a decade working in international development for mostly global NGOs (nongovernmental organizations) primarily in West Africa.

Doing a PhD Degree in Political Science

After a decade of working in international development (1996–2006), I returned to graduate school at University of Toronto in my home city. There I found quite a few Black and racialized graduate students in political science compared to other places, and that is why I chose to attend this school. A few of us were uneasy because the professoriate at the time was generally white. While I was a graduate student (2006–2012), I found refuge with African-born Canadians from Sudan, Kenya, and Uganda. We were all mature students, well into our thirties and forties, because of our nontraditional pathways of doing a PhD. We were also married, and some of us had children and a prior career for a decade or more.

The APSA task force report (2011) indicated that the representation of Black women scholars in the discipline of political science was meager. In 2006, when Black friends in the doctoral program and I met, we discussed how we not only were not seen by others but were told that what we studied was not standard political science work. It seemed that certain kinds of research by racialized students mattered and that those students would be supported. Some of us being mature students and older than most, as well as coming from "working-class roots" (where neither parent went to any college), meant that we would need to navigate the university differently than many of our peers. To some extent, we also self-excluded and formed our own close-knit group to be able to function and to flourish. I vowed from that day forward that I would assist and share my materials with students and early career faculty, particularly those of Caribbean immigrant backgrounds.

Think Strategically and Go Where Your Work Is Valued

In Canada, some of the established Black political scientists I remember from when I was a graduate student were Dickson Eyoh, Abbas Gnamo, Malinda Smith, Richard Iton, Wisdom Tettey, Carla Norrlöf, Pablo Idahosa, and Andy Knight. The late Richard Iton (who had just left Toronto for a position with Northwestern) had chaired my panel at the National Conference of Black Political Scientists (NCOBPS) conference back in 2008, and he also spent time giving me advice, which included making connections to people outside of the field. To broaden my academic goals, I did a number of my courses outside of political science, in the Women and Gender Studies program as well as the Social Justice program at the Ontario Institute for Studies in Education. My department at this time had no courses in Black feminist theory, and I received permission to take Black feminist thought.

Choosing to be the Unicorn and to Read Black Feminist Writing

Coming from more than a decade of international development experience at a senior level and landing into a doctoral program, I found the process frustrating because my race, age, and work knowledge made it difficult to find faculty who could work with a student like me. As I mentioned earlier, I eventually found a few fellow students who were excluded, and we formed a group of sorts. With time, the reality that I faced of "not fitting in anywhere" in political science actually emboldened my research agenda. I had two choices: I could adapt and try to work within the theoretical and methodological confines of the discipline, or I could excavate thinking from alienated Black scholars writing on my subject matter.

I chose to do the latter, knowing the risks that would entail for my career because I was reading beyond political science. The works of Black and Brown feminist scholars have helped me to find my voice through their writing. These included political scientists such as Lisa Aubrey (1997), Tiffany Willoughby-Herard (2015), and Sharon Wright Austin (2007, 2018); political economists Nina Banks (2020) and Jessica Gordon Nembhard (2014); economic geographer Beverley Mullings (2021); and gender and development scholar Naila Kabeer (1994). I was fortunate to have a supervisor, Judith Ann Teichman, who was also on the margins in the department because, as a development expert, she read widely, particularly in history. Her antiracist feminist stance in support of global development studies as a major field and her standing in the department provided shelter for me so that I could take risks in terms of the works I read and cited and methods that I used.

Reading widely with an emphasis on Black and Caribbean feminist political economy writings can make one a unicorn in the field. One such work, which was the centerpiece for my own learning about Black feminist thought, was by Patricia Hill Collins (2000). Her work provided an entire framework to guide my thinking in my first book, *Politicized Microfinance*, which grew out of my doctoral research on the topic. To succeed as a Black graduate student in this department and to use new theories meant that I had to work with a diverse group of scholars who could support unorthodox methods and theories in the study of politics.

Many mainstream disciplines do not value theories by women such as Hill Collins (2000) and Wane and Deliovsky (2002) from the Global South or empirical methods that listen to people. Professor Oyeronke Oyewumi (1997) demonstrated to me that biased colonial systems that exclude African people, and especially women, had to be cited and shared. These "objective" methods used in fields like comparative politics and development studies were framed in such a way as to make African women inferior (Oyewumi 1997). This meant that sometimes those who coached you and supported you were not Black, but they were people who do not buy into the differentiation of people's identities. It was an unlikely group of scholars assembled on my committee, and they each served a function in terms of formal finance, feminist theory, mixed and empirical methods, and regional expertise—and all of them had the gravitas needed to help me advance what I wanted to do.

Staying Focused on Why We Do What We Do

One point worth mentioning is that when I received a US Fulbright to support a full year of study in Jamaica, I was not recognized for this achievement, while other students getting less prestigious awards were being celebrated. I learned early on that celebration was reserved for those students, including model minorities, who conformed and engaged with faculty in ways that I was not ready to do. This was hurtful. And I also noted that those same students were able to tap into resources and support in ways I could not because of the access they had with their white male supervisor. Regardless of all of this, I finished in a timely manner. The lack of distractions also kept me focused on my project, and I was able to self-fund through consulting given my years of fieldwork in several Caribbean countries.

People will not stay in places where they are not valued. It was not that Black women were not studying politics—it was just that they would move into the industry or other disciplines for a job. I knew the lack of Black women hired in political science meant that my finding a tenure-track position in political science in Canada was going to be near impossible. So, before I submitted my thesis in 2012, I combed every page to make sure that I captured the broader concepts in "political economy," "feminist theory," and "development" so that I could be hired into interdisciplinary departments. It was very important to cast myself across different fields to increase the likelihood of getting hired. This meant that I also started to position my articles in an array of feminist, development, and political economy academic journals so that I could teach in multiple and cross-disciplinary departments.

My commitment to study the community was not going to be derailed because political science could not see what I did as "standard" political research. I knew why I came to academe for a PhD in political science. My work was to be a paradigm shifter and to change the way things are going in the field of politics. In a field concerned with power dynamics, rights, and unequal development, the fact that we are not making room for Black women academics to contribute fully was not acceptable. Many of us come to the academe from working-class roots, from families without anyone who ever went inside a university, and it is this lived experience that enables us to treat data and the theory in unique ways from many of our peers.

We also have access to communities in ways that others do not. I know from my work with hundreds of people known as the banker ladies, who organize informal cooperative banks, that one must come from within community to be able to go underground to do this work. People are aware of the ties, rooted in trust, required for me to be able to reach these women, and these relationships are built on a decade of trust (see Mondesir's *The Banker Ladies* 2021).

My work examining Black women cooperators in Canada and the Caribbean region is about politics, power, and violence, issues that are at their core political science research. Yet, this research, which has important policy implications, was not viewed as such. The dissertation turned book *Politicized Microfinance* (2016) went on to win two major prizes from prestigious academic organizations known for work in Black politics and feminist economics. Black women scholars are prolific workers, doing worldly research that is too threatening to those who adhere to the status quo. Yet we are often presumed to know nothing, and what we study is labeled as too narrow (Gutiérrez y Muhs et al. 2012).

Black women studying politics in informal arenas is often not regarded as standard political research. Nor was the idea that Black women's lived experience can teach the discipline what it means to be human, and still today peer review will reply to an article as "narrow" and "subjective." Development scholar Arturo Escobar (2020) in his recent work acknowledges that the pluriversal is how we will save the planet and that Black and Indigenous citizens in the Americas have insight on how to do this locally. It is this lived experience that actually matters in development politics. Escobar (2012) points out that this obsession with an "objective operation" in terms of how we organize the economy and life has only validated white, Western systems. Everything else has been seen as inferior. The act of relying on Black women who choose world-making that is rooted in mutuality and cooperation is despised even by those who ascribe to some kind of reform but are not ready for complete transformation.

My Personal Experience at a "Social Justice" University

Studying informal institutions, Black women, and issues in the Global South, I knew I was not going to be "seen" as a political scientist. I realized that applying for political science jobs seemed "easier" in the United States because the United States had more jobs on offer than Canada did. But I was not ready to uproot my family and move back again after being away from home for sixteen years, living in the United Kingdom, the United States, and parts of West Africa. This time I came home married and starting a family, so we decided to stay in Toronto, Canada, and this meant that I would apply to positions beyond political science.

My first job offer came while I was still a PhD student, and it was for a three-year contract position at York University. I was the only trained political scientist, racialized person, and woman hired as a contractual into an all-white male program outside of my discipline because of the interdisciplinary nature of my research. Being in a program with white tenured men focused mostly on firms, economics, and business ethics was not comfortable. There was a lack of diversity in many ways.

Being in an All-White Male Academic Program

As soon as I was hired, I realized I was in hostile territory. Shortly thereafter, I sought out a therapist because of the everyday abuse I endured on campus. One of my colleagues was banned from my tenure file because of his interference in my placement course—for example, he wanted students to work on his special projects rather than work in local community-based organizations. I was opposed to this way of thinking so I told him this and then later ignored his messages and hallway lectures. He was a tenured professor and a spousal hire. This was my entry into the social science department.

Later, upon being hired for a tenure-stream position at the school, a white male colleague invited a British consultant writing on microfinance to give a lecture in my department. I was told that I had to organize the talk because the colleague was traveling to South America. I said no to this tenured white man. These microlevel aggressions were commonplace because I was the only woman of color in the unit and I was viewed as the "disruptor."

One positive aspect of the position was that I actually connected well with the student body, which was mostly immigrant children and first in their family to attend university. But in the program, I was viewed as a "problem." The program was required by the administration to attend mediation with regular sessions over a one-year period at a very expensive law firm on Bay Street. I was the only woman and Black person in that room and was untenured. One of the tenured men in this mediation was an associate dean (a family member of Ontario's former attorney general and former chancellor of the same university).

I felt completely vulnerable and afraid in those mediation sessions. They were triggering for me and interfered with my ability to have a proper work/life balance. I overworked myself out of fear. Listening to white men who were tenured speak about their "structural exclusion" in the unit was offensive to me. But I could do very little and sought additional therapy because of those sessions.

Speaking Up

As a coping mechanism, I tried to affiliate with graduate programs outside of my unit, in social political thought and political science; doing so is a process that usually takes weeks to confirm. In my case, it took more than two years and several emails and meetings with chairs and directors for me to get approval to affiliate with both programs. It was also difficult for me to wait while colleagues would discuss whether I was competent enough or not to be appointed to a graduate program (Gutiérrez y Muhs et al. 2012). I also found access to graduate teaching hard because only certain new professors have this privilege. It was not until two years after being tenured and complaining to my union that I was able to teach a PhD methods course in a different school. As Black women in political science, we must ask those tough questions to show how conscious this bias is, but speaking up is never easy.

Most insulting to me was that my program would not let me create my own course at the undergraduate level. I was only allowed to service courses already on the books. In Gutiérrez y Muhs et al. (2012), so many women of color recount over and over again the alienation one feels in academia. Meanwhile, sessional white teachers, many with no doctorate, were able to teach in units with ease and flexibility, even at the graduate level. My work has been winning prizes for articles and books, and I publish with top-tier book publishers, such as the University of Toronto Press and Oxford University Press.

Achieving global recognition as a research chair does not stop white men, including those with no qualifications, from being difficult to us. In two human rights applications that I filed, I allege that a white male—who had no PhD, no expertise in the field, no publications, and no relevant work experience—would confront me on a downtown street because he felt my tenure-track hire ousted him from his appointments. What I saw was that some contract faculty were protected by their white professoriate.

The challenges I have experienced also arise from my research. I study informal institutions and work with Black people in the community who are not respected. For years, York has had a troubled history with the Jane & Finch community, one of the poorest urban peripheral communities in Canada. I know this community firsthand because my father's business has been there for at least forty years and I live a seven-minute drive from it. In 2021, a woman from a partner organization of mine in a low-income community called me. A finance officer had followed up with her directly, believing her work to be a "fraud." As a result, I had to deal with the partner. I also reported the incident so it would not happen again.

Legal Action as Another Form of Therapy

As Black women harmed by colleagues, we spend a lot of time on actual therapy but the legal process has helped me address some of my suffering. It is expensive and one must set aside a lot of money to pay lawyers on retainer, but it is what keeps us safe in this academic system. My union was only helpful to a certain point and was limited on how to address intersectional matters for Black women. The time came when I had to hire outside counsel.

With my own counsel, I knew that my interests were the priority. Table 14.1 lists some of the issues I document in my human rights applications. It outlines ten issues I endured over a nine-year period as a

Table 14.1. Selected Issues for the Period 2012–2021, as Documented in an Application

Alleged Issues	Description
Denial of graduate teaching	I allege that I was not appointed to any graduate program besides gender studies because of the influence of white administrators and, at times, contractuals or new faculty with fewer publications taught courses I was qualified for.
Not allowed to create my own courses	In my view, I saw white men with a limited research file create courses for a mostly racialized student body.
Mediation while untenured	I attended mediation sessions over the course of more than a year at which I was the only Black person and the only woman. I believe that this mediation (which failed) was more to manage me than it was to resolve the issues.
Pay inequity	Over the years I applied for salary anomalies because I earned substantially less than many white male colleagues, and this can be proven through the Sunshine List, a public list of salaries.

Alleged Issues	Description
Altercations and not being believed	On a downtown street I was confronted by a colleague with the statement that "I took his job" by getting a tenure-track position. The chair at the time would not believe my complaint when I filed it until a white woman professor who witnessed the event confirmed it was true (and there are emails attesting to this matter). After teaching my course, a white male lecturer was angry that I was late ending my class and insulted me numerous times. The university gave this person tenure despite my lodging a complaint to his then chair.
Bias in assigning courses	The norm is to allow for tenured faculty to have first choice of courses during the main part of the year. Nevertheless, I was denied a course because I would not coteach with a person with whom I had a conflict and who had no PhD or publications in the field.
Internal human rights center	As my lawyer explained in a letter, the center failed to do the one thing they are supposed to do: investigate and interview people. A center like this makes Black women even more vulnerable because it interviews us over a period of time, triggering unpleasant memories.
Retaliation and financial reports	Ten months after leaving the university, a white male administrator accused me of ineligible claims for a grant they failed to reconcile when claims were first submitted. Following a refusal to transfer the balance of my grant, my lawyer had to write a letter and the ministry had to intervene to resolve the issue.
Disciplined for participating in the collegial process	I was written up by a senior administrator and have the letter for going public on social media about the hiring process and a problematic hire.
Politicized research chairs	Though I was denied twice for an internal research chair for unverifiable reasons, white women faculty (including one who voted against my proposal for a chair) asked me to join their research project. Based on their email, the project looked at African women and their relationship to vervet monkeys, and they thought my project on the financial exclusion of Black Canadians was a fit.

tenure-track professor.[4] I choose not to go into too many details or name people because this case is moving through the legal process.

The issues above are largely why I had to leave a school that I worked at for nine years and was planning on retiring at. I felt even though I was tenured I was still vulnerable to microlevel aggressions and denied opportunities and sometimes felt that less qualified men would have access to things that I did not have access to. How would the parents of the mostly immigrant students feel if they knew that their money for tuition was paying for their children to be taught by less qualified people (often with no PhD degree)?

What I learned while at York was that branding mattered. Universities can market your work for the external awards and deny you any internal awards. I found that awards from internal committees were often given to "certain" scholars who are connected to the administration in ways they find appropriate. A number of awards would go to those active in the administration, and I have seen that some were even spouses of administrators. And those of us who report abuses by white colleagues were ignored and told to coteach with hostile men.

The issues I list in table 14.1 do not include many of the everyday racist encounters I experienced—for example, colleagues mistaking me for a secretary and asking me to get supplies or someone to fix the photocopier, or telling me that my hair would look more "professional" if it was straightened, or interrupting my meetings because they did not see me as their peer. Many faculty hide behind the concept of collegiality as a way to discipline certain colleagues.

Positive Disruption: Fighting for a New Way in Political Science

After a decade of being an academic, I'm finally in a place where I am happy. I am trained in international development and comparative politics, and I am working in fields for which I have the requisite expertise. For years, academics assumed that I was an economist because of the department I worked in and the work I do, straddling both politics and economics. I also have been ashamed that I am a political scientist. The androcentrism and whiteness that dominate the discipline are abysmal, and when one is not wanted, one will not identify with that group, if they can avoid it. Luckily, I found a home for my work in feminist economics.

In fact, I have noticed that many Black and racialized women studying politics or economics choose to be called political economists, hearkening to the time before silos existed between political science and economics. I am one of those academics that calls herself a political economist.

Know Your Worth

I will never forget when a full professor (a white male) called me into his office and told me that he could not understand why I received so many job talks, that it must be that "something" on my paper resume was interesting because that was not the case for me in person. I was in a contractual position when I was told this. I confided in others, who told me to ignore him. It was then and there that I knew I was worth more than this man insulting me and that I would build my own community.

I urge Black women to join associations and collectives where you can grow and do well. I did join a Black political science association called the NCOBPS and one called the International Association for Feminist Economics (IAFFE), where I serve on the global board of directors and am active in the membership and publication committees because I am valued. The mainstream political science organizations in the United States and Canada did not think about politics in the way that I was doing it. Given that I was a mature student, I also could not find mentors and allies within those organizations.

At NCOBPS I found a support system. Early on in graduate school (2007) and thanks to Professors Lisa Aubrey, Russell Benjamin, James Taylor, and Sharon D. Wright Austin, I felt like I belonged in political science. I was grateful for NCOBPS, as it pushed the boundaries of political science to think about issues that mattered to excluded people around the world. There, I found other women scholars who had been negatively impacted by the tenure process at their university. I remember that one stood up in a room of people and shared her tragic story of being denied tenure: this stayed with me. It was that sharing moment when I also felt it was okay for me to be very public about the harms from the university. NCOBPS has been my only connection to the politics field—a conference led by Black scholars dedicated to the study of Black politics. I met many NCOBPS colleagues who shared my class background and who could understand how trying it was to be a scholar in any academic department. NCOBPS saw me as a political scientist and often referred to me as their "Canadian" sister.

In 2017, I won the Helen Potter award for my article at the Association for Social Economics, and this changed my role from being unknown in social economics to having a Black feminist voice in the field. Around this time, my unit was in formal mediation. In 2018, I was a cowinner of the W. E. B. Du Bois Distinguished Book Award from NCOBPS, and these external awards were being shared widely through York's social media outlets.

A strong feminist network gave me the refuge I needed most. Many IAFFE scholars have endured various forms of misogyny and have been able to do powerful work and continue to uplift one another. I tell junior scholars to find the global academic organizations that fit their research and attend those meetings and find mentors and friends there. When I won the Agarwal Book Award from IAFFE and was flown to Glasgow to receive my award, York promoted this win from one of the world's best feminist economist organizations. I learned that to be a disruptor, we need to spread our wings and build academic communities outside of where we work.

And as you meet other people you learn that what you are enduring is not acceptable. It was during the pandemic in 2020 that I decided it was enough, and I hired my own legal counsel to represent me against my university and two male colleagues. At the same time, I won the Emerging Scholar Award from the Comparative and International Education Society–African Diaspora Special Interest Group, recognizing innovative research, and the Rodney Higgins Award for the best faculty paper on Black epistemologies for the solidarity economy; meanwhile, I suffered in my unit. Every year since being tenured (2017–2021), I was recognized as a York Research Leader, but I boycotted the recognition events because all my awards came from the outside and I never received any major award within York. I know that going outside of one's university is vital for Black women scholars in more ways than one.

Teaching as Activist Pedagogy

It was feminist scholar bell hooks (2015 [1981]) who made it clear that Black women are never seen—neither by feminists nor within the patriarchy. In *Teaching to Transgress*, bell hooks (1994) used the classroom as a powerful site for teaching about social change. Though I did not create my own courses in my own unit, I serviced the existing courses by infusing my own knowledge-making. I had students read literature that white men would not (could not) teach on the social economy. I also ensured that in the placement course I taught, the students worked mainly with Black- and women-led organizations.

Through teaching, within the confines of what I was "allowed" to teach, I rebelled and made sure that what I was doing was Blackening the curriculum to appeal to my mostly Black and racialized student body. I made sure to organize events in the classroom and invited Black activists to speak to the students, to change their minds, and to demand that the university consider their educational needs.

Fight the Racial Patriarchy: Figure Out How to Hire Black Women

In 2017, my program was allocated a hire. I was finally, as tenured faculty, "permitted" to sit on the hiring committee. I wanted to be on the committee to ensure no bias in the hires and eventually chaired it. The result was that, instead of making just one hire, three exceptionally qualified women—two of them women of color—were hired.

It is my personal opinion that when I became the new chair of the job-hiring committee, I positively "disrupted" the process. The conversations that took place among the committee were difficult, but I can ultimately sleep easily knowing that those women were hired. I also know that that process changed me. I saw so-called capital F "feminists" silence the only two Black faculty members of the hiring committee. I saw how a mainly white male voting committee diverted from the script for questions, especially for a Black woman, and how colleagues make themselves absent at dinners for certain job candidates. Each job talk was taped so that administrators could see the quality of lectures in the field and the level of the candidates' English for themselves. I wanted to make sure they had every bit of evidence that these three women deserved to be hired.

A few years earlier, the department had had a failed search. In my letter to the administration as committee chair, I justified the new hires on those grounds. They could either hire all three women or have another failed search. Other committee members questioned my tactic. I was successful though. Overnight, the program had shifted from being a white male program to one with gender equity and three full-time women of color. This change in the faculty was a positive disruption. Eventually we must all do the work to ensure that we, as faculty members concerned with equity and social justice, continue to disrupt the field and institutional processes for the better.

In Closing: Being a Unicorn in the Academe

Still, many departments of political science tokenize Black women scholars, and they are often ready to hire Black men, but usually not Black diaspora women. The graduate students, many of them male, do far too much grandstanding. They refuse to accept our evaluations and send "reminders" and "tips" on how to do our jobs, even though we are tenured. The recruitment of graduate students is based on the assumption that we share this notion of what is "the best." Some of the most renowned schools have had a troubled past and rely too much on corporate funders. White faculty who are favored want to be the ones to decide on how knowledge is being reproduced, even those we put into these departments. So, they collude with one another to ensure that their students have a place to continue moving along their own research agendas while leaving others without students. Being a positive disruptor means finding ways to expose those systems that appear to be "inclusive" but are (un)consciously biased.

No one admits to targeting Black women scholars. The exclusion and erasure are often attributed to unconscious bias. Bailey and Trudy (2018) coined the term "misogynoir" to refer to a deliberate exclusion of Black women. Being a Black feminist in the field of political science is very much like being the Black unicorn: one that is different and despised for no reason. Being Black is one thing, but being Black and feminist in the field of political science to study power is threatening. Audre Lorde (1978) writes about the Black unicorn as being depicted as evil and dangerous, one that deserves no place or attention and that suffers over and over again. Black feminists in political science are maltreated and vilified without reason—simply for being Black and female.

Even after a decade of being called out for failing to hire Black women, the racial patriarchy is intact. Departments still hire mainly Black men, and Black women political scientists are still largely missing. While I can see some changes afoot, with the hiring of new faculty who are from the Global South, Indigenous, or Black, there is still a need to hire Black women and to make sure more get through the pipeline. Departments need deliberate plans not only to hire Black women scholars but to listen to promote their work and to listen to their ideas on advocating certain kinds of changes.

Notes

1. This article was supported by the Canada Research Chair program and the Social Sciences and Humanities Research Council, and I used funds to hire legal technical assistance to limit any risks.

2. I self-identify as a Black woman (and specifically a Dougla) of Caribbean heritage born in New York City and raised in Toronto, Canada.

3. We use the term racialized in Canada, but for consistency in this book I will mostly use the term people of color as many of the authors are American.

4. I am willing to share redacted copies of these complaints with any reader if it can help them pursue justice through the legal process; find me on Twitter @carolinehossein.

References

American Political Science Association (APSA). 2011. Political Science in the 21st Century: Task Force Report. https://www.apsanet.org/portals/54/Files/Task%20Force%20Reports/TF_21st%20Century_AllPgs_webres90.pdf.

Aubrey, L. M. 1997. *The Politics of Development Co-Operation: NGOs, Gender and Partnership in Kenya.* London: Routledge.

Bailey, M., and Trudy. 2018. "On Misogynoir: Citation, Erasure, and Plagiarism." *Feminist Media Studies* 18, no. 4: 762–68.

Banks, N. 2020. "Black Women in the United States and Unpaid Collective Work: Theorizing the Community as a Site of Production." *Review of Black Political Economy* 47, no. 4: 343–62.

Douglas, Delia D. 2012. "Black/Out: The White Face of Multiculturalism and the Violence of the Canadian Academic Imperial Project." In *Presumed Incompetent: The Intersections of Race and Class for Women in Academia*, edited by Gabriella Gutiérrez y Muhs, Yolanda Flores Niemann, Carmen G. Gonzalez, and Angela P. Harris, 51–64. Salt Lake City: Utah University Press.

Escobar, A. 2012. *Encountering Development: The Making and Unmaking of the Third World.* Princeton, NJ: Princeton University Press.

———. 2020. *Pluriversal Politics: The Real and the Possible.* Durham, NC: Duke University Press.

Few, A. L. 2007. "Integrating Black Consciousness and Critical Race Feminism into Family Studies Research." *Journal of Family Issues* 28, no. 4: 452–73.

The Fifth Estate. (2021, February 26). *Black on campus: Students, staff and faculty say universities are failing them* [Video]. YouTube. https://youtu.be/y1CQRi76nho?si=HXB7bxTvQr91sY1n

Gordon Nembhard, J. 2014. *Collective Courage: A History of African American Cooperative Economic Thought and Practice.* University Park: Pennsylvania State University Press.

Gutiérrez y Muhs, Gabriella, Yolanda Flores Niemann, Carmen G. Gonzalez, and Angela P. Harris. 2012. *Presumed Incompetent: The Intersections of Race and Class for Women in Academia*. Salt Lake City: Utah University Press.

Henry, Frances, Enakshi Dua, Carl E. James, Audrey Kobayashi, Peter Li, Howard Ramos, and Malinda S. Smith. 2017. *The Equity Myth: Racialization and Indigeneity at Canadian Universities*. Vancouver, Canada: University of British Columbia Press.

Hill Collins, P. 2000. *Black Feminist Thought: Knowledge, Consciousness, and the Politics of Empowerment*, 2nd ed. New York: Routledge.

hooks, bell. 1994. *Teaching to Transgress: Education as the Practice of Freedom*. New York: Routledge.

———. 2015 (1981). *Aint I a Woman: Black Women and Feminism*. New York: Routledge.

Hossein, C. S. 2016. *Politicized Microfinance: Money, Power and Violence in the Black Americas*. Toronto, Canada: University of Toronto Press.

James, C. E. 2012. *Life at the Intersection: Community, Class and Schooling*. Halifax, NS: Fernwood.

Kabeer, Naila. 1994. *Reversed Realities: Gender Hierarchies in Development Thought*. London: Verso.

Lorde, A. 1978. *The Black Unicorn Poems*. New York: Norton.

———. 2007 (1984). "The Master's Tools Will Never Dismantle the Master's House." In *Sister Outsider*, 110–14. Berkeley, CA: Crossing Press.

Mensah, Joseph. 2010. *Black Canadians: History, Experience, Social Conditions*. 2nd ed. Halifax, NS: Fernwood.

Mondesir, E. dir. 2021. *The Banker Ladies*. Produced by DISE Collective. [Film]. https://www.filmsforaction.org/watch/the-banker-ladies/.

Mullings, B. 2021. "Caliban, Social Reproduction and Our Future Yet to Come." *Geoforum* 118: 150–58.

Oyewumi, O. 1997. "Gender and Colonialism." In *The Invention of Women Making an African Sense of Western Gender Discourses*, 121–56. Minneapolis: University of Minnesota Press.

Pinderhughes, D. 2009. "Presidential Address: The Challenge of Democracy: Explorations in American Racial Politics." *Perspectives on Politics* 7, no. 1: 3–11.

Rodriguez, C. O. 2018. *Decolonizing Academia: Poverty, Oppression and Pain*. Halifax, NS: Fernwood.

Tomlinson, A., L. Mayor, and N. Baksh. 2021. "Being Black on Campus." CBC Fifth Estate. February 24. https://www.cbc.ca/news/canada/anti-black-racism-campus-university-1.5924548.

Wane, N., and K. Deliovsky. 2002. *Back to the Drawing Board: African Canadian Feminisms*. Minneapolis, MN: Sumac.

Willoughby-Herard, T. 2015. *Waste of a White Skin: The Carnegie Corporation and the Racial Logic of White Vulnerability*. Oakland: University of California Press.

Wright Austin, S. D. 2007. *The Transformation of Plantation Politics: Black Politics, Concentrated Poverty, and Social Capital in the Mississippi Delta*. Albany: State University of New York Press.

———. 2018. *The Caribbeanization of Black Politics: Race, Group Consciousness and Political Participation in America*. Albany: State University Press of New York Press.

15

Journey of a Young Black Woman Political Scientist

Lauhren Olivia McCoy

Introduction to Political Science

During my time at my undergraduate institution, I was required to take a multitude of political science courses to satisfy my degree requirements. Being that the political science department was rather compact, I quickly became familiar with many of the professors within the department as well as other political science majors within the program. With such a tight-knit community, I was able to identify the majority opinions and ideologies of most of my counterparts and saw firsthand how their beliefs would influence my experiences at my institution. Coming from a rural area to one of the largest universities in my state, I was able to experience a different outlook through courses, including American government and women in politics that gave me the most insight into the differing opinions and values that I had with many of my classmates. I was able to get a better understanding of how important Black women are to political science and how imperative it is to make our voices heard in society. I am grateful to have learned a variety of course material that not only made my experience in college informative but also gave me a guidebook to navigate being a Black woman political scientist in the twenty-first century.

Course Expectations

When I first began college in 2016, it marked a new election year, with the presidential candidates being Hillary Clinton and Donald Trump. Being raised in a Black liberal household, I was taught to "lean blue" because liberals were "for the people." Going into my political science courses, I expected most of my classmates to have been taught the same principles; however, I was wrong. Although I felt as if most of the department were considerably liberal, the masses were overwhelmingly conservative, to the point it almost felt like a religious ideology/practice. My first political science course, Introduction to American Government, was focused solely on the bases of familiarizing us with concepts, policies, and the origins of the American government. We discussed the framework of elections, the basis of democracy, and the essentials of the American political system. Oddly enough, we refrained from speaking on the election during this course even though most of what we were learning during this time was very relevant to the course material. Going into this class I was certain we would spend a considerable amount of time watching election updates and discussing each political candidate and the policies that each candidate was running on. I was taken aback for a few weeks because my expectations were not being met, but as time progressed, I understood why during some of our class discussions. As the semester progressed and I became more aware of my professors' teaching styles, which ultimately gave me a glimpse into their political stances, I realized not only how the institution they were teaching for shaped the verbiage of their lectures but also how the majority opinions somewhat restrained them from having open dialogue within their classroom. One of the first lessons I learned at my institution within the political science department was that people have differing views on certain policies. However, how they choose to operate within disagreement speaks more to their character than it does policy. Having a Black woman professor, who was liberal, I understood the scrutiny she may have faced if she were to open a dialogue that would make most of my white classmates feel as if they were being targeted, which at the time was a huge issue for me being part of a marginalized group within the classroom. I remember laughing to myself about how ludicrous it was for us to refrain from certain conversations because it would result in a race debate, which ironically is the framework this country was built upon. Imagine being a minority within a group and constantly having to be mindful of what you say or how you feel because the majority will invalidate your thoughts and views solely based on your race and even your gender. I quickly realized how my experience as a Black woman student would continue for the rest of my time at my institution.

Black Women's Representation in Political Science

The summer of my freshman year of college I had an internship with Congresswoman Terri Sewell of the seventh congressional district of Alabama. I was tasked with writing mail memos, creating a small business booklet, gathering constituents' concerns, and collaborating with other interns to bring suggestions to the congresswoman. Of all the opportunities I was fortunate enough to have during college, this by far was the most influential on my political science career. Ever since high school my goal was to become an attorney, and majoring in political science was typically the route to take to ensure it. I remember discussing our ambitions of attending law school after undergrad with the congresswoman, and she suggested that we make sure of our decision because to go to law school was too major a financial decision to subsequently be unsure of our career after completion. Most politicians have a juris doctorate and are barred attorneys, so her advice was sound. I then took the time to figure out if I could enter the realm of politics and all that comes with public administration and government. I became more attentive to our local election procedures and the candidates running in my jurisdiction. I quickly noticed the false interest many of the candidates had in their constituents before and after they were elected. Many of the predominately Black neighborhoods were pandered to by local officials and promised results that they never received after their preferred candidate was in office. I remember a constituent from an outside district calling our office and explaining how a train was blocking a neighborhood entrance that housed mainly elderly people and how they tried to contact their representative, but their calls were not going through. We assured them that we would get in touch with their representative, and they responded with how politicians are always present when they need their vote but, once they have it, they are nowhere to be found. That resonated with the experiences I had had during my internship, and it opened my eyes to what it truly means to be a Black woman in politics. Most times you are either a token who uses your identity for personal gain with no intentions of helping your people or you get in a position of power and realize just how little you truly have, and the system changes your views on the political system entirely. Not to mention the constituents who invalidate your qualifications based on your race and gender. Being an intern for a representative today includes maintaining and checking social media for any live updates that may have happened in the house. I remember reading the comments following some of the congresswoman's tweets that dispelled her ability to lead and represent her people because she was a Black woman.

Black Women's Gaze

There's a quote by Anna Julia Cooper that states "when and where I enter . . . the whole negro race enters with me" ("Anna Julia Cooper" 1970). This is one of the most powerful quotes I ever came across in undergrad. This quote was introduced to me by my African American studies professor, and I am thankful for this important piece of literature because it is the epitome of my journey as a Black political scientist. In undergrad, I had a course that was built around a simulation that required us to act as if we were government officials within a small town. We covered a variety of issues, including abortion, taxes, racial injustice, and climate change, and with each scenario, based on whatever position we held within the town, we had to make decisions that best fit the people we governed. During this course, I had an interesting outlook on how many people view politics and policy. Most people vote in their best interest; however, most Black women vote with others in mind. Most of my classmates, who were majority white men, would back policies that solely benefited them and even in some cases voted against policies that had absolutely nothing to do with them. For instance, one of the issues we faced in the simulation was to defund planned parenthood. Many of the white men in my course believed it was an unnecessary financial decision to fund planned parenthood even after hearing all the benefits and resources it has to offer. Most of them, and women as well, defended their decision based on religious beliefs, completely disregarding the separation of church and state. It was saddening to see how my counterparts were so quick to make decisions that only affected them, and I could see how our elected officials would do the same.

Black women historically have been at the forefront of justice for several groups demanding equality and justice for all. That is why the quote from Anna Julia Cooper is so powerful: it explains the framework of intersectionality, a theory later explained by Kimberlé Crenshaw. Black women fall within the framework of intersectionality because we fall into two categories of discrimination being a woman and Black, not to mention sexual preference, disabilities, and nationality. These categories automatically put us behind, yet we still prevail despite the unfair disadvantages that are placed before us. Hence why it is so important that our voices be heard and our presence felt because even with so much against us somehow, someway we create real change even if we are not able to see it right away. That is why even during a simulation with made-up scenarios I made sure that I spoke up and out on prejudice because I need to be conscious of not only what benefits me but benefits those around me as well.

Gender Politics

One of the classes that I took in undergrad was a gender politics course, more specifically women in politics. I went into this class expecting to hear about the racial divide among women political figures during the women suffragist movement, a historical look into Hillary Clinton's campaign structure and how women trailblazers paved the way for her position in politics, and how many policies that disenfranchise women are enacted and voted on by women. In my gender politics class, we discussed how women have shaped our political system for the advancement of marginalized groups, an opposite viewpoint from what I expected to learn in this class. Most of the rhetoric used when describing these women completely evaded how their political standpoints and ideologies excluded Black women from such advancement. This became a prominent theme in this course because most of the women we discussed throughout the semester created platforms and advocated policies that disenfranchised Black women while promoting advancement for white women. Although the professor who taught this class was exceptional, and overall a very progressive and fair woman, there were many instances where she would teach only from her level of perception, which coming from a white woman can cause dissonance between Black and other women of color in the classroom.

One of the topics we covered in this course was Hillary Clinton's campaign and how historic it was for her to be one of the first women to run for president. We attributed her success to women trailblazers such as Victoria Woodhall, the first woman to run for president, and Susan B. Anthony and Elizabeth Cady Stanton, who advocated for women's rights;

however, we glossed over Shirley Chisholm. Even during Clinton's campaign, she made little to no emphasis on Chisholm's historic achievements not only as a member of her political party but as a woman, which made her campaign for the presidency so historic. White women in politics have a habit of refusing to acknowledge Black women for many of their accomplishments, while Black women give credit when it's due. During the women's suffragist movement, white women activists rallied together to demand rights for women with an emphasis on only other white women. The women's suffrage movement of the nineteenth century dates to the exclusion white women have regarding acknowledging the need for equal rights for all women. In 1866 Susan B. Anthony and Elizabeth Cady Stanton were members of the American Equal Rights Association, which was created to gain voting rights for both women and Black Americans. The issue behind this organization was that white women activists such as Anthony and Stanton used the Black voice and support to aid in their demand for equal rights and the right to vote but fell silent regarding and even disagreed with the right for Black Americans to vote. They even argued that if white women were given the right to vote, their votes would overshadow those of Black men, which is another reason they excluded Black women from many of their efforts to obtain women's rights. Stanton is even quoted as saying, "we educated, virtuous white women, are more deserving of the vote." This historical context speaks volumes about Clinton's lack of appreciation for Black women who came before her. Like many other white women activists, it is always best to look out for themselves and their best image.

In an interesting exercise, we were divided into groups and asked to read an excerpt from *Incidents in the Life of a Slave Girl* by Harriet Jacobs (1861). We were tasked with interpreting her feelings within the text and relating them to modern issues that women face today. To summarize the passage, we were given the enslaved woman was afraid for her and her children's lives, so she decided to escape to protect them. I was amazed at how the white women in my group regarded the enslaved woman as brave and unwavering when asked their opinions on the passage and began to relate it to instances in their own lives where they had to make a "difficult decision" when mine differed tremendously. Deciding whether you want your children to be sold off to different plantations and having little to no idea what will happen to you should never be classified as a "difficult decision." I was almost insulted at how trivial they made the matter seem. In a society that has capitalized on Black suffering, I quickly began to realize how my white counterparts viewed racism in America but also the gender solidarity/women empowerment constructs that are placed on Black women specifically. Black women are expected to be the phoenix that rises from the ashes. Whatever life throws at us, we are inherently supposed to overcome all obstacles with superhero characteristics. This is an extremely dangerous perception because it gives the illusion that Black women are nonhuman and, therefore, we should be able to deal with insane amounts of prejudice, discrimination, and the struggles of simply being Black and a woman all because we are considered "strong." I vividly remember telling my classmates that I strongly disagreed with their perception of this text and how dangerous to Black women it was and still is to view us in such a manner. I regarded Harriet Jacobs as a scared woman who had no other choice but to leave because her and her children's lives depended on it.

Ultimately what are considered acts of bravery come from fear, and historically that is a reoccurring theme within the Black community. Black women are hailed as these figures who can withstand the struggles that men face but lack the same support and power that comes with being a man, but they are also not viewed with the same respect and delicacy as a white woman. Sojourner Truth said it best at the Women's Convention in Akron, Ohio, in her "Ain't I a Woman" speech (1851). Truth details how the women during that time were pushing for equal rights and that the men around them should take their demands seriously because, after all, woman created man. She posed the question "Where did your Christ come from . . . man had nothing to do with him" (Truth). To make such a bold and thought-provoking comment during her time speaks volumes about her inherent ability to lead and set precedent for women to come. She is the epitome of Black women in politics. This was such a fascinating speech because during her marginalization she still spoke for all women as if the women of her time were doing the same for her.

The Black Woman's Vote

In 2017, I worked on the Doug Jones for Senate campaign as a field organizer. I was responsible for recruiting volunteers, training recruits on how to campaign and phone bank, and providing literature for potential supporters. This election was one of the most historic elections in Alabama. Given Alabama's history and reputation of being a red state, the election between the candidates, Doug Jones (Democrat) and Roy Moore (Republican), was very close. While working on this campaign I realized just how important the Black vote, especially the Black woman's vote, was in politics. Our field director expressed the importance of campaigning in predominantly Black areas because statistically those votes were needed to obtain the victory. We spent hours phone banking members of these disenfranchised communities and creating avenues to register voters and provide them transportation to the polls. Once election day came, I worked after hours for a data organization that acquired election results for media outlets, political organizations, and financial firms. I was able to see which counties voted Democratic and Republican in real time. When all the ballots were counted and analyzed, Black women contributed significantly to Doug Jones's winning a seat in the Senate. Without them it would have been impossible for him to win; this election alone proved how important Black women are to politics. Whether we are candidates, politicians, elected officials, or simply supporters, our voices and votes truly matter. The same is true for the Biden/Trump election of 2020, where Black women contributed en masse to Biden's victory.

Life as a Black Woman Political Scientist

Navigating life after undergrad and being a political scientist have been a struggle for me. I know how much work needs to be done in my community; however, finding the right avenue to bring about change is quite challenging. After undergrad, I moved to Chicago, where I began working at one of its inner-city schools that taught mainly Black and Hispanic kids. Being that 98% of my students were minorities, I took it upon myself to align my course material to reflect not only their respective histories but issues that they may face day-to-day. I ran into a lot of opposition as to how I should run my classroom and what was "appropriate" to teach my students. And it became very discouraging after a while, to the point where I felt that nothing I wanted to teach my students was effective to not only their learning but their identity as well. I decided to leave that job and focus on my aspirations of getting into law school and studying for the LSAT. I spent numerous hours using free prep tools and resources online, but I was not achieving the score that I wanted. I then decided to look up the history of the test, and by doing so I came across a few articles that highlighted inequalities between white and Black test takers.

According to a report by the National Association for Law Placement, minority women are overwhelmingly underrepresented in law school, and upon completion of the bar exam Black women account for less than any other minority group in law firms, both on the associate and partnership level. After reading more about the misrepresentation of Black women in the legal field, I question if this data is intentional. Because Black women have contributed to political science and government historically and have created change through voting and protest, one would think that the need for Black women in law would be greater. Even though the data may not be on my side, it is imperative that I and other Black political scientists optimize our place within the realms of political science—because to be a Black woman in the realm of political science is to be overlooked, underappreciated, and undervalued. But that should never be a reason to not have a seat at the table. Historically, Black women have contributed so much to the political framework of this nation that to not include us and recognize our contributions would be to erase the structure of the American government.

References

Andrews, Evan. "Who Was the First Woman to Run for President?" History.com, May 6, 2015. https://www.history.com/news/who-was-the-first-woman-to-run-for-president.

"Anna Julia Cooper." *Smithsonian Libraries*, January 1, 1970. https://library.si.edu/ahwi/outbox/cooper.

Coaston, Jane. "The Intersectionality Wars." Vox, May 20, 2019. https://www.vox.com/the-highlight/2019/5/20/18542843/intersectionality-conservatism-law-race-gender-discrimination.

Gadoua, Renée K. "State of Democracy Lecture Marks Centennial of Women's Suffrage." *SU News*, October 3, 2017. https://news.syr.edu/blog/2017/10/03/state-of-democracy-lecture-marks-centennial-of-womens-suffrage/.

Ginzberg, Lori D. "For Stanton, All Women Were Not Created Equal." NPR, July 13, 2011. https://www.npr.org/2011/07/13/137681070/for-stanton-all-women-were-not-created-equal.

Little, Becky. "How Early Suffragists Left Black Women Out of Their Fight." History.com, November 8, 2017. https://www.history.com/news/suffragists-vote-black-women.

Truth, Sojourner. "Ain't I a Woman?" Rutgers University. https://tag.rutgers.edu/wp-content/uploads/2014/05/Aint-I-woman.pdf.

Tucker, Jennifer. "Shirley Chisholm Paved the Way for Hillary Clinton." *Washington Post*, August 5, 2016. https://www.washingtonpost.com/opinions/shirley-chisholm-paved-the-way-for-hillary-clinton/2016/08/05/468dcf52-58e7-11e6-8b48-0cb344221131_story.html.

16

A Word of Advice to the Doctoral Sisters Who Just Graduated

Leave Hungry, Not Starving

Ashley C. J. Daniels

To my newly minted sister-doctors and sister-doctors to be:
Congratulations on one of the biggest accomplishments of your life! I won't go down the list of everything that it took for you to get here; you already know that better than anyone. Instead, I encourage you to reflect on being *here*. Take pride in your presence, standing in the midst of the moment you worked hard to have. You earned your place here; reflect on that. For those who have yet to reach this milestone, I invite you to reflect on the idea that your time is coming. There will come a time when you, too, will be *here*. Keep moving forward!

As you reflect on being *here* or getting *here*, I know that there will be tons of advice you receive along your journey. The advice will cover all kinds of things, including self-care, impostor syndrome, professional development, and the like. I offer another piece of advice that is a blend of all those things that you may not hear as often–when it comes to pursuing your future, ***go hungry, but not starving***. Allow me to explain.

As a church kid growing up in Baltimore, one of the staples of my childhood summers was attending Vacation Bible School. Whether I was with my mother or grandparents, I knew that at some point between family reunions, vacations, and countless days outside, I would wind up sitting in a small church classroom listening to Bible stories for a week. For those who may not be familiar with this world as much or need a reminder, every year Vacation Bible School, or VBS as we affectionately called it, had a theme. With the theme came a toolkit (usually available at your local Christian supply store) with all kinds of games, prizes, activity sheets, songs, and stories set to entertain kids of all ages in the various classrooms throughout the church. One year, the theme focused on the life of Jacob, known as the father of the twelve tribes of Israel. As the children snacked on small stacks of butter ring cookies and drank room temperature red juice, we listened to our teacher tell us the story of Genesis 25:29–34 about how Esau, Jacob's older twin brother, lost his inheritance as the first heir to their father's fortune (his birthright). As the story goes, Esau spent the entire day hunting and gathering in the field when he returned home exhausted and starving. Jacob was in the kitchen cooking a large pot of stew. Desperate to eat after a long day, Esau begged his brother for a bite to eat. Sensing the desperation of his brother at that moment, Jacob makes the proposition that he will only share the meal with his brother if he gives him his birthright. Overcome with starvation, Esau agreed to trade his birthright for the meal. Later in the chapter, we learn how Jacob reinforced his swindle from Esau with the help of his mother, Rebekah. During the course of the lesson, my teacher framed the story as Esau being wrong for "giving away" his birthright. While she was right on some accounts of Esau being at fault, there was always something about the story where my young mind could not totally put *all* the blame on Esau. After all, it was *Jacob* who coerced his brother in his time of need, right? As I was also taught in the same church space, it is wrong to manipulate others to get the things you want. Where was the condemnation for Jacob? Though I pondered this heavily as my teacher told the story, my limited life experience as a seven-year-old did not provide me with the language to describe how I was feeling. That moment would not come until nearly thirty years later as a newly minted PhD when my mind would revisit this story, and the moral of the story for me would be again to **go hungry, but not starving**.

From where I stand today, the job market for young doctoral graduates is very similar to this Bible story. In some ways, we are like Esau. As doctoral students, we spent many days wandering the academic forest hunting for new knowledge. We spent countless days and nights trapping new ideas, cleaning data, hauling sources, sorting through materials, crafting our research, and performing every other action that can serve as a comparable metaphor between being a huntsman and a doctoral student. And as soon as we reach the end of our academic journey with great joy, we are also often filled with great exhaustion. The constant process of writing and rewriting, thinking and rethinking, researching and (re)researching has left us worn out physically, mentally, emotionally, and spiritually. For those of us who may not have worked jobs outside of academia while matriculating through our programs, we may also be extremely hungry for the next opportunity that comes after being doctoral students. We are anxious about how we will sustain ourselves in the next chapter of our life. In fact, we may be hungry to the point of starvation so that, like Esau, we are willing to feast on whatever opportunity presents itself *at any cost*. And it is here where we may run into a *Jacob*.

Now in the Bible, *Jacob* is an actual person who appears before Esau. Within the confines of this . . . advice, I suppose . . . *Jacob* can be seen as a metaphor for a person *or an opportunity*. In either scenario, it is clear that the key defining attribute of a *Jacob* is anyone or anything that makes a small offer for things of great value or potential based on the person's assumed level of desperation. As noted in the biblical story, Jacob wanted to have the birthright of Esau so bad but was cunning enough to only take it at the most opportune time for little to nothing. Speaking softly but firmly, Jacob waited until Esau was extremely tired and desperate to take his most prized gift away—all before Esau could fully enjoy the gift himself. Connecting this to the subject matter at hand, in the midst of these new waves of battle-worn doctors coming from the academic woods as former students, there are plenty of *Jacobs* waiting to hustle their intellectual gifts away in the form of stolen scholarship, exploited labor, and other forms of common academic abuse among junior scholars. And again, these things do not always look like specific individuals. In my talks with other new PhDs who were also unconventional students like I was (many of us held jobs outside of our institutions that were not academic related), some of the *Jacobs* we've encountered looked like underpaying job offers for which we were overqualified, requests for copies of our dissertations to mine our intellectual property, and people wanting to "just pick our brains" with no compensation. They come in the form of nice emails, gentle compliments, or friendly introductions. They look like senior scholars, junior scholars, nonprofit managers, conference goers, or network attendees. They come in the form of white men, white women, Black men, and Black women. In any case, their primary goal is that of the biblical Jacob: to play on your desperation as a new scholar and to take whatever gift you may have. This issue has left many in pain and fear of enjoying the full academic life they worked so hard to achieve. It causes some to leave academia altogether, leaving the world a lesser place without their beautiful brilliance. Black women seem to be the most susceptible to this problem—being the *Esaus* in a range of ways, from coping with alienation in academia (Collins 1986; Jackson 2019; Blackshear and Hollis 2021; Harbin and Green 2022) to more serious challenges such as emotionally, financially, and professionally taxing legal battles for tenure (Ward and Hall 2022).

But despite this issue, my dear sister-doctors, there is hope. There is a way to protect yourself and your gift in this time of great uncertainty. Granted, it is not 100 percent foolproof; no solution ever is in this life. But hopefully, it is a solution that may give you peace as you navigate this new season of your life. It is the mantra and the charge that I started with at the beginning of this love letter to you: **go hungry, but not starving**.

As I reflected more on the Jacob/Esau saga over time, I realized that one of the problems (of many) in the story was not that Esau was hungry but how he responded to the feeling. Naturally, when you work for something tirelessly and for a long period of time, you develop a hunger for something to satisfy your appetite, physical or otherwise. The problem arises when you try to meet that need with a starvation mindset. What is a starvation mindset? For me, a starvation mindset is when you will do anything by any means necessary to fulfill your appetite, even if it is at a conscious or unconscious detriment to others and/or yourself. A starvation mindset is what drove Esau to give away his gift for a morsel of food. So in considering this, my newest mantra for the next phase of my life is that it's good to be hungry for the next chapter, but not at the expense of giving away my intellectual gifts. As the elder women in my life used to always say: everything that looks good *to* you may not always be good *for* you. When offered something that directly impacts my career, there is nothing wrong with weighing my options carefully to see if it truly adds value or if it could be a potential and unnecessary hazard along my life journey. So sure, I may get strange glances, weird responses, and such because no so-called young scholar in their "right mind" would turn away any opportunity to publish or be employed. But that's been part of the problem. We as an academic society have normalized this exploited behavior for so long that it's become almost standard for young academics to grab any morsel of opportunity available to them, even those that are not good *for* them. And while one part of addressing this problem is telling the *Jacobs* of the world to stop exploiting, another part to this is letting the *Esaus* of the world know how valuable their intellectual gift is and how much it should be cherished and protected.

And that is the advice I am giving you, sister-doctors and sister-doctors to be. When you make the transition from student to scholar, **go hungry, but not starving**. Always look for opportunities to advance your career, but know that you don't have to TAKE every opportunity either. Be vigilant about opportunities and people that tell you that you don't have to do "too much work." Be mindful of those people who may name-drop all kinds of folks to get ahold of unpublished copies of your intellectual property (never do this; HUGE red flag). Do not feel pressured by people "in power" to take whatever they offer you. While you are in school, take opportunities to hone skills outside of being in the academy. Sharpen your administrative skills. Seek internships and fellowships in other fields where your degree is welcomed as you learn a new skill set. That is how you can curb starvation once you graduate so you are thinking more clearly and carefully about the many opportunities that will be shoved in your face. Don't be afraid to question the personal benefit of someone adding your name to a task or project. There is *always* a personal benefit. You have the right to know what it is. And above all else, don't let the hunger pangs of others dictate how you nourish your career. Yes, you may be looked on as weird, or strange, or whatever. But in the end, you will be well fed.

References

Blackshear, Tara, and Leah P. Hollis. 2021. "Despite the Place, Can't Escape Gender and Race: Black Women's Faculty Experiences at PWI's and HBCUs." *Taboo: The Journal of Culture and Education* 20, no. 1: 3.

Collins, Patricia Hill. 1986. "Learning from the Outsider Within: The Sociological Significance of Black Feminist Thought." *Social Problems* 33, no. 6: s14–s32.

Harbin, M. Brielle, and Stacy A. Greene. 2022. "Navigating the Discipline in this Moment: Considering What It Means to Be Women of Color Political Scientists in the Current Political Space." *PS: Political Science & Politics* 55, no. 2: 376–379.

Jackson, Jenn M. 2019. "Breaking Out of the Ivory Tower: (Re)Thinking Inclusion of Women and Scholars of Color in the Academy." *Journal of Women, Politics, & Policy* 40: 1, 195–203.

Ward, LaWanda W. M., and Candace N. Hall. 2022. "Seeking Tenure While Black: Lawsuit Composite Counterstories of Black Professors at Historically White Institutions." *The Journal of Higher Education* 93, no. 7: 1012–1036. https://doi.org/10.1080/00221546.2022.2082760

Contributors

Dr. Nikol G. Alexander-Floyd is professor of political science at Rutgers University, New Brunswick. Her interdisciplinary work and teaching focuses on Black feminist thought, law and politics, and psychoanalysis. Her most recent book, *Re-Imagining Black Women: A Critique of Post-Feminist and Post-Racial Melodrama in Culture and Politics*, was awarded the 2022 W. E. B. DuBois Distinguished Book Award by the National Conference of Black Political Scientists. She is also author of *Gender, Race, and Nationalism in Contemporary Black Politics* (2007) and coeditor, with Julia Jordan-Zachery, of *Black Women in Politics*. Her articles have appeared in leading journals such as *Contemporary Psychoanalysis, Feminist Formations, Frontiers: A Journal of Women's Studies, The International Journal of Africana Studies, Meridians: Feminism, Race, Transnationalism, The National Political Science Review, Politics & Gender, PS: Political Science & Politics*, and *Signs*. She is a recognized leader, being asked to serve for two years as cochair of the annual meeting of the national Women's Studies Association and serving as chair of the American Political Science Association's Committee on the Status of Women and the Profession. She has cochaired the Rutgers University Salary Equity Appeal Committee to promote pay equity and serves as vice-president for tenured faculty and member of the Executive Council of Rutgers Association of University Professors-American Federation of Teachers.

Dr. Sharon D. Wright Austin is a professor of political science at the University of Florida. Her research focuses on African American women's political behavior, African American mayoral elections, rural African American political activism, and African American political behavior. She is the author of *Race, Power, and Political Emergence in Memphis* (2000); *The Transformation of Plantation Politics in the Mississippi Delta: Black*

Politics, Concentrated Poverty, and Social Capital in the Mississippi Delta (State University of New York Press, 2006); *The Caribbeanization of Black Politics: Race, Group Consciousness, and Political Participation in America* (State University of New York Press, 2018); *Beyond Racial Capitalism: Cooperatives in the African Diaspora* (2023 and coedited with Caroline Shenaz Hossein and Kevin Edmonds); and most recently *Political Black Girl Magic: The Elections and Governance of Black Female Mayors* (2023). She has also published several book chapters and articles and is the colead editor of the *American Political Science Review*.

Dr. Lakeyta M. Bonnette-Bailey is a professor of Africana studies at Georgia State University and the codirector for the Center for the Advancement of Students and Alumni. Her research interests include hip-hop culture, popular culture, political behavior, political attitudes, African American politics, Black women and politics, political psychology, and public opinion. Her current research examines the relationship between political rap music and racial attitudes in a book (with Adolphus Belk Jr.) tentatively titled, *Check the Rhyme: Political Rap Music and Racial Attitudes.*
She recently published a coedited volume with Jonathan Gayles titled *Black Popular Culture and Social Justice: Beyond the Culture* (2023). Dr. Bonnette-Bailey has also published a coedited volume with Adolphus Belk Jr. titled *For the Culture: Hip-Hop and Social Justice* (2022) examining the relationships between hip-hop culture and social justice. Additionally, Dr. Bonnette-Bailey published a book titled *Pulse of the People: Rap Music and Black Political Attitudes* (2015).

Dr. Ashley C. J. Daniels (she/her) is a presidential postdoctoral fellow at the University of California, Irvine. She conducts research in the areas of Black politics, Black feminist and womanist theory, public opinion, and popular culture. Her writing has been featured in the *Washington Post*, the *Washington and Baltimore Afro-American Newspaper*, the blog *For Harriet*, the *PHILLIS Journal for Research on African American Women*, *Political Science Today*, and the *National Review of Black Politics*. In addition to her academic work, Dr. Daniels is the project director for the Black Girls Vote Research Network, the academic arm of Black Girls Vote, Inc. She is currently working on a book based on her doctoral dissertation from Howard University exploring the how Black sorority women evaluate and support Black women candidates.

Dr. Terri R. Jett is currently a professor in the Political Science/Peace and Conflict Studies Department and affiliate faculty member of the Race, Gender, Sexuality Studies Department at Butler University. Originally from Richmond, California, she has a BA in ethnic studies, an MPA from California State University-Hayward (now California State University-East Bay), and a PhD in public policy and public administration from Auburn University. Dr. Jett is also the founding and current faculty director of the Butler University Hub for Black Affairs and Community Engagement created in 2020 in response to the killing of George Floyd Jr. and as a re-imagining of the abolitionist roots of Butler University. Her book, titled *Fighting for Farming Justice: Diversity, Food Access and the USDA*, was published in December 2021, and she is working on another book, *Talking about Race: James Baldwin and Margaret Mead Then and Now*. Dr. Jett is also the Emmy-nominated moderator of WFYI Simple Civics and serves on a number of boards, including the Indianapolis Land Improvement Bond Bank Board (as a mayoral appointee), the Board of Indiana Humanities, and the Board of the Federation of State Humanities Councils (as vice-chair).

T. D. Harper-Shipman is the John D. and Catherine T. MacArthur Assistant Professor of Africana Studies at Davidson College. Prior to Davidson, she was a postdoctoral fellow in the Institute for Politics and Strategy at Carnegie Mellon University. Her first book, *Rethinking Ownership of Development in Africa* was published in 2019. She has published in *Third World Quarterly*, *Journal of Asian and African Studies*, *Philosophy and Global Affairs*, and *International Studies Review*. She has also published public-facing work in *Pambazuka*, *The Global African Worker*, *Miami Institute of Social Sciences*, and *Africa Is a Country*.

Caroline Shenaz Hossein is associate professor of global development studies and political science at the University of Toronto, Scarborough, Canada. She holds a Canada research chair tier 2 in Africana development and feminist political economy and an Ontario Early Researcher Award. She is the author of the award-winning *Politicized Microfinance: Money, Power and Violence in the Black Americas* and the editor of *The Black Social Economy, Community Economies in the Global South and Beyond Racial Capitalism*. She is a founding member of the international Diverse Solidarity Economies Collective (DISE), highlighting the need to amplify culturally diverse community economies to counter the systemic economic exclusion of marginalized populations. See more at Twitter @ carolinehossein and www.africanaeconomics.com.

Dr. Tara Jones holds a PhD in depth psychology, specializing in community, liberation, indigenous, and ecopsychologies from Pacifica Graduate Institute. She earned a master's in the science of teaching, a master of arts in counseling psychology, a master of arts in depth psychology from Pacifica Graduate Institute, and a bachelor of arts in sociology and Black studies from University of California, Santa Barbara. She has served as a public school teacher, social-emotional learning facilitator for teens and young adults, psychotherapist, community mental health expert, and employment specialist. She currently coordinates the African diasporic Cultural Resource Center at the University of California, Santa Barbara and serves as an Academic Achievement Counselor for UCSB's Educational Opportunity Program, supporting first-generation and income eligible students' retention and matriculation. Her scholarship explores the topics of the ecology of well-being in public education, teacher well-being, cross-professional applications of counseling to teaching, pan-African traditions of educational fugitivity, Black womxn's activism as a response to Black maternal necropolitics, legacies of transnational African diasporic research, reggae epistemologies, and African-centered psychologies. Her scholarly work has been published in *Meridians: Race, Feminism, Transnationalism*. Her visual art has been featured on the covers of the *National Political Science Review*, a publication of the National Conference of Black Political Science. She is the 2023 winner of the Caribbean Philosophical Association's Anna Julia Cooper Award.

Dr. Julia S. Jordan-Zachery is professor and chair of the Women's, Gender and Sexuality Studies Department at Wake Forest University. Her interdisciplinary research focuses on African American women and public policy. She is the author of the award-winning books *Black Women, Cultural Images and Social Policy*, *Shadow Bodies: Black Women, Ideology, Representation, and Politics*, and *Erotic Testimonies: Black Women Daring to be Wild and Free* and several articles and edited volumes, including "Black Girl Magic beyond the Hashtag," "Black Women and da 'Rona" and "Lavender Fields: Black Women Experiencing Fear, Agency, and Hope in the Time of COVID-19." Jordan-Zachery also produced the documentary *Healing Roots*.

Dr. Angela K. Lewis-Maddox is a professor of political science and assistant dean of student engagement in the College of Arts and Sciences, University of Alabama at Birmingham. She is an established scholar in Black politics, publishing in nationally recognized journals, including the *National Political Science Review, PS: Political Science & Politics, American Review of Politics, International Journal of Africana Studies,* and *Polity.* She has also provided political commentary and analysis for local, state, national, and international media outlets. Her work examines Black political opinions and Black political behavior. Most notable among her research is *Conservatism in the Black Community: To the Right and Misunderstood,* which examines the existence of conservatism in the Black community. Her teaching focuses on social justice and encompasses wellness practices to enhance student learning.

Dr. Lewis-Maddox has received numerous awards, including the Anna Julia Cooper Teacher of the Year from the National Conference of Black Political Scientists, University of Alabama at Birmingham Black Student Awareness Committee Faculty Award, and the Southeastern Association of Educational Opportunity Program Personnel, TRIO Achiever Award. In political science, she has served in leadership in various professional associations, including the American Political Science Association, the National Conference of Black Political Scientists, and the Southern Political Science Association.

As a first-generation college graduate and an alum of the Ronald McNair Post Baccalaureate Program, she completed the BA in political science from the University of Alabama and the MPA and PhD from the University of Tennessee. She is also a 2023 Higher Education Resource Service Leadership Institute graduate. Her leadership philosophy is equity centered, and she believes that to whom much is given, much is required.

Lauhren Olivia McCoy was born on September 25, 1997, to a single mother in rural Alabama. She is a graduate of the University of Alabama at Birmingham with a degree in political science and African American studies. During her time at the University of Alabama at Birmingham she interned for Senator Doug Jones and Congresswoman Terri Sewell; she assisted constituents with local concerns, aided the congresswoman in meetings and campaigns, and labored on numerous projects for the Birmingham area. Currently Lauhren is an intern for Viola at Chicago, where she assists the marketing team with brand-consumer relationships and marketing brand attributes.

Dr. Desireé R. Melonas is an assistant professor in the departments of Political Science and Black Study at the University of California, Riverside. She researches and teaches in the areas of Black political thought, critical geography, new materialism, and Black feminist thought, and she is working on her book to be titled *Place in Black: Moving Racial Geographies*. Her work has appeared or is forthcoming in *Theory & Event*, *Meridians*, *Women Studies Quarterly (WSQ)*, *National Review of Black Politics*, the *Journal of Women, Politics, & Policy*, *The Routledge Companion to James Baldwin*, and *The Routledge Handbook to the Lived Experience of Ideology*. Desireé is a 2020–2021 Woodrow Wilson Career Enhancement Fellow and is currently a co-principal investigator on a $1.25 million National Academies of Sciences grant to assist in developing environmental justice-focused, service-learning based curricular interventions in an Africatown, Alabama, middle school as well as in neighboring schools.

Dr. Sherice Janaye Nelson is a speaker, author, and researcher and has a decade of higher education experience. She has taught at the University of California, Berkeley and other premier institutions in the San Francisco Bay Area and in Los Angeles, California. She was the inaugural director for the Jewel Limar Prestage Public Policy, Polling, and Research Center, which preforms mixed methods research that tells the stories of Blacks with data at Southern University. Dr. Nelson is only historically Black colleges and universities educated and earned her masters of public administration focusing in public management at the University of the District of Columbia. She graduated magna cum laude with a dual degree in history and English from Stillman College in Tuscaloosa, Alabama.

Dr. Clarissa Peterson is professor of politics and African and African American studies and special advisor to the vice provost for Diversity, Equity, and Inclusion for Faculty Affairs at Sewanee: The University of the South, where she teaches American politics and African and African American studies.

Dr. Peterson's research focuses on the role that race plays in American political behavior. Her research has been published in journals such as *The National Review of Black Politics*, *The Journal of Black Studies*, and *the Journal of Race and Policy*, and she has written several book chapters. Her book, coauthored with Emmitt Y. Riley III, *Racial Attitudes Today: One Nation Still Divided*, focuses on the relationship between racial resentment and American politics. Dr. Peterson has also authored several grants, including a GLCA Global Connections Grant to investigate racial attitudes in Australia. Professor Peterson has served as both the Frank L. Hall Endowed Professor of Political Science and the Lenard B. and Mary E. Howell Endowed Professor of Political Science at DePauw University and held the Schaenen Faculty Fellowship.

Dr. Adaugo Pamela Nwakanma is a postdoctoral fellow at the Stavros Niarchos Foundation Agora Institute at Johns Hopkins University. She earned her PhD in political science and African and African American studies from Harvard University in 2022 and will be joining University of California, Irvine as an assistant professor of political science in the fall of 2024. She studies international development and democratic politics in Africa and Afro-diasporic communities in the Americas. Previously, she was a Leading Edge Fellow with the American Council of Learned Societies, where she coordinated research strategies for People Powered. Her work has been published in journals such as *Perspectives on Politics* and *Politics, Groups, and Identities*, as well as edited volumes such as the *Palgrave Handbook of African Women's Studies* and Routledge's *African Scholars and Intellectuals in the North American Academy: Reflections of Exile and Migration*. Her interdisciplinary research thus far has won multiple awards from the American Political Science Association, the Society for the Study of Social Problems, and the African Studies Association. Her work has also been featured in public media outlets such as *Break the Boxes*, *Collateral Benefits*, and *Voyages Africana*. She is currently working on a book project that examines the relationship between women's economic mobility and political stagnancy in Africa's largest economy.

Dr. Stephanie A. Pink-Harper is an associate professor in the Master of Public Administration Program in the Department of Political Science and Public Administration at the University of Alabama at Birmingham. She obtained her Doctor of Philosophy from Mississippi State University in public policy and administration.

The aim of her interdisciplinary research agenda is twofold. One area explores comprehensive economic development theoretical frameworks that enhance the quality of life for rural local communities. The other explores human resource management theoretical frameworks that enhance the quality of life for public servants in the workplace. Specifically, she focuses on identifying ways that the workplace environment can enhance the quality of life for public servants from marginalized groups.

Her research has been published in the *American Review of Public Administration, Journal of Public Management and Social Policy, Public Budgeting and Finance, Canadian Journal of Administrative Sciences, Journal of Health and Human Services Administration*, the *International Journal of Public Administration*, and *Economic Development Quarterly*.

Dr. Evelyn M. Simien is professor of political science at the University of Connecticut. She is also interim director of the Africana Studies Institute. Simien received her BA in political science from Xavier University of Louisiana, along with her master's degree and PhD in political science from Purdue University. Simien is the author of two books: *Black Feminist Voices in Politics* (State University of New York Press, 2006) and *Historic Firsts: How Symbolic Empowerment Changes U.S. Politics* (2016); she was the editor of *Gender and Lynching: The Politics of Memory* (2011) and *Historic Firsts in U.S. Elections: Trailblazing Candidates in Gubernatorial, Congressional, and Mayoral Campaigns* (2022). She has published in such peer-reviewed journals as *Political Research Quarterly, American Politics Research, Perspectives on Politics, Politics & Gender, Politics, Groups, and Identities, Social Science Quarterly, DuBois Review, Journal of Women, Politics, and Public Policy, PS: Political Science & Politics, Frontiers: A Journal of Women's Studies, Women & Politics, Political Science Quarterly*, and *the Journal of Black Studies*.

Dr. Kira Tait is an assistant professor in the Department of Politics at the University of California, Santa Cruz. She teaches courses on constitutional law, legal studies, and the politics of sub-Saharan Africa. She earned her doctoral degree in political science from the University of Massachusetts, Amherst and was the 2021–2022 Chancellor's Postdoctoral Fellow at the University of California Irvine in the Department of Criminology, Law and Society. In her research, she explores ordinary Black South Africans' perceptions of the law and how they impact their views of the desirability and appropriateness of appealing to courts when they have problems accessing constitutionally guaranteed services. Specifically, she studies why people choose not to use courts to secure access to water, healthcare, education, and housing when it is both legal and possible to do so. Kira's research has been funded by the US Fulbright Program, the National Science Foundation, and the American Political Science Association. Her work has been published in *Law and Social Inquiry*.

Dr. Robin L. Turner is an associate professor of political science at Butler University, an honorary research associate of the Society, Work, and Politics Institute at the University of the Witwatersrand, South Africa, and a cofounder of the Black Women Writing African Politics Collective (previously Transnational Black Womxn Scholars of African Politics). Her research focuses principally on how public policies shape rural political economies, influence identities, and affect people's behavior in southern Africa. She has published on topics ranging from the politics of tradition; dispossession, property, and nature tourism; and field research to decolonial pedagogy in journals including *Africa Spectrum*, *Development and Change*, *Journal of Modern African Studies*, *Peacebuilding*, and *Qualitative and Multi-Method Research*. Currently chair of the Butler Department of Political Science, director of the Peace and Conflict Studies Program, and African Studies minor coordinator, Dr. Turner teaches courses that help students better understand the perspectives, experiences, and political strategies of historically marginalized people in Africa, the United States, and elsewhere in the world.

Dr. Tiffany Willoughby-Herard is associate professor of global and international studies at University of California, Irvine and professor extraordinarius in the Chief Albert Luthuli Research Chair at University of South Africa. Their research explores Black political thought and the material conditions of knowledge production in radical movements; South African historiography; blackness in international relations and diaspora; third-world feminisms; decolonizing theory; feminist pedagogy; Black and African feminisms; and racial capitalism/gendered racisms/sexuality in international relations.

Their forthcoming book, *'I meant for you to be free': Winnie Mandela's Love Letter to Young South Africans, the Post-1994 Generation* explores political education, contemporary youth-led movements, and Fatima Meer, Motsoko Pheko, and Winnie Mandela as South African feminist and pan-Africanist architects of the present. Willoughby-Herard authored *Waste of a White Skin: The Carnegie Corporation and the Racial Logic of White Vulnerability* (2015); coedited *Sasinda Futhi Siselapha: Black Feminist Approaches to Cultural Studies in South Africa's Twenty-Five Years since 1994* (2021) with Dee Marco and Abebe Zegeye; and edited *Theories of Blackness: On Life and Death* (2011). Their scholarship has been published in *Palimpsest: A Journal on Women, Gender, and the Black International*;

African Identities; Journal of Women Politics, and Policy; PS: Political Science and Politics; Critical Ethnic Studies Association; Frontiers: A Journal of Women's Studies; Abolition Journal; Contemporary; Journal of Contemporary Thought; Politics, Groups and Identities; Race & Class; National Political Science Review; National Review of Black Politics; Social Justice; Theory & Event; and *Kroeber Anthropology Society Papers.*

Index

1619 Project, 163–64

Abrams, Stacy, 37
abuse, 148, 202–3, 238, 242, 263–64
academia: Black women in, xii–xiv, 67–69, 74–75, 80, 82–83, 91–95, 99–103, 109–10, 120, 130, 147–60, 163–66, 169, 201–2, 214–15, 225–30, 245–46, 263–65; class in, 21, 31, 228–30, 233–34; diversity in, 149–50, 164–66, 170–71, 213–14, 237–38; gender in, 25–26, 27–28, 79–80, 82–83, 88, 150–51, 153–54, 200–1, 229–31, 244; joy in, 95–99; microaggressions in, 213–23, 225–26, 238–42; power structures of, 97–98, 100–4, 113–14, 123–24, 149, 150–53, 165, 170–71, 181–82, 246; racism and racial hierarchies in, 21–24, 27–28, 31, 49, 55, 132–33, 138–39, 150–54, 156–57, 159–60, 170–71, 194–95, 213–14, 217–18, 229–31; representation in, 67–71, 73–74, 80–83, 88, 109–10, 165, 169, 172–73, 176–78, 188–89, 233–34; violence in, 92; wellness in, 203–5; whiteness and white supremacy in, 228–29, 231

activism, 21–22, 51–52, 112–13, 117–18, 122, 232; scholar-activism, 19–22, 74–75, 113–16, 118, 120, 123–25, 229; teaching as, 244–45; white women and, 255–56
affect, 113–14, 138–39
affirmative action, 199–200, 215–16
African American studies. *See* Black studies
African Heritage Studies Association, 112–14, 118–19, 139–41
African studies, 109–13, 116–18, 120–22, 125–31, 135, 142n5; knowledge production in, 136–41, 226; whiteness in, 130, 139–41
African Studies Association, 130, 135–36, 139–41
Africana feminism, 69–70, 112–13, 115
Africana studies, 139–41, 206
Africana women's studies, 113–14, 139–41
agency, 192–93, 231
aggressiveness, 155–56. *See also* microaggressions
Ahmed, Sara, 25–26, 53n9
Alcoff, Linda, xii–xiii
Alexander-Floyd, Nikol G., 5–7, 9, 12–13, 14, 101, 139–41, 204–5
Ali, Magda, 233

278 | Index

alienation, 32, 50–51, 102–3, 229, 234, 239
Allman, Jean, 130, 135–36, 138–41
allyship: performative, 70–71; pseudoallies, 157–58; whiteness and, 135
American Equal Rights Association, 255–56
American National Election Survey, 174–75
American Political Science Association (APSA), xi–xii, 2–4, 6–9, 23–25, 67–68, 95, 112, 127–28, 200–1, 204–5, 227; African Politics Conference Group, 120–22; Centennial Center, 118–19, 125–26; "Political Science in the 21st Century" report (2011), xii, 2, 7–9, 42–43, 46, 53n5, 60, 67–68, 225, 233–34; Race, Ethnicity, and Politics (REP) section, 11–12, 13; Ralph Bunche Panel, 126–27; "Systemic Inequalities in the Discipline" report (2021), xii, 7–8; Women, Gender and Politics section, 11–12, 13
American Political Science Review (APSR), 10–12
American Society for Public Administration (ASPA), 81
Anthony, Susan B., 255–56
anti-Blackness, 100, 104, 106n5, 118, 122–23, 132–33, 139, 229–30
apartheid, 123–24, 138
approval, 57–62. *See also* prestige
Arbery, Ahmad, 3–4
area studies, 135–36
Arscott, Jane, 231–32
Association for Social Economics, 244
Association for the Study of Black Women in Politics (ASBWP), 2, 6–7, 13, 118–19, 127–28

Association of Caribbean Studies Conference, 122–23
Aubrey, Lisa, 225–26, 234–35, 243
Austin, Sharon Wright, 234–35
authenticity, 65–66, 70, 72, 74
autoethnography, xiii–xiv, 14–15, 103
Azikiwe, Nnamdi, 135–36

Bah, Khadija, 233
Bailey, Moya, 246
Bairros, Luiza Helena, 122–23
BAMA-Kids, Inc., 22–23
Bambara, Toni Cade, 92–93
Banks, Nina, 231, 234–35
Belessis, Stephen, 233
Belk, Adolphus, Jr., 36
belonging, 1, 25, 32, 56, 95–96, 115–16, 130–31, 150, 243–44
Benjamin, Russell, 243
Berger, Michele Tracy, 204–5
Beyoncé, 37
Bible, 167–68, 223, 261–65. *See also* Christianity; spirituality
Biden, Joe, 257–58
Big Boi, 35–36
Black Doctoral Network, 73–74
Black feminism, 12–13, 14, 35–36, 93, 95–98, 112–13, 115, 165–72, 200–1, 204–6, 226, 234–35, 244–46; in academia, 101; care and, 65–66, 70, 94–95; difference in, 128–29; space-making and, 93–94, 96–97, 99
Black Girl Blueprint, 15, 92–95, 97–99
Black girls, girlhood, 19–20, 94–95, 142n3, 188, 190, 191–96, 201–2
Black Graduate Student Association, 199
Black Lives Matter movement, 36
Black Power, 119
Black studies: interdisciplinarity and, 61, 71, 129–30; knowledge

production in, 139–41; political science and, 49; tenure and, 61; as transnational, 112–16
Black Studies Association, 139–41
Black women: in academia, xii–xiv, 67–69, 74–75, 80, 82–83, 91–95, 99–103, 109–10, 120, 130, 147–60, 163–66, 169, 201–2, 214–15, 225–30, 245–46, 263–65; as disruptors, 147–49, 153–54, 157–58, 226–27, 229, 244–46; health of, 67, 152–53, 156–58, 166–68, 188–89, 202–3, 213–14; as important electorate, 257–58; joyful resistance of, 72, 95–97; knowledge production by, 94–95, 98–99, 101–3, 106n5, 110–11, 126–27, 130, 132–35, 139–41, 142n10; in leadership positions, 171–72, 181–82, 188; in legal field, 258–59; in political science, xi–xiii, 1–7, 9–16, 19–20, 23–28, 31–32, 42–43, 45–48, 50–53, 56–62, 67–71, 91–95, 98–105, 109–22, 125–26, 128–31, 139–41, 159, 187–88, 200–2, 205–9, 214, 216, 225–28, 233–44, 246, 251–59; research by and of, 29–31, 61–62, 95–98, 112–16, 120–22, 125–29, 133–35, 204–9, 231, 235–37, 239–40; scapegoating, 3–4, 5–6; service of, 24–26, 51, 55–56, 68–69, 82–83, 119–20, 150–52, 166; social justice movements and, 254–55; as space invaders, 12–15, 139–41; stereotypes of, 4–6, 9–10, 41–42, 68, 151, 160, 171–72, 188–89, 199–200, 219, 256–57; tenure and promotion of, 8, 27, 46, 60–62, 86–87, 110, 149–50, 163–64, 176–77, 178–80, 182, 205–7, 217–18, 220–22, 243–44, 263–64; visibility of, 169, 244–45

Black Women and Girls Collaborative, 94–95
Black Women's Initiative, 13
Black women's studies, 204–5
Black Women's Studies Association, 73–74
blackface, 194–95
Boas, Franz, 132–34
body, 43–44, 73–74, 95–96, 142n7, 169; care for, 72–73, 96–97, 120; disembodiment, 93–95, 99–101, 104–5, 105n2; violence toward, 92, 130
bootstrap mentality, 188
Bottoms, Keisha Lance, 37
British Teachers for East Africa Program, 127
Brown, Nadia E., 74, 117
Bunche, Ralph, 3, 126–28
Burgess, John W., 4
busing policy, 19–23
Butler, Kim, 122–23

Campos, Patricia, 233
capitalism, 96–98, 105n2, 166–67; settler colonial, 133, 138–39; slavery and, 135; violence of, 115–16
care, 65–66, 94–95, 120–22, 139–41, 154–55, 203–4. *See also* self-care
Caribbean, 225, 228, 230–37, 247n2
Caribbean feminism, 235
Caribbean studies, 67–68, 122–23
Carnegie Corporation, 135
Carter, Sydney, 169
caste, 4–7, 10–12
Chandler, Nahum, 126–27
Chapelle, Dave, *Block Party*, 32–33, 38n1
check-ins, 120
childhood. *See* Black girls, girlhood
Chisholm, Shirley, 255–56

280 | Index

Christian, Barbara, 101
Christianity, 66–67, 195–96, 261–64. *See also* spirituality
citation, 8, 114–15, 118, 120–22, 125–26, 128, 225–26, 235
#CiteBlackWomen, 128
Civil Rights Act, 22–23
Clarke, John Henrik, 135–36, 139–41
class, classism, 21, 31, 68–69, 187, 190–99, 228–30, 233–34
Clawson, Rosalee, 200–1
climate, 8, 24, 69, 71, 151–52
Clinton, Hillary, 252–53, 255–56
Cohort Sistas online network, 74
collaboration, 115, 117–18, 120–24
collectivity, 25, 44–45, 104–5, 120, 231–32
collegiality, 8, 159, 229–30, 241, 242
Collins, Patricia Hill, 43, 235
colonialism, 232, 235; knowledge production and, 123–25, 138–39; racial, 115–16, 130, 135; rhythm of, 44–45, 52–53; settler colonialism, 138–39
color-blind policies, 170
Commission of Interracial Cooperation, 135
community, 52–53, 65–66, 72–73, 195–96, 236–37, 243–44
community colleges, 58–59, 229
Comparative and International Education Society, African Diaspora Special Interest Group, 244
comparative politics, 2, 30–31, 126–27, 182n1, 235, 242–43
competition, 61–62, 128–29, 204
complicity, 132
Conaghan, Joanne, 232
Cone, James, 45
conferences, 37, 60, 61, 95–96, 116–18, 122–23, 125–27, 139–41, 159, 200–1, 203, 243–44. *See also* professional associations
Congressional Black Caucus, 119, 127–28
Cooper, Anna Julia, 254–55
COVID-19 pandemic, 3–4, 14, 83, 94–95, 116–18, 244
Covin, David, 122–24
creativity, 65–66, 71, 74, 98, 129–30
Crenshaw, Kimberlé, 254–55
criminal justice, 30–32
critical race theory (CRT), 12–13, 165–66, 170–72, 182, 226
Cross-Generational Echoes International Conference on Intersectionality, 97
cultural retentions, 132–33
cultural taxation, 68–69
culture, 33–36; dominant, 150–52
curriculum, curriculum development, 7, 23–24, 42–43, 46–50, 81, 113–14, 245. *See also* teaching
Curtin, Philip, 130–32

dancing, 41, 43–44, 72–73, 104, 167–68
Davis, Angela, xii–xiii, 50–52
Dawson, Michael, 33–34
DeBarge, "The Rhythm of the Night," 43–44
debt, 191, 198–99
decolonialism, 73–74, 115–16
Delgado, Antonio, 35–36
Deloria, Ella, 134–35
Delta Sigma Theta Sorority, 29–30, 173
democracy, democratization, xi–xiii, 3, 22–23, 35–36, 73–74, 165
Desselle, Shane, 85, 88
diabetes, 67, 188–89, 202–3
diaspora, diasporic thinking, 110–15, 117–19, 122–23, 127–28, 135–36, 230–32

Diesfeld, Kate, 232
difference, xi, 6–7, 25–27, 30–31, 59–60, 100, 113–14, 124–25, 128–29, 173–74, 205–6
disability, 254–55
discipline, disciplining, 97–99, 101, 103–4, 105n4; undisciplining, 101–5, 106n5
disembodiment. *See under* body
diversity, xi–xiv, 7–13, 27, 61, 67–69, 83, 88, 103–4, 147–50, 156–57, 164–66, 170–71, 213–14, 237–38; diversity statements, 100–1; in leadership, 181. *See also* equity; inclusion
Dotson, Arch, 232
Dougé-Prosper, Mamryah, 112
Douglas, Delia D., 227
Drezner, Daniel W., 79–80
DuBois, W. E. B., 4
Duke University, Ralph Bunche Summer Research Program, 29–30
Dunbar, Paul Laurence, 167–68

egalitarianism, 62, 120–21, 170–71
emancipation, 69
embodiment. *See* body
empathy, 26–27, 120, 156
epistemology of being, 93
Epstein, Joseph, 79–80
equality, 12–13, 101, 254–55
equity, xii–xiv, 27, 68–69, 100, 164–66, 245–46; evaluation of, 8, 25. *See also* diversity; inclusion; inequity
erasure, 113–14, 133–34, 138–39, 140–41, 231, 246
erotics, 96–97
Escobar, Arturo, 237
ethnicity, 128–29
ethnic studies, 20–24, 61
Eurocentrism, 58, 123–24, 151–52, 226

exclusion, 5–6, 47–48, 69, 101, 102–3, 109–10, 113–14, 124–25, 170–72, 181–82, 188–89, 199–200, 226–29, 246. *See also* inclusion; *under* power
exhaustion, 180, 202–4, 261–63
exploitation, 5, 74–75, 188–89, 202–3, 263–65
Eyoh, Dickson, 225, 234

faith. *See* spirituality
family, 20, 121–22, 132, 152–53, 158–59, 187–94, 204–5, 209, 223, 237–38
Fanon, Frantz, 142n5; *La Damnés de la terre*, 44–45, 52–53
fathers, fatherhood, 187–94, 209
feminism. *See* Africana feminism; Black feminism; Caribbean feminism
Feminist Africa Network, 125–26
Few, April, 226
fit, 170–72. *See also* hiring
Floyd, George, 3–4, 118
folklore, 133–34
Ford Foundation, 6, 135
friendship, 130–31, 157–58, 159, 228–29, 233, 244
Fujii, Lee Ann, 104
Fulbright scholarship, 235–36

gatekeepers, 139, 166, 170–72, 206–7
gender: in academia, 25–26, 27–28, 79–80, 82–83, 88, 150–51, 153–54, 200–1, 229–31, 244; knowledge production and, 115–16, 132–33; mentorship programs and, 84–88; in political science, 10–14, 46, 53n5, 56–57, 59–61, 110–11, 204–6; power and, 59–60, 123–24; racialized, 9–10, 192, 194–95, 204–5, 229–31, 246, 252–57;

gender *(continued)*
  representation and, 81–83; service and, 82–83; socialization and, 188, 192–94; ungendering, 123–24; whiteness and, 255–57; womxn, 110–11. *See also* Black women; sexism
gender studies, 112–13, 115
General Education Fund, 135
Getachew, Adom, 118–19
Gilliam, Angela, 122–23
glass ceiling, 82
Glover, Maggie, 29–30
Gnamo, Abbas, 234
"go hungry, but not starving," 261–65
Gonzalez, Jovita, 134–35
Graduate Records Examination (GRE), 172–73
graduate school, 8, 16, 30–34, 37–38, 172–75, 197–99, 214–17, 228, 233–36, 262–63
Great Migration, 20
grounding, 120
Gutiérrez y Muhs, Gabriella, 239

Hall, K. Melchor, 112
Hamilton, Charles, 126–27
Hanchard, Michael, 122–23
Hancock, Ange-Marie, 204–5
Hannah-Jones, Nikole, 163–64
Harlem Renaissance, 132–33
Harper-Shipman, Takiyah, 112, 116, 118–20
Harris-Lacewell, Melissa, 33–34
Harris-Perry, Melissa, 69, 204–5
Harris, Adam, 74–75
Harris, Kamala, 165
Harris, Rose M., 6–7
Hartman, Sadiya, 130–31
Harvard University, Nasir Jones Hiphop Fellowship, 36–37

Hassan, Salah, 232–33
healing, 66, 92, 129–30, 166–68
health, 12–13, 117, 152–53, 156–58, 202–3; inner well-being, 73–74; isolation and, 92–93; mental health, 166–68, 188–89
heart disease, 188–89, 202–3
Henderson, Errol, 33–34
Henry, Charles P., 33–34
Henry, Frances, 225–26
Herskovits, Melville, 130, 132–35
heteronormativity, 97–98, 188
hierarchy: challenging, 101, 188–89; class, 193; gender, 59, 130–31, 193; knowledge production and, 115, 123–25, 129–31, 135–39, 142n10; racial, 4–6, 59, 123–25, 130–31, 135–39, 193; university structure as, 4–6, 85–86, 101
Hine, Darlene Clark, 94–95
hiring, 9–10, 46–47, 74–75, 85–86, 149–50, 171–72, 175–76, 201, 206, 216, 217–18, 225, 228, 230, 236, 238, 240–42, 245–46, 262–64. *See also* retention
historically Black colleges and universities (HBCUs), 56, 58–59, 196–97; African studies in, 135–36, 138
HIV/AIDS, 3–4
Hochschild, Jennifer, 56–57, 62
homophobia, 58–59, 219–20
hooks, bell, 14, 73–74, 98–99, 166–67, 171–72, 244–45
hunger, 261–65
Hunter, Thea, 74–75
Hurston, Zora Neale, 132–35
hypertension, 67, 188–89
hypervisibility. *See* visibility

Idahosa, Pablo, 234

Index | 283

identity, 19–20, 66–67, 132; ascriptive, 110–11; multiple axes of, 71, 187–89, 193–95, 204–6
identity politics, 30–31, 37–38
immigrants, immigration, 91, 92, 98–99, 128–29, 230–31, 233–34, 238, 242
impact, 208–9
imperialism, 112–13, 115–16, 124–25, 139
imposter syndrome, 31–32, 169, 261
inclusion, inclusiveness, xii–xiii, 7, 8, 16, 27, 32, 35–36, 37–38, 50–52, 67–69, 73–74, 80, 81, 88, 100–1, 112–13, 156–57, 164–66, 177, 229, 246. *See also* diversity; equity; exclusion
indigenous scholarship, 46–47
individualism, 52–53, 65–66, 93, 99, 105n2
inequity, inequality, xii, 7–8, 34, 61, 68–69, 123–24, 128, 152, 170, 231, 258–59; pay inequity, 240–42
integration, 190, 230
interdisciplinarity, 21–24, 26–27, 35, 60–61, 69–73, 236–38
interest conversion, 170
interiority, 94–95
International Association for Feminist Economics (IAFFE), 243–44
International Association of Black Professionals in International Affairs, 127–28
International Meeting on African Studies, 139–41
International Political Science Association (IPSA), 2–3, 6
intersectionality, 19–20, 27–28, 68–69, 97–98, 204–6, 254–55
invisibility. *See under* visibility

isolation, 102–3, 112–13, 119–20, 147–48, 151, 155–56, 159, 199–200
Iton, Richard, 234

Jackson, Ketanji Brown, 165
Jackson, Melanie Njeri, xii–xiii
Jacobs, Harriet, 256–57
Jacobs, Sarah, 85
James, Carl E., 225–26, 230–31
Jeffries, Leonard, 135–36, 139–41
Jewish identity, 20–21
Jim Crow, 123–24, 128–29, 138
job market. *See* hiring
Joint Center for Political and Economic Studies, 119
Jonah, Ibe Ibeike, 233
Jones, Doug, 257–58
Jones, Mack, xiii–xiv
Jordan-Zachary, Julia, 12, 14, 204–5
Journal of New Political Science, 35
Journal of Politics (JOP), 12
Journal of Race and Ethnic Politics, 122
joy, 65–67, 70–73, 75, 95–99

Kabeer, Naila, 234–35
Kagobe, Melina, 135–36, 139–41
Keeble, Edna, 231–32
Kempadoo, Kamala, 225–26
King, Mae, xii–xiii, 4–6, 13, 126–28, 138, 170–71, 214
kinship. *See* family
Knight, Andy, 234
knowledge production: Africanizing, 123–24; Black radical tradition of, 139–41; Black women and, 47–48, 61–62, 69–70, 94–95, 98–99, 101–3, 106n5, 109–11, 126–27, 130, 132–35, 139–41, 142n10; commodification of, 202–3; democratizing, 73–74; hierarchies

knowledge production *(continued)*
of, 115, 123–25, 129–31, 135–39, 142n10; interiority and, 94; joy and, 96–99; spaces of, 43
Kobayashi, Audrey, 225–26
Kola, Ijeoma, 74
Kuumba Singers (Harvard College), 72–74

Larkin, Byrdie, 214
Laura Spelman Rockefeller Fund, 135
law school, 170, 172–73, 232, 253–54, 258–59
Law School Admissions Test (LSAT), 172–73
leadership, 24–25, 27–30, 59, 60–61, 164–66, 170–72, 181, 188, 199
legal action, 240–42, 244
Lennear, India, 117
Lewis-Maddox, Angela K., xi–xiv
Lewis, John, xii–xiii
Lewis, Shelby, 112–13, 125–27, 135–36, 138–41
LGBTQ+ scholars, 8, 46–47, 142n3
Li, Peter, 225–26
liberal arts, 26–27
liberalism, 170, 182, 252–53
liberation, 51–52, 65–66, 71, 139
Lincoln, Abraham, 5
lived experience, 6–7, 22, 49, 58–59, 98, 187, 230–31, 236–37
Locke, Alain, 135–36
loneliness, 113–14, 150–51, 157–58
Lorde, Audre, 14, 65–66, 94, 96–97, 167–69, 226–27, 246
Lusane, Clarence, 33–34

Mama, Amina, 125–26
Marable, Manning, 132
marginalization, 2–7, 8, 257; in academia, 68, 86, 98–99, 100, 102–4, 149, 151–52, 155, 171–72, 181–82, 252–53; in political science, 7–8, 33–38, 46–50, 56–57, 60, 70–71, 81, 112, 119–20, 124–25, 156–57, 227
marriage, 152–53
Mason, Monica, 233
mass incarceration, 36
maternal mortality, 203
matrix of domination, 113–14
McClain, Paula, xi–xiii, 3–7, 29–30, 214
McClaurin, Irma, 164, 169
McNair (Ronald E. McNair) Postbaccalaureate Achievement Program, 172–73
meditation, 120, 129–31, 203
Mensah, Joseph, 230–31
mentorship, 32, 68, 75n1, 82–88, 118, 200, 231–32, 244
meritocracy, 170, 172, 182
methods, methodology, 173–74, 226–27, 235
#MeToo, 142n7
microaggressions, 31–32, 37–38, 62, 68, 194–95, 198–99, 213–23, 225–26, 238–42
Midwest Political Science Association, 2
misogynoir, 68–69, 110–11
misogyny, 68, 226, 229–30, 244, 246
Morrison, K. C., 122–23
Morrison, Toni, 105n1
mothers, motherhood, 19–20, 152–53, 188, 193–94, 202–3
Mullings, Beverley, 234–35
multiculturalism, 66, 69
music, 32–36, 43–44
mutuality, 120, 237

National Association for Law Placement, 258–59

National Association for the Advancement of Colored People (NAACP), 215, 234
National Black Feminist Study, 204–5
National Black Politics Study, 201
National Center for Faculty Development and Diversity (NCFDD), 73–74; Faculty Success Program, 83–84, 87–88, "WriteNow," 83–84
National Conference of Black Political Scientists (NCOBPS), 2, 6–7, 13–14, 73–74, 110–13, 116–24, 126–28, 139–41, 159, 200–1, 243–44
National Council of Black Studies, 119, 122–23
National Council of Negro Women, 127–28
National Defense Education Act Title IV (1958), 135–36
nationality, nationalism, 35–36, 254–55
Ndulo, Muna, 232
Nelson, William "Nick," 33
Nembhard, Jessica Gordon, 225–26, 234–35
neoliberalism, 93, 99, 105n2
Network of Schools of Public Policy, Affairs and Administration (NASPAA), 84–85
networks, networking, 83, 200–1, 244; research networks, 109–23, 125–26, 128–29, 142n2
neutrality, 22, 24, 62, 101, 172, 182
New York Colonization Society, 135
norms, 124–25; in academia, 71, 79–80, 86–87, 101, 148, 150–51, 170–71, 169; in political science, 1, 12–13, 56–61, 130–31
Norrlöf, Carla, 234
Norwood, Chris, 233

Obama, Barack, 3, 35–37, 176–77

objectivity, 116–17, 130, 132–33, 172, 182, 235
Ohito, Esther O., 96–97
Onyawu, Nicholas, 135–36, 139–41
Opportunity Doctoral Fellowship, 198–99
Orfield, Gary, 29–30
organizing, 35–36, 61, 112–13, 117–18, 120, 122–23
outsider, 31–32
Oyěwùmí, Oyèrónké, 115–16, 126, 235

Padilla, Elena, 134–35
Paige-Pointer, Barbara, 20
Pala, Achola, 126
Pan-Africanism, 112, 115–16, 117
Pateman, Carole, 3
paternalism, 101
patriarchy, 69–70, 93, 132–33, 188, 246
Peck, M. Scott, 166–67
peer review, 207–8
personal life, xv, 19–20, 67, 74–75, 158–60
Phelps Stokes Fund, 135
Phillips, Layli, 24
Philpot, Tasha, xiii–xiv
Pinderhughes, Diane, xi–xiii, 3, 7, 25, 42–43, 214, 225, 227
pipeline programs, 201–2
plagiarism, 225–26
podcasts, 37
poetry, poetics, 130–31, 138–39
police, policing, 80, 113–14, 151–52, 169
political science, 2; Black women in, xi–xiii, 1–7, 9–16, 19–20, 23–28, 31–32, 42–43, 45–48, 50–53, 56–62, 67–71, 91–95, 98–105, 109–22, 125–26, 128–31, 139–41, 159, 187–88, 200–2, 205–9, 214, 216, 225–28,

political science *(continued)* 233–44, 246, 251–59; as caste system, 4–7, 10–12; culture and, 33–36; ethnicity in, 128–29; gender in, 10–14, 46, 53n5, 56–57, 59–61, 110–11, 204–6; identity politics in, 30–31, 37–38; interdisciplinarity in, 23–24, 26–27, 60–61, 205–6; knowledge production in, 30–36, 58–59, 61–62, 69–70, 97–98, 109–10, 130–31, 139–41; liberal arts and, 26–27; marginalized groups in, 7–8, 33–38, 46–50, 56–57, 60, 70–71, 81, 112, 119–20, 124–25, 156–57, 227; methodology in, 173–74, 226–27, 235; neutrality in, 22, 24, 62; power and, 59–60, 113–14, 130–31, 152–53; publishing in, 34–36; race and racism in, xi–xiii, 3–14, 22–24, 37–38, 46–50, 56–60, 110–11, 116–17, 119–20, 139–41, 142n5, 204–6, 252–53; representation in, 12–14, 46, 53n5, 70–71, 112–13, 119–20, 233–34, 253–54; teaching, 26–27, 46–50

Political Science Graduate Student Association, 199

Political Science Quarterly, 4

Politics, Groups, and Identities, 58

positionality, 109–10, 115, 128–29, 202–3

poverty, 190, 194–95, 198–99, 219

power, 2, 5–6, 59–60; exclusion and, 100–3, 113–14, 165, 226–27, 246; in knowledge production, 115, 130–31; institutional violence and, 9–10; language and, 97–98; maintenance of, 123–24, 149, 152–53, 170–71, 181–82

predominantly white institutions (PWIs), 24, 170–71, 217–18

Prestage, Jewel, xii–xiii, 6, 13, 214

prestige, 57–62

productivity, 7, 68–69, 150–51, 193–94

professional associations, 2–3, 6–14, 60, 73–74, 112–14, 118–19, 122–26, 200–1, 243–44

professional development, 83, 200–1, 203, 261

professionalism, 242

PS Sistah Scholar virtual community, 74

public administration, public policy, 2, 19–20, 22–23; Black women in, 80–81, 88

publishing, 34–36, 176–77, 179–80, 204–5, 207–9

race, racism, 3, 20, 58–60, 68–69, 104, 132–33, 151–52; in academia, 21–24, 27–28, 31, 55, 132–33, 138–39, 150–54, 156–57, 159–60, 170–71, 194–95, 213–14, 217–18, 229–31; gender and, 9–10, 192, 194–95, 204–5, 229–31, 246, 252–57; health and, 67, 117, 152–53, 188–89; hierarchy and, 4–6, 59, 123–25, 130–31, 135–39, 193; knowledge production and, 58–59, 68, 115–16, 132–33; mentorship and, 84–88; in political science, xi–xiii, 3–14, 22–24, 37–38, 46–50, 56–60, 110–11, 116–17, 119–20, 139–41, 142n5, 204–6, 252–53; power and, 5–6, 59–60, 139; stereotypes and, 4–6, 139; teaching and, 153, 159, 218–20

Race and Democracy in the Americas Project, 122–26, 142n3

Ramos, Howard, 225–26

rational choice theory, 57–59, 61

Rauseo, Elizabeth, 233
reflexivity, 97
relationality, 115–16, 118
representation: in academia, 67–71, 73–74, 80–83, 88, 109–10, 165, 169, 172–73, 176–78, 188–89, 233–34; burden of, 198–99; in political science, 12–14, 46, 53n5, 70–71, 112–13, 119–20, 233–34, 253–54
representative bureaucracy, 80–83, 88
research, 2, 32–36, 58–59, 68; African studies in, 136–38; by and of Black women, 29–31, 61–62, 95–98, 112–16, 120–22, 125–29, 133–35, 204–9, 231, 235–37, 239–40; collaborative, 115; engaged, 69–70, 73–74; experimental, 129–31; as forward facing, 36–37; healing and, 129–30; quantitative methods in, 61; transnational, 116–19, 122–24
resiliency, 45, 71, 192
retaliation, 240–42
retention, 8, 68–69, 85–86, 88, 165–66, 201–2, 203–4, 223. *See also* hiring
rhythm, 41–46, 50–53
Robinson, Cedric, 135
Robinson, Pearl, 126–27, 132–33, 135–39
Rockquemore, Kerry Ann, 83, 87–88
Rodney, Walter, 132
Rodriquez, Clelia, 229
role models, 25, 201–2
Rosenwald Fund, 135
Rubin, Marilyn, 81
Russell, Tonya, 79–80

safety, safe spaces, 33, 37–38, 142n3, 220, 240
Sanders, Bernie, 35–37
#SayHerName, 169

scapegoating, 3–4, 5–6
scholar-activism. *See under* activism
Scott, Jill, 29–30
segregation, 128–29, 138
self-care, 65–67, 70–72, 83, 204–5, 223, 261. *See also* care
self-determination, 115–16
Semmes, Clovis, 177
Sen, Shayan, 233
service, 24–26, 51, 55–56, 68–69, 82–83, 119–20, 150–52, 166
Sewell, Terri, 253–54
sexism, 166–67; in academia, 68–69, 79–80, 93, 97–98, 154, 157–58, 159–60, 229–31, 244; health consequences of, 67, 188–89; in political science, xi–xiii, 58–60, 93; in teaching, 153. *See also* gender
sexuality, xii, 205–6, 254–55
Shklar, Judith, 3
silencing, 156, 167–70
Sistah Scholar, 117
Skinner, Elliott, 126–27
slavery, 3–4, 20–21, 45, 115–16, 123–24, 132, 135, 166–67
Smith, Malinda S., 225–26, 234
Smith, Roger, 10
Smith, Steven Rathgeb, 10
Smooth, Wendy, 13, 204–5
social justice, 25, 36–37, 245–46; self-care and, 65–66
social reproduction, 123–24
Social Science Research Council, 135
sociality, 115–16, 120–22
Southern Christian Leadership Council, 127–28
Southern Political Science Association, 2, 200–1
space invaders, 1–2, 12–15, 139–41
space-making, 93–94, 96–97, 99, 109–13, 122–23

speaking up, 159–60
spirituality, 180, 223, 261–64; joy and, 72–73; resistance and, 93
spirituals, 45
Stanton, Elizabeth Cady, 255–56
starvation mindset, 264–65
stereotypes, 4–6, 9–10, 41–42, 68, 139, 188–89, 194–95, 198–200, 219; angry Black woman, 160, 171–72; Mammy, 151; strong Black woman, 256–57
storytelling, 97, 106n5; counterstorytelling, 170, 182
stress, 156–58, 166–67, 188–89, 199, 202–3, 216–17
stretching, 120
Stromile-Golden, Kathie, xii–xiii
student evaluations, 9–10, 68. *See also* teaching
subjectivity, 94, 205–6
success, 37–38, 73–74, 152–53
suffering, 99, 256–57
suffragist movement, 255–56
survival, xii–xiii, 115–16, 148
syllabi, 126. *See also* curriculum, curriculum development

T. I., 35–36
Tait, Kira, 112, 116, 122
Taylor, Breonna, 3–4
Taylor, James, 243
teaching, 26–27, 46–50, 62, 153, 156, 159, 175–76, 218–20, 239–42, 258–59; engaged scholarship and, 69–70, 73–74; social change and, 244–45
TedX, 36–37
Teichman, Judith Ann, 234–35
tenure and promotion, 8–10, 23–26, 36, 61–62, 69, 154, 163–66, 169–71, 176–82, 205–9, 217–18, 220–22, 243. *See also* hiring; retention
Tettey, Wisdom, 234

therapy, 238, 240
Thornton, John, 130–32
Threadgill, Thomas L., 22–23
Threadgill, Sheryl, 22–23
thriving, xii–xiii, 71, 74–75, 158–60
time management, 83–84, 203–4
tokenism, 169, 199–200, 246
Transnational Black Womxn Scholars of African Politics Research Network, 112–13
transnationalism, 69–70, 109–26, 128–29, 132
trauma, 20–21, 66, 97, 225–26
Trudy, 246
Trump, Donald, 252–53, 257–58
truth telling, 166–70, 172, 213–14
Truth, Sojourner, 257
Tsikata, Dzodzi, 126
Turner, Robin L., 112, 116, 120, 122, 142n3

unicorns, 114–15, 200–1, 226–27, 230, 235, 246
unions, unionizing, 120, 239–40

Vacation Bible School, 261–62
value systems, 101, 125–26
violence, 132; against Black women, 5; domestic, 66; institutional, 9–10; race-gender, 92–94, 97, 115–16, 118–20
visibility, 12–14, 169; invisibility, 12–14, 154, 244–45
vulnerability, 169, 238

Walker-Barnes, Chanequa, 100–1
Walker, Alice, 24, 132–33
Walton, Hanes, 177
We Won't Stop! workshop, 94–95
weathering, 67, 119–20, 188–89, 202–3
wellness, wellness retreats, 92–93, 201–3. *See also* health
Wells-Barnett, Ida B., 213–14

West, Cornel, 51–52
West, Kanye, 37
Western Political Science Association, 58
White, Deborah Gray, xii–xiii
whiteness, white supremacy, xi–xii, 20–21, 24, 56–57, 130, 132–33, 135, 139–41, 153, 166–67, 10, 228–29, 231
Williams, Linda, xii–xiii
Williams, Serena, 169
Willoughby-Herard, Tiffany, 13, 15, 112, 116, 122, 130–31, 135–38, 142nn2–7, 234–35

Wilson, Sherée, 152–53
Wilson, David, 22–23
womanism, 24, 112–13
women and gender studies, 61, 220, 234
Woodhall, Victoria, 255–56
work ethic, 200
work-life balance, 83
World Health Organization, 116
world-making, 133, 237
Wright Austin, Sharon D., 243

yoga, 120
youth organizations, 22–23